JÜRGEN MÜLLER (ED.)

MOVIES
OF THE 50s

IN COLLABORATION WITH defd
AND CINEMA, HAMBURG;
BRITISH FILM INSTITUTE, LONDON
BIBLIOTHÈQUE DU FILM, PARIS

BARNES & NOBLE

NEW YORK

THE THING FROM ANOTHER WORLD

1951 - USA - 87 MIN. - B & W - SCIENCE FICTION, HORROR FILM

DIRECTOR CHRISTIAN NYBY (1913–1993)
SCREENPLAY CHARLES LEDERER, based on the short story *WHO GOES THERE?* by JOHN W. CAMPBELL JR.
DIRECTOR OF PHOTOGRAPHY RUSSELL HARLAN EDITING ROLAND GROSS MUSIC DIMITRI TIOMKIN PRODUCTION HOWARD HAWKS for
RKO RADIO PICTURES INC., WINCHESTER PICTURES CORP.

STARRING KENNETH TOBEY (Captain Patrick Hendry), MARGARET SHERIDAN (Nikki), JAMES ARNESS (The Thing),
DOUGLAS SPENCER (Ned Scott), JAMES R. YOUNG (Eddie Dykes), ROBERT CORNTHWAITE (Doctor Carrington),
DEWEY MARTIN (Bob), EDUARD FRANZ (Doctor Stern), JOHN DIERKES (Doctor Chapman), SALLY CREIGHTON
(Mrs. Chapman), EVERETT GLASS (Professor Wilson), WILLIAM SELF (Corporal Barnes).

"No pleasure, no pain ... no emotion, no heart. Our superior in every way."

The Thing From Another World tells the story of a crashed UFO and its surviving pilot – a blood-guzzling Martian who threatens a U.S. research base at the North Pole. It could have been a typical trashy and forgettable run-of-the-mill B-movie, if it hadn't been for two things: the political climate of the U.S. in the early 50s and Howard Hawks' involvement as a producer.

The film is directed by Christian Nyby, who had worked with Hawks as an editor for many years. Yet although the old master took a back seat to his protégé, Hawks' influence on the movie is quite unmistakable. The dialog, often fiery and sometimes witty, reminds us of his screwball comedies such as *Bringing Up Baby* (1938). The fast-paced, frequently overlapping verbal exchanges are so engrossing that the near-total absence of special effects is easily forgotten. Only occasionally is the war of the words interrupted by the grotesquely inarticulate grunting of the "creature" in its rubber suit. Much of the film's humor comes from the contrast between the wisecracking soldiers' bawdy talk and the anemic language of the scientists. Typically for Hawks, there's also a woman in the midst of it all, adding endless complications because she refuses to behave like a lady. And here's another very Hawksian irony: ordered by their superiors in Washington to spare the alien's life, the two "camps" react quite unexpectedly. The scientists, normally interested only in the future, turn out to be compliant conservatives, ready to follow the

"*The Thing* has turned out to be the best thriller ... since *King Kong*."

Films in Review

1   Hawks and predators: With a gun in one hand and a woman in the other, Captain Patrick Hendry (Kenneth Tobey) investigates all things alien. Margaret Sheridan as Nikki.

2   The tip of the iceberg: What looks like a shark fin is actually something more ominous – intergalactic debris peaking out of frozen tundra.

3   She blinded them with science: But is Nikki's intellectual prowess enough to knock the monster back into deep space?

4   Technical difficulties: State-of-the-art gizmos can't
    give the research team the upper hand against the
    cosmic being.

5   The trap is set: But they've got their picks, axes,
    and cleavers ready to go just in case something
    goes wrong.

government line and do their appointed duty. The soldiers, by contrast, throw all military discipline overboard, defying their commander-in-chief and doing their damnedest to settle the monster's hash. This movie is one more proof that a limited budget and a sparing use of the means available can result in highly creative solutions. The claustrophobically narrow environment of the research station is a case in point: there's no way out of there, except to certain death in the eternal Arctic ice.

The powerful effect of *The Thing From Another World* also has a lot

the political zeitgeist, this sci-fi spectacle is actually a parable on the vicissitudes of contemporary history. From the frozen wastes of the Cold War, an unknown creature emerges, and it's nothing like you or me: it has the physiology of a plant and the skin of an insect, it's asexual and unfeeling, it's more than two meters tall, it can't speak, it's bloodthirsty and it has the strength of a bear. Though vaguely humanoid in appearance, The Thing is clearly very far from human; we are faced, of course, with a creature from another planet. And though its intentions are unclear, one fact is obvious: The Thing wants into that research station double quick, because it can only

survive by drinking human blood. We hear about atmospheric disturbances, an explosion in the East, radioactive contamination … and without a doubt, we're deliberately being served up stereotypes of the communist enemy. This is disarming. Unlike many sci-fi B-movies, *The Thing From Another World* never becomes ridiculous, simply because it never takes itself too seriously. If sci-fi movies are often artless to the point of fatuity, then this movie makes a virtue of the genre's vices. It takes a clichéd situation seriously – a dumb monster threatening a bunch of frightened humans – and goes on to make a highly ironic statement about a country driven half-crazy by fear of Red infiltration.

Thank you, Howard Hawks, for a minor masterpiece of subversive Hollywood filmmaking! BR

CUTTER / EDITOR

In the early days of the cinema, the editor's tasks were relatively simple: to cut the exposed film mechanically, and to piece it together according to the wishes of those in charge. The finished version was expected to provide an elementary continuity of time, place and narrative – no more and no less. Very quickly, however, film editing became an art form with its own expressive possibilities. "Cutters" began to acquire respect as artists, and were increasingly expected to play a creative role in the filmmaking enterprise. By analogy to the profession of journalism, the lowly cutter-and-paster was transformed into an editor. And far from simply sticking the stuff together, artists such as Edwin S. Porter (*The Great Train Robbery*, 1903), David W. Griffith (*The Birth of a Nation*, 1915) and Sergej Eisenstein (*Battleship Potemkin*, 1925) developed highly expressive new techniques, from continuous montage to parallel, rhythmic, tonal, metric and "associative" montage. Though they tend to be less conspicuous than directors and cameramen, film editors have a very significant influence on the final form of the movies we see on the screen.

---

6 Little shop of horrors? The scientists try to cultivate an alien offspring as a means of studying the species.

7 The iceman cometh: The Martian awakes from within a block of solid ice and heats up the scene.

8 Taking on the unknown: There's no telling what horrors lie in store for the romantic leads – apart from a happy ending.

8

"Chris Nyby had done an awfully good job as the cutter on
Red River and he'd been a big help to us too, so I let him do it.
He wanted to be a director and I had a deal with RKO that
allowed me to do that. I was at rehearsals and helped them
with the overlapping dialog – but I thought Chris did a

QUO VADIS?

1951 - USA - 171 MIN. - COLOR - HISTORICAL EPIC

DIRECTOR MERVYN LEROY (1900–1987)
SCREENPLAY S. N. BEHRMAN, SONYA LEVIEN, JOHN LEE MAHIN, based on the novel of the same name by HENRYK SIENKIEWICZ DIRECTOR OF PHOTOGRAPHY WILLIAM V. SKALL, ROBERT SURTEES EDITING RALPH E. WINTERS MUSIC MIKLÓS RÓZSA PRODUCTION SAM ZIMBALIST for MGM.

STARRING ROBERT TAYLOR (Marcus Vinicius), DEBORAH KERR (Lygia), LEO GENN (Petronius), PETER USTINOV (Nero), PATRICIA LAFFAN (Poppaea), FINLAY CURRIE (Petrus), ABRAHAM SOFAER (Paulus), MARINA BERTI (Eunice), BUDDY BAER (Ursus), FELIX AYLMER (Plautius)

"Now indeed, Nero has his place in history."

Quo vadis? ushered in the last great era of sword-and-sandal sagas. Long before the appearance of *Ben-Hur* (1959) and *Spartacus* (1960), this third film adaptation of Henryk Sienkiewicz's famous novel set new standards for the historical epic. Though the movie's overt "message" was unmistakably Christian, the spectacular crowd scenes and the unprecedented extravagance of the sets bore witness to the moviemakers' pagan delight in excess for excess's sake. And it was a small, podgy, barely-known actor who embodied this excess to perfection: Peter Ustinov, as the cruel tyrant Nero. Was overacting ever as brilliant as this? Has it ever seemed so perfectly *right*? Nero is a self-appointed Artist-God, and his music is as dodgy as his divinity. As a ruler, he's prone to outbursts of rage and childish defiance, and when he reaches for his lyre, his lackeys break out in a cold sweat. He orders the killing of his own mother and wife, and then goes on to sing at an orgy. He sings the praises of his last great work of art, the burning of Rome itself, while shoving the blame onto the Christians. Only once is he ever reduced to silence: when the followers of this obscure upstart sect are thrown to the

Boring is the only word for the wooden love story between the famous general Marcus Vinicius (Robert Taylor) and the pious Christian slave Lygia (Deborah Kerr). Stiff, stolid and po-faced, Vicinius could hardly be more unlike the man who gives him his orders. Whether he's wooing Lygia or threatening her – before ultimately adopting her peculiar religion – Vicinius' Roman heroism remains quite unshakeable. Only a mediator with the wisdom of Solomon could bridge the gap between Vicinius and Nero; and director Mervyn LeRoy provides him in the shape of Petronius (Leo Genn), an amused and devious cynic. As a long-serving senator and a master of rhetoric, Petronius is capable of flattering and criticizing the Emperor in the same breath. As Rome burns, he damns Nero with ambiguous praise: "You will be worthy of the spectacle – as the spectacle is worthy of you." Together with Vicinius, he plots to disempower the tyrant, who is clearly quite mad. This will be the first good deed of Petronius' life – and the last, before he kills himself in a great final ceremony. The age of decadence is past, and the old Empire falls to make way for a new one. Nero too falls on his sword, but not without com-

2

1   A lyre and a coward: Emperor Nero looks death in the eye and Peter Ustinov comes face to face with super-stardom.

2   State of affairs: Nero's mistress, Poppaea (Patricia Laffan), has got a few aces up her robe that'll trump this king of conundrum.

3   Architect of madness: Nero lets his senators in on his urban renewal program and prepares to set the night on fire.

**PETER USTINOV
(1921–2004)**

Universal genius or all-round dilettante? Sir Peter Ustinov, a Briton of Russian, French, German, Italian and French descent, never saw the need to give priority to any one of his innumerable talents. Actor, director, writer, producer, dramatist, master of the bon mot and international talk-show guest, Ustinov was simply good at everything he did. His most memorable films roles included Nero in *Quo vadis?* (1951), the ringmaster in Max Ophüls' *Lola Montes* (1955), a fugitive prisoner in *We're No Angels* (1955), the cowardly slave-owner Batiatus in *Spartacus* (1960) and a helpless crook in *Topkapi* (1964). Even when he repeated himself, his audience loved him. In three Agatha Christie adaptations, including *Death on the Nile* (1978), he played the quirky master detective Hercule Poirot.

Ustinov began his fabulous career shortly after the war – not as an actor, but as a film and theater director. In 1962, he directed *Billy Budd* (1962), a highly acclaimed film adaptation of Hermann Melville's novella. From 1968 onwards he also worked as a UNICEF ambassador. On 28 March, 2004, Peter Ustinov died of heart failure in Switzerland, his adopted home.

"The scenes of Roman gatherings in Nero's decadent reign to honor triumphant heroes or to watch Christians clawed to death by lions are rendered intoxicating by the magnificence of the sets and the massing of thousands of extras, which shooting in Italy has allowed Metro to afford. On the strength of its crowds and architecture, this *Quo vadis?* would tip any scales." *The New York Times*

4 For the love of God! Lygia (Deborah Kerr) wants to die for her faith, but Marcus (Robert Taylor, left) has livelier plans for her …

5 Hell on earth: Nero paints the town red and credits the Christians with the blaze.

Originally, John Huston was supposed to direct *Quo vadis?* Had he done so, the world would presumably have missed out on a bombastic cult movie. LeRoy takes his bearings more from Cecil B. DeMille's *The Sign of the Cross* (1932) than from Sienkiewicz's novel: he is never afraid of going over the top, nor does he let his respect for the Easter message get in the way of a good, meaty scene. In the catacombs of the Eternal City, the apostle Paul (Abraham Sofaer) delivers a breathtaking five-minute summary of the Gospel; and in the arena, he comforts his desperate brothers and sisters in Christ for the very last time. It's a truly dignified spectacle, though it gains in authenticity partly by means of its very excessiveness. In fact, most of the events depicted did actually take place. (Nero, however, did not take his own life in 64 B.C., but four years later.)

Films like *Quo vadis?* had a significance that went beyond their mere commercial success. Many scholars of the cinema see the wave of Roman epics after WW II as an attempt by Hollywood to come to terms with the experience of European fascism. These movies depict Imperial Rome as a cruel dictatorship, and they oppose it with a smorgasbord of Christian and humanist ideals. Rome's ideology is condemned, but its fatuous perpetrators – such as Marcus and Petronius – are given their chance to see the light. This is how a new world power gives expression to its sense of political mission. Sir Peter Ustinov, however, took a somewhat more sober view of things. In his memoirs, he described the Romans as a pragmatic people with a relaxed attitude to power and the dubious taste of the *nouveau riche*. And this, he suggested, was why the Americans were best at making Roman epics. PB

A STREETCAR NAMED DESIRE

1951 - USA - 125 MIN. - B & W - LITERARY ADAPTATION, DRAMA

DIRECTOR Elia Kazan (1909–2003)
SCREENPLAY OSCAR SAUL, TENNESSEE WILLIAMS, based on Williams' play of the same name
DIRECTOR OF PHOTOGRAPHY HARRY STRADLING SR. EDITING DAVID WEISBART MUSIC ALEX NORTH
PRODUCTION CHARLES K. FELDMAN for CHARLES K. FELDMAN GROUP, WARNER BROS.

STARRING VIVIEN LEIGH (Blanche DuBois), MARLON BRANDO (Stanley Kowalski), KIM HUNTER (Stella Kowalski),
KARL MALDEN (Harold "Mitch" Mitchell), RUDY BOND (Steve Hubbell), NICK DENNIS (Pablo Gonzales),
PEG HILLIAS (Eunice Hubbell), WRIGHT KING (Cashier), RICHARD GARRICK (Doctor), EDNA THOMAS (Mexican woman).

ACADEMY AWARDS 1951 OSCARS for BEST ACTRESS (Vivien Leigh), BEST SUPPORTING ACTRESS (Kim Hunter),
BEST SUPPORTING ACTOR (Karl Malden), and BEST ART DIRECTION (Richard Day, George James Hopkins).

IFF VENICE 1951 BEST ACTRESS (Vivien Leigh).

"Hey, Stella!"

Film adaptations of stage plays have a bad reputation. Only one of them can be said to have given a new direction to the performing arts of the 20th century, including both theater and film: Elia Kazan's *A Streetcar Named Desire*, based on Tennessee Williams' play of the same name.

A blood-chilling yell pierces the sultry heat of a New Orleans summer night: "Hey, StellAAAH!" Stanley Kowalski (Marlon Brando) doesn't have to wait for long. Stella (Kim Hunter) will come into his strong arms, magically drawn by an animal virility that makes her forget all the times he hurt her. Another woman will be shipwrecked by this merciless love: Stella's sister Blanche DuBois (Vivien Leigh), who is driven mad by Stanley's coarse attacks. She's an ageing Southern belle, and she hates the impoverished milieu of the Kowalskis. Blanche has lied to herself all her life, for she's convinced she deserves better. Stanley will drum the truth into her, expose her bitter past and ruin her life by raping her.

This is more than a battle of the sexes, though; it's a struggle between two fundamentally different styles of acting. The Method actor Brando, fresh from Lee Strasberg's Actors' Studio, *is* Kowalski, with body and soul. This was the role that made him famous. In his proletarian directness, he seems wholly unaware of the camera's presence. He talks with his mouth full, he fills the entire room with his physical presence, and while he's at it, he makes the t-shirt fashionable. The tattered army-surplus item on his muscular torso was probably a major factor in the film's success. What's

2

"Brando's performance as Stanley is one of those rare screen legends that are all they're cracked up to be: poetic, fearsome, so deeply felt you can barely take it in. In the hands of other actors, Stanley is like some nightmare feminist critique of maleness: brutish and infantile. Brando is brutish, infantile and full of a pain he can hardly comprehend or express. The monster suffers like a man." *The Washington Post*

1 Treasure trove: Stanley Kowalski (Marlon Brando) holds the keys to Stella's (Kim Hunter) heart.

2 Wife beater: Only Blanche (Vivien Leigh) is immune to Stanley's animal magnetism.

3 Fox and sable: Brando and Leigh are contradictory breeds – the former is Method, the latter Old Hollywood.

meant by the "Method" is a little harder to say; classical actors suspected the Method was no more and no less than Marlon Brando himself. All we can say with any certainty is that Vivien Leigh's performance as Blanche is the opposite of Method acting; yet her nervous theatricality is the perfect embodiment of a woman who lives in a dream world and cannot survive reality. And there's something truly tragic in the casting of this former screen goddess as poor Blanche DuBois: 12 years after *Gone With the Wind* (1939), Scarlett O'Hara is finally blown away. By 1951, Old Hollywood was on its way out.

For director Elia Kazan, *Streetcar* also signified a transition to a new creative phase, as he moved away from the theater and into the movies. When one compares it to his later Tennessee Williams adaptations (*Cat on a Hot Tin Roof*, 1958 and *Sweet Bird of Youth*, 1962), *Streetcar* still looks very much like the work of a man of the theater. Most of his actors had already been acclaimed for their performances in his Broadway production of the play, while the English Vivien Leigh had played Blanche in London. Moreover, the film itself is basically theatrical in conception: Kazan keeps his focus narrow and concentrated, and evokes a claustrophobic atmosphere by means

4   The end of the line: Stanley's friend Mitch (Karl
Malden) backs Blanche into a corner and sees
through her shadow and fog allure. Director Elia
Kazan said that Method actor Malden was his
brightest protégé.

5   For whom the 'belle' tolls: Stanley pushes Stella to
the limit and forces her to decide between him
and her sister.

of short panning shots. Yet he does use thoroughly cinematic means in order to create the impression of unreality so expressive of Blanche's worldview, making effective use of indirect light filtered through lanterns and the eerie shadows cast by ceiling fans. In New Orleans, the night belongs to the dead, and only the nocturnal loudmouth Stanley Kowalski is capable of bringing it to life.

Brando's performance has often been copied, but never been matched. At the time, however, many critics felt his acting was exaggerated, overstat-ed, and simply *too much*. This was not just because Brando's style was so radical and so unfamiliar. In fact, censorship had a lot to do with it, as was made clear by a reconstructed version of the movie released in 1992. Just a few brief sequences had been cut, but the effect was to rob the "animal" Stanley of his full humanity, while Stella's wild desire was carefully tamed for a 50s audience. The difference between the two versions is enormous. In 1951, apparently, the world was not yet ready for the full spectrum of human emotions. Reality would have to wait just a little bit longer.   PB

**ELIA KAZAN
(1909–2003)**

When Elia Kazan picked up his Lifetime Achievement Oscar in 1999, many guests and members of the Academy remained seated in protest. His statement to the House un-American Activities Commission had made him the bad boy of Hollywood. Kazan, a former member of the Communist Party, had collaborated with McCarthy's witchhunters, and he had never publicly expressed any regret about it. In fact, the role of the outsider seemed to suit him: Elia Kazan, the son of Greek-Anatolian immigrants, was a socially critical realist whose films repeatedly examine the contra-dictions at the heart of American society.

In *Gentleman's Agreement* (1947), for example, he had already criticized the pervasive, latent anti-Semitism in the U.S. But in the 50s, he found his best "material" in the plays of Tennessee Williams, a writer whose work excited huge controversy at the time. With *A Streetcar Named Desire* (1951) and *Baby Doll* (1956), Kazan started a veritable boom in Williams adaptations for the cinema. Kazan himself came from the theater. In 1947, he and Lee Strasberg had opened the famous Actors' Studio together. The actors he discovered there included Marlon Brando and James Dean, both of whom played a huge role in Kazan's rise to fame. For *On the Waterfront* (1954), both he and Brando won an Oscar. Kazan's Steinbeck adaptation *East of Eden* (1955) marked his final departure from the visual and dramaturgical constraints of the theater. Though the 50s were Elia Kazan's great decade, he did make some remarkable films in later years, including *Splendor in the Grass* (1961), *America, America* (1963) and *The Arrangement* (1969).

"The haunting performance of England's great Vivien Leigh in the heart-breaking role of the deteriorating Southern Belle, and the mesmerizing moods Mr. Kazan has wreathed make this picture as fine, if not finer, than the play. Inner torments are seldom projected with such sensitivity and clarity on the screen." *The New York Times*

THE AFRICAN QUEEN

1951 - USA/GREAT BRITAIN - 105 MIN. - COLOR - DRAMA, LITERARY ADAPTATION

DIRECTOR JOHN HUSTON (1906–1987)
SCREENPLAY JAMES AGEE, JOHN HUSTON, based on the novel of the same name by C. S. FORESTER
DIRECTOR OF PHOTOGRAPHY JACK CARDIFF **EDITING** RALPH KEMPLEN **MUSIC** ALLAN GRAY **PRODUCTION** SAM SPIEGEL for ROMULUS FILMS LTD., HORIZON PICTURES.

STARRING HUMPHREY BOGART (Charlie Allnut), KATHARINE HEPBURN (Rose Sayer), ROBERT MORLEY (Samuel Sayer), PETER BULL (Captain of the 'Louisa'), THEODORE BIKEL (First Officer), WALTER GOTELL (Second Officer), PETER SWANWICK (First Officer of the 'Shona'), RICHARD MARNER (Second Officer of the 'Shona'), GERALD ONN (Petty Officer).

ACADEMY AWARDS 1951 OSCAR for BEST ACTOR (Humphrey Bogart).

"Could you make a torpedo, Mr. Allnut?"

Had things gone according to plan, this film as we know it today would have never been made at all. MGM had secured the rights to C. S. Forester's novel (which based on a true story) 13 years before successfully producing it, having hoped for a screen adaptation starring Bette Davis and David Niven. But the pampered Miss Davis shuddered at the thought of an on-location shoot, especially in the most remote corner of the big bad African continent. She was a studio girl and that was that. The project was thus pushed back indefinitely on the MGM production schedule and nothing came of it until film noir great John Huston got hold of the script. Immediately clear about who would fit the bill for the unshaven, ornery and somewhat sauced riverboat captain Charlie Allnut, Huston contacted old pal Humphrey Bogart. "The hero is a common Joe," the director told him, "and you're the commonest Joe this town's got."

A happy marriage was born. Bogey threw everything he had into the role, endowing it with dramatic virtuosity and sardonic wit, and walked away from the film with a much overdue Oscar – the only one of his entire career. Acting at his side was the equally brilliant Katharine Hepburn as the matronly Methodist missionary Rose Sayer. Credit must also be given to master of ceremonies John Huston, the man who dreamed up the best mismatched pairing in the history of romantic adventure. His vision proved to be box-office gold, and today the AFI rates *The African Queen* as the 17th best film of all time.

The story begins with Rose Sayer, a progressive-thinking, God-fearing Englishwoman who in 1914 finds her calling in German East Africa after imperialist troops kill her beloved brother (Robert Morley) and destroy a Methodist mission. She feels compelled to confront the evildoers face to face. Her only means of doing so is to board a rickety mail and transport steamboat called the African Queen and journey down the Ulanga river with the vessel's Canadian skipper, Charlie Allnut.

Surrounded by the enemy and somewhat distrustful of each other, Charlie and Rose seem to be headed on a one-way trip up the creek without a paddle. With the chips stacked against them, they flee downstream through a torrential rainstorm and past a German fort. The pair eventually arrive on a large lake patrolled by a German gunboat, which they intend to sink with two homemade torpedoes.

"Well I ain't sorry for you no more, ya crazy, psalm-singing, skinny old maid!"

Film quote: Charlie Allnut (Humphrey Bogart)

1. **Oscar for a grouch:** From eternal hangovers to devoted husband, the role of boatsman Charlie Allnut supplied Humphrey Bogart with his sole Academy Award.

2. **Mission impossible:** Rose Sayer (Katharine Hepburn) plays the organ, while her brother Samuel (Robert Morlay) spreads the word of the Lord in the African jungle.

3. **River regalia:** The African Queen may not look like much, but she gives it her all against those nasty Germans.

4 Virgin forest deflowered: Soldiers overrun a new population of imperial subjects in a war that knows no boundaries.

5 Prohibitionist: An old maid does a little housekeeping in an effort to keep Charlie sober.

While acclimatising to the endless obstacles of bush life, Rose gradually softens to Allnut's unconventional charm. About halfway into their odyssey, she blossoms with the gossamers of love, eclipsing the colors of even the most tropical flowers Africa has to offer. Likewise, Allnut abandons the bottle at Rose's stern request and reforms himself from an incor-rigible drifter into a courageous and responsible human being. Although Allnut can hardly believe it himself, he and Rose become a couple.

In terms of storyline and acting styles, Katharine Hepburn and Humphrey Bogart complement each other perfectly. Both the actors themselves and the characters they portray represent opposing views on life that are drawn together over time. Huston gave the actors total freedom in developing the character dynamics as they saw fit, allowing for the relationship to veer into comic waters. The result was a love story that is neither forced nor far-fetched. The unique on-screen chemistry gave rise to one of the mos

HUMPHREY BOGART

Much has been written about New York City native Humphrey Bogart (b. January 23rd 1899 – despite dissenting opinion). As time goes by, philosophies continue to spring up that try to pinpoint just what it was about his presence that set him apart. John Huston once made an indirect attempt at solving the mystery, remarking facetiously about his good friend and colleague that "the trouble with Bogart is he thinks he's Bogart." Having directed him in three films, Huston himself had a hand in creating the Bogey myth. When film noir was born with *The Maltese Falcon* in 1941, Bogart became the genre's foremost icon. From then on the name Bogart became synonymous with the image of detective Sam Spade's snugly belted trench coat and downward tilted fedora; and Sam Spade likewise was forever associated with Bogey's gestures, with hands that dug deep into his coat pockets and a mouth that turned up at one side as a snow-white Chesterfield cigarette dangled from its lips. Although portraying a rawer and more differentiated character in the 1948 adaptation of Traven's novel *The Treasure of the Sierra Madre*, Bogey's performance remained true to the image he'd created. In *The African Queen* (1951) indomitable humor added body to his rough-around-the-edges, no-nonsense persona. Different from the quick quipped brand humor he'd mastered in Michael Curtiz' *Casablanca* (1942), Allnut's rye humor mirrored Bogart's rather cynical take on himself. The actor summed up his approach to the character saying "I've got an image of someone in my mind who drove me to drink and cost me many a sleepless night." According to *The African Queen*'s screenwriter James Agee, the secret to his success lay in his ability to "be always the same, and yet surprise us every time. He's naturally charming and doesn't waste any of his energy by trying to act ... His facial expression never changes, whether he's looking at the woman he loves, the corpse of someone he killed, or an ordinary bug."

The bottom line is that Bogart was Bogart because he was an original. He lost his life to cancer in 1957. Although it wasn't as spectacular a depar-ture as that of James Dean or Marilyn Monroe, it was just as jolting, if only because it was

"Bogart ... does the best acting of his career as the badgered rumpot who becomes a man and a lover against his will. Katharine Hepburn is excellent as the gaunt, freckled, fanatic spinster. Their contrasting personalities fill the film with good scenes, beginning with Bogart's tea-table agony as the indelicate rumbling of his stomach keeps interrupting missionary Robert Morley's chitchat about dear old England." *Time Magazine*

6   Method to his madness: Director John Huston pushed his leading actors to their limits. Particular demands were made of Bogart, who had to swim in crocodile-infested waters.

7   Bushwhackers: By the film's end, Charlie and Rose have ripped through the convictions that once confined them. At long last, their travels through the swamp are steered by common goals.

beautiful and endearing romances ever to come out of Hollywood. In the original script the protagonists were to meet with an untimely demise; but the ending was changed to better suit the dramatic arc born out of the acting as well as to preserve the dignity of Charlie and Rosie's love. Had they died in the jungle, the film's humor and the carefree nature of their affair would have perished along with them.

Instead, the characters succeed in the impossible. They triumph over the river and send the Germans packing. It is a metaphor for the cinema's own aptitude for having illusion emerge victorious over reality. The implicit message is that courage and love conquer all – no matter what the odds. The audience feels the power of this mystical principle in the exotic imagery of the river wild, which serves throughout the picture as a living mirror of Charlie and Rose's feelings for one another. And like any good odyssey, this heroic quest meets love story is actually an allegory for life itself. One can only imagine what sort of monsters might have inhabited the jungle, had Bette Davis been a sun worshipper or nature lover and adhered to the terms of the MGM contract she so nonchalantly signed.

SR

AN AMERICAN IN PARIS

ↀↀↀↀↀↀ

1951 - USA - 114 MIN. - COLOR - MUSICAL

DIRECTOR VINCENTE MINNELLI (1903–1986)
SCREENPLAY ALAN JAY LERNER DIRECTOR OF PHOTOGRAPHY ALFRED GILKS, JOHN ALTON (Ballet Sequences) EDITING ADRIENNE FAZAN
MUSIC GEORGE GERSHWIN, SAUL CHAPLIN, JOHNNY GREEN PRODUCTION ARTHUR FREED for MGM.

STARRING GENE KELLY (Jerry Mulligan), LESLIE CARON (Lise Bouvier), OSCAR LEVANT (Adam Cook),
GEORGES GUÉTARY (Henri Baurel), NINA FOCH (Milo Roberts), EUGENE BORDEN (George Matthieu),
MARTHA BAMATTRE (Mathilde Matthieu).

ACADEMY AWARDS 1951 OSCARS for BEST PICTURE (Arthur Freed), BEST SCREENPLAY (Alan Jay Lerner),
BEST ART DIRECTION (Cedric Gibbons, E. Preston Ames, Edwin B. Willis, F. Keogh Gleason),
BEST CINEMATOGRAPHY (Alfred Gilks, John Alton), BEST COSTUMES (Orry-Kelly, Walter Plunkett, Irene Sharaff),
and BEST MUSIC (Johnny Green, Saul Chaplin).

"Brother, if you can't paint in Paris, you better give up and marry the boss' daughter."

Destiny comes knocking and yanks our protagonist from a deep slumber. Still shrouded in a veil of sleep, he opens the door just enough to retrieve his morning croissant delivery from the hallway. He gets up, tugging on a rope that gently raises his bed to the ceiling. Continuing, he reaches for his cabinet and removes a table and chair from within. Like poetry in motion, his left hand pulls open a drawer containing a cup and knife, whilst his right selects a jacket from the armoire. The jut of his knee sends the drawer sliding shut as he turns to face the table. And voilà! breakfast is served.

Opening with melodic gusto, An American in Paris makes it perfectly clear that even the tight French living quarters of ex-patriot painter Jerry Mulligan (Gene Kelly) can't cramp his style. Here, we witness Kelly doing what he did best, gliding across the screen in flying colors. The awesome actor/dancer as well as – in this case – choreographer gives new meaning to "going through the motions" of everyday life. It is a celebration of movement, grace and the human body.

As is often the case with musicals, the function of the plot is to provide the film with a more or less transparent shell for stunning song and dance numbers. The gist is as follows: Jerry is an American artist, who resides in post-war Paris and just can't get his life on track. Although he paints day and night, he relies on the handouts of his friends for survival. These include people like fellow American Adam Cook (Oscar Levant), a concert pianist who has yet to get his first professional engagement. Money, it seems, presents no real concern to the film's characters. It follows that An American in Paris is an old-fashioned Hollywood fairytale, which shuts out the burdens of the real world with a wave of its magic wand. This is underscored by the way Jerry prioritizes the women in his life; although the wealthy Milo Roberts (Nina Foch) is wild about the young artist's work and eager to patronize the penniless artist, Jerrry only has eyes and time for Lise Bouvier (Leslie Caron) – a beauty beyond compare. Needless to say, Lise has already promised her heart to another man.

It would be misleading to just call the opening scene of An American in Paris a celebration of the electric energy maintained throughout the picture. It might be the light-footed chemistry between Gene Kelly and Leslie Caron (a ballet dancer Kelly had discovered two years previously on the Champs-

3

1. Matron of the arts: Jerry's sugar mama, Milo Roberts (Nina Foch) compares notes with down-and-out pianist Adam Cook (Oscar Levant).

2. Paris when it sizzles: Painter Jerry Mulligan (Gene Kelly) and his muse Lise Bouvier (Leslie Caron).

3. Gay Paris! Artists in their own right Henri Baurel (Georges Guétary), Adam Cook and Jerry Mulligan dream of the life less lived.

"Kelly's dance numbers are spectacular and unforgettable, reflecting his genius as a choreographer and dancer of grace and joie de vivre, a unique talent equalled only by Fred Astaire." *Motion Picture Guide*

Elysées) or the luminous attractions of Paris, but for whatever reason, there's a sense that love is in the air. This also has more than a little to do with a soundtrack full of George and Ira Gershwin classics (music and lyrics respectively). Titles like "Our Love Is Here To Stay" and "S'Wonderful" top the list. And absolutely priceless is Kelly's rendition of the Gershwin classic "I Got Rhythm," performed alongside a chorus of Parisian urchins whilst the dancer extraordinaire teaches France's youth a bit of English.

Fairy tale or not, the picture thrives on the sheer joy of storytelling. Director Vincente Minnelli and screenwriter Alan Jay Lerner (*My Fair Lady*, 1964) let their imagination run wild as they tweaked narrative conventions. The movie starts with no fewer than three off-screen narrators, consisting of Jerry Adam and a French revue performer named Henri Baurel (Georges

Guétary). Playful whims such as these are woven many times over into the story's fabric, as when Adam fantasizes about his first virtuoso concert and sees himself not only at the piano, but also conducting the orchestra while simultaneously playing several other instruments. Indeed, the film gradually departs from all plot-driven conventions, concluding with an 18-minute ballet sequence which ate up almost twenty percent of the picture's 2.7-million dollar budget. Accompanied only by instrumentals, Kelly and Caron skate and twirl in a mélange of modern dance and classical ballet. Set against highly stylized backdrops inspired by the works of French painters such as Renoir and Toulouse-Lautrec, the choreography is an allegory of their love and a ode to Parisian beauty. It all makes for a dazzling finale that is without a doubt the film's *pièce de résistance*.

4 French Impressionism: From his Parisian picture window, penniless Jerry soaks up inspiration from the streets of Montmartre.

5 May I have this dance? Jerry glides through a fairytale Paris with Lise and ease.

6 Thank heaven for little girls: Lise was Leslie Caron's breakout role. The dancer-actress went on to spellbind audiences as a leading lady in pictures like *Lili* (1952), *Daddy Longlegs* (1955) and *Gigi* (1958).

7 Foreign exchange: Jerry steals kisses from the lovely Lise, a Parisian engaged to another man.

"The real reasons to see *An American in Paris* are for the Kelly dance sequences, the closing ballet, the Gershwin songs, the bright locations, and a few moments of the ineffable, always curiously sad charm of Oscar Levant." *Chicago Sun-Times*

VINCENTE MINNELLI (1903–1986)

Having directed musical masterpieces like *Meet Me in St. Louis* (1944), *Brigadoon* (1954), and *Gigi* (1958), the name Vincente Minnelli will ring bells for all time to come. Minnelli was born into show business, and first appeared on stage at the age of three. As a filmmaker, he reshaped Hollywood musicals by allowing them to transcend the realms of reality – as was the case with *An American in Paris*. Calling upon his vast experience as a Broadway musical director, as well as his sense of spectacle, pageantry and style, Minnelli brought the stage to the cinema, giving his films a signature all his own.

Remarkably, most of Minnelli's pictures were non-musicals. He directed timeless comedies like *Father of the Bride* (1950), starring Spencer Tracy as a father who just doesn't want to lose beloved daughter Elizabeth Taylor to her future husband, a picture that proved so popular Minnelli directed a sequel the following year entitled *Father's Little Dividend* (1951). With *The Bad and the Beautiful* (1952) and *Two Weeks in Another Town* (1962) he brought two of the most notable movies about movies to the screen. And demonstrating a *Lust for Life* (1956), he shot a lush Vincent van Gogh biography.

But musicals were his passion. Both his wife, singer-actress Judy Garland, and his daughter Liza were Broadway and Hollywood musical sensa-

HIGH NOON

ↀↀↀↀ

1952 - USA - 85 MIN. - B & W - WESTERN

DIRECTOR FRED ZINNEMANN (1907–1997)
SCREENPLAY CARL FOREMAN, based on the short story "The Tin Star" by JOHN W. CUNNINGHAM
DIRECTOR OF PHOTOGRAPHY FLOYD CROSBY EDITING ELMO WILLIAMS, HARRY W. GERSTAD MUSIC DIMITRI TIOMKIN
PRODUCTION STANLEY KRAMER for STANLEY KRAMER PRODUCTIONS.

STARRING GARY COOPER (Marshal Will Kane), GRACE KELLY (Amy Kane), THOMAS MITCHELL (Mayor Henderson), KATY JURADO (Helen Ramirez), LLOYD BRIDGES (Harvey Pell), IAN MACDONALD (Frank Miller), LEE VAN CLEEF (Jack Colby), LON CHANEY JR. (Martin Howe), OTTO KRUGER (Judge Mettrick), JACK ELAM (Charlie).

ACADEMY AWARDS 1952 OSCARS for BEST ACTOR (Gary Cooper), BEST EDITING (Elmo Williams, Harry W. Gerstad), BEST MUSIC (Dimitri Tiomkin), BEST SONG: "Do Not Forsake Me, Oh My Darlin'" (Music: Dimitri Tiomkin; Text: Ned Washington).

"A man's gotta do what a man's gotta do."

By 1880, the Wild West was taking it easy. Particularly on Sundays. But today is an an exception: between 10.34 AM and 12.15 PM, the life of Will Kane (Gary Cooper), Hadleyville's resident marshal, will be turned on its head. Just moments after marrying Amy Foster (actress Grace Kelly was incidentally 30 years younger than her on-screen husband Gary Cooper) and ending a career in law enforcement, he gets word that murderer Frank Miller (Ian MacDonald) is coming to town and decides to hold onto his badge just a bit longer. Miller, eager to settle a score with Kane, is scheduled to arrive on the noon train, and the outlaw's three old cohorts are already waiting at the station.

Kane's initial impulse is to leave with Amy, but having "never run away from anybody" he soon makes his way back to Hadleyville to face the bandit. He seeks out reinforcements, but the only men willing to help him are a half-pint, a half-ass, and a guy who's half-blind. And even they are prepared to ditch him at the drop of a hat. With no-one to rely on but himself, Kane drafts a will, heads out to Main Street, and waits for the four outlaws to show up. The confrontation gets underway from behind the building crevices, with Kane laying two of the posse to rest. Amy does away with a third, coming to her husband's aide just in the nick of time. She, in turn, is taken hostage by Miller, who is soon eating lead at Kane's hand. Peace is restored, and the town denizens appear from their homes with a sigh of relief. Too little, too

Within its first six minutes, *High Noon* pulls out all the stops and hits just about every Western convention in the Hollywood bible. "Do Not Forsake Me, Oh My Darling," the title song performed by country music's Tex Ritter, establishes a link between Hadleyville's opposing forces as Miller's cronies mosey through town toward the train station, while Will Kane and his Quaker bride say "I do." The wedding and the marshal's shedding of his star take place with the audience fully aware that Will Kane has another law enforcement challenge lying in store. When he receives word of Miller's return, the newly retired Kane decides to stick it out one last time. 'Cause as the old saying goes, "a man's gotta do what a man's gotta do." And that goes double in the West, Bucko.

Shooting on the project began in 1951, temporally coinciding with gung-ho efforts to combat sedition during the Cold War. Communist witch-hunter, Republican Senator Joseph McCarthy and the House un-American Activities Committee were smearing the dossiers of public figures who had anything resembling a pink past. And the Committee's efforts weren't lost on *High Noon*. Screenwriter Carl Foreman was called before the Committee to disclose names, but refused to testify. His name was promptly blacklisted, creating both tension and discord on the project. Producer Stanley Kramer and leading actor Gary Cooper severed all ties to Foreman, whereas director Fred Zinnemann stood by him. Broader opposition formed throughout Holly-

1 Star couple: Amy Foster (Grace Kelly) and Marshal Will Kane (Gary Cooper) are forced to put love on hold when outlaw Frank Miller returns to town.

2 Model citizens: Propriety gets a foothold in the West when Amy and Will tie the knot. No-one seemed to object to the fact that Grace Kelly was 30 years Cooper's junior.

3 Veto power: Even the mayor (Thomas Mitchell) refuses to support the marshal's cause.

"Loaded with interest and suspense, *High Noon* is a Western to challenge *Stagecoach* for the all-time championship." *The New York Times*

president of the Motion Picture Alliance for the Preservation of American Ideals, he and others banded together against Foreman. A point of note: Wayne later signed onto Howard Hawks' *Rio Bravo* (1959), still referred to by Western buffs as the "anti-*High Noon* movie."

High Noon enjoys the distinction of being a classic Western with a message that transcends the storyline. Political and moral yardsticks have inspired a wide range of critical interpretations. There's no overlooking the traditional debate of integrity, conscience, commitment, and duty pitted against opportunism, self-interest, easy outs, and cowardice. Some might go so far as to say that the film casts a critical eye on democracy, at least the form it has taken in the United States. Also striking is that Zinnemann's lifelong motto can be readily applied to *High Noon*'s underlying philosophy: a man's character is his destiny. It was an endeavor steered by individual-ists, each of whom was a master in his own right: from producer Stanley

Kramer, via Fred Zinnemann, screenwriter Carl Foreman, cinematographer Floyd Crosby (1931 Oscar recipient for Friedrich Wilhelm Murnau's *Taboo* (*Tabu*), composer Dimitri Tiomkin, to editors Elmo Williams and Harry W. Gerstad. Sadly, the collaborative efforts of these men came to a halt in the early 1950s; but each of them was instrumental in contributing to *High Noon*'s success.

Still, the actors were the ones to thank for an enthusiastic audience. A stunningly silver Gary Cooper, aged 50, plays the stoic Will Kane, a former hero of the Wild West ready to reassume his duty for good measure. He is beautifully countered by 21-year-old Grace Kelly as Amy Kane, the character that propelled Kelly on a light-speed career, however short-lived it was; a star-studded supporting cast with players like Thomas Mitchell as the mayor, Lloyd Bridges as the deputy, and Katy Jurado as Kane's former love gave the film its finishing touches. All of their roles economically serve the progression

"A man's character is his destiny." *Fred Zinnemann*

of the story; there is little hint of a private life beyond what we see, and no tinge of comic relief. Indeed, the film is earnest to the point of being bone dry – often a cinematic liability, but not here.

Severe and laconic in style and narrative, its 100 minutes of action is compressed into an actual 85 minutes of celluloid. The magic of this documentary feel and the acting talents of the cast gave *High Noon* its status as a seminal Western. Kane is not a lonesome dove, he's socially isolated. His manner isn't cool, it's cautious and fear-ridden. He's on the verge of tears as

he makes out his will. This aside, he's preyed upon and compelled to fight dirty for survival with all he's got.

Finally, mention must also be made of the breathtaking photography. Director and cameraman wanted the film to have the aesthetic of a news broadcast. The coarse grain of the black-and-white imagery is set off by Dimitri Tiomkin's marvelous score; it doesn't push the story forward per se, but rather layers the film with a new rhythm altogether, making for a gripping viewing experience more than 50 years strong. R

3

4 A woman's gotta do what a woman's gotta do: When this Quaker must decide between her life and her principles, she momentarily forgets what the Good Book says.

5 Death trap: Westerns are studies in masculinity and willpower; the first guy to flinch gets to push up the lilies.

GARY COOPER (1901–1961)

Even those born well after Gary Cooper's relatively early death still readily recognize the name and the face of this legendary actor. An American film critic once dubbed Coop's angular face "a map of America," and Jean-Luc Godard viewed it as a timeless "geological artifact." Born in Montana, Cooper got his start in film around 1925, working as a stuntman in Hollywood Westerns. His rise to fame got underway in 1929, when he played the title role in *The Virginian*, a Western about life on a frontier void of judges and jail cells – and the Easterner who tried to change it all. In 1937, *The New York Times* reported Cooper to be the highest-paid American actor. He enjoyed a sterling career that included collaborations with Paramount's brightest directors and the industry's sultriest leading ladies, including Marlene Dietrich, Jean Arthur and Claudette Colbert. Often playing characters in uniform, be it in military or Western garb, Cooper became the quintessential image of bygone America and traditional values. In 1947, he testified in front of the House un-American Activities Committee, although he didn't speak out against any of his associates. He was awarded an Oscar for lifetime achievement in February 1961, which James Stewart accepted on behalf of the critically ill actor. Cooper lost his battle with cancer in Beverly Hills in May of that year.

SINGIN' IN THE RAIN

1952 - USA - 103 MIN. - COLOR - MUSICAL

DIRECTORS GENE KELLY (1912–1996), STANLEY DONEN (b. 1924)
SCREENPLAY BETTY COMDEN, ADOLPH GREEN DIRECTOR OF PHOTOGRAPHY HAROLD ROSSON EDITING ADRIENNE FAZAN
MUSIC NACIO HERB BROWN, LENNIE HAYTON PRODUCTION ARTHUR FREED for MGM.

STARRING GENE KELLY (Don Lockwood), DONALD O'CONNOR (Cosmo Brown), DEBBIE REYNOLDS (Kathy Selden),
JEAN HAGEN (Lina Lamont), MILLARD MITCHELL (R. F. Simpson), RITA MORENO (Zelda Zanders),
DOUGLAS FOWLEY (Roscoe Dexter), CYD CHARISSE (Dancer), MADGE BLAKE (Dora Bailey),
KING DONOVAN (Rod).

"Of course we talk! Don't everybody?"

Cupid's arrow strikes Don Lockwood (Gene Kelly) like a heart-seek-ing missile. Moments previously, the movie star dropped off girlfriend Kathy Seldon (Debbie Reynolds) at her doorstep and was bid farewell with a good-night kiss. Long forgotten are the gray skies looming over the silent screen heartthrob's uncertain career brought on by a preview audience's rejection of his first talkie, "The Dueling Cavalier." An evening of romance and artistic inspiration has set world on fire for Don, Kathy, and mutual friend Cosmo Brown (Donald O'Connor). For the unstoppable trio are about to corner the market on the new motion picture medium by turning tired period pieces into a radically new genre – the Hollywood musical.

Tonight, even Mother Nature's fury couldn't rain on Don's parade. Pulling his umbrella shut, he defiantly welcomes a downpour and opens his arms to its cathartic effects. With a skip here and a splash there, Don glides from sidewalk to puddle "just singin' and dancin' in the rain."

It is a scene that would immortalize Gene Kelly and the spirit of opti-mism inherent in great Hollywood fairy tales – thus explaining its current sta-tus as the most readily identifiable musical sequence in cinematic history. If you go by Kelly's story, making it happen was as easy as one, two, three. When producer Arthur Freed asked him whether he had a concept for the title song's staging – a piece written by composer Nacio Herb Brown and lyricized by Freed himself – Kelly simply said, "Sure. When it rains, I sing."

Sounds simple enough, but there's a bit more to this sweet little snippet of film history: screenwriters Betty Comden and Adolph Green had originally conceived the number as a invigorating trio for Kelly, Reynolds and O'Connor, intended to follow the Dueling Cavalier's failed preview. This was a role even-tually delegated to the song "Good Morning," and "Singin' in the Rain" was reserved for Kelly's show-stopping magic alone.

Comden and Green's original task – however vague – was to structure a story around as many existing Arthur Freed and Nacio Herb Brown songs as possible. Given that the majority of the tunes were written in the late 1920s and early 30s, the dawn of sound in Hollywood, the screenwriters built a plot around the technical difficulties that arose during these transitional years.

Singin' in the Rain does this without taking a cheap stab at the era. Full of fondness and ironic insight, the picture recreates a time that began with director Alan Crosland's partially sound-synchronized classic, *The Jazz Singer* (1927), the first film with audible dialog and the one that paved the way for art features with embedded musical soundtracks. In its infancy, syn-chronization was a hit and miss business, and the audience was expected to bear with the unbearable during screenings whenever sound and picture went their separate ways. In a tongue-in-cheek montage sequence entitled "Beautiful Girl," *Singin' in the Rain* revisits the aesthetics of the first singing talkies as an overhead camera shot – culminating with chorus girls in kalei-

1 Gotta Dance! Don Lockwood (Gene Kelly) trips all the lights of his imagined Broadway.

2 Sheets and sheets: After composing all night, Don is showered with Kathy's affections and spends the dawn just singin' and dancin' in the rain.

3 Anyplace I hang my hat is home: The long-legged gangster moll (Cyd Charisse) kicks off the show-stopping "Broadway Melody" – one of the grandest dream ballets Hollywood ever created.

doscopic formations – a homage to musical director Busby Berkeley's self-coined "top shot."

The film's depiction of the countless mishaps ushered in by the advent of sound are by no means fabricated. Nor is the crisis that faced the histrionic screen acting rooted in mugging and heavy gesticulation – a style that had served the silent screen so well. Many beloved stars found that their careers had come to an abrupt end either because they had "no voice" or one that clashed with audience expectations. *Singin' in the Rain* brilliantly references this in the Lina Lamont character (Jean Hagen in an Oscar nominated performance), a sultry diva who sounds like a rusty door whenever she opens her trap.

The predominant tones of the film's comic sensibility emerge along similar lines of characterization: dizzy blonde Lina can't remember where the microphone is hidden; star-struck Kathy garishly brands the film industry as morally reprehensible, then embarrasses herself at a Hollywood party by jumping out of a cake; and at the top of the film, a self-absorbed Don casually forgets his former career as a third-rate vaudevillian entertainer while looking back on his journey to super-stardom.

Without question the musical numbers themselves also keep the picture light and breezy: Donald O'Connor's high-energy "Make 'Em Laugh" – a flagrant copy of Cole Porter's "Be a Clown" with a new set of lyrics – is a slapstick circus come to life; Kelly and O'Connor's synchronized tap danc-

ing routines in numbers like "Fit as a Fiddle" and "Moses Supposes" are as energetic as they are intoxicating, with the athletic Kelly and plastic acrobatic Connor coaxing each other to new heights.

The way in which these pre-existing musical numbers were seamlessly integrated into the plot reflects the artistic genius of the creative pairings of Comden & Green and Donen & Kelly. We get a taste of this when Don must avow his love for Kathy via song and dance in "You Were Meant For Me," because, once again, the eloquent actor just can't limit his emotions to words alone.

As the sole song that does little to further the action, "Broadway Melody" stands in clear opposition to *Singin' in the Rain*'s other numbers. A sequence that ate up a sizable chunk of the picture's total budget, it features Kelly/Lockwood as a naive dancer thwarted into Broadway's deadlier throes vis-a-vis leggy mob commodity Cyd Charisse, a dancing sensation in a money-colored dress. The piece is a climatic dream ballet in the same vein as those from movie musicals like *On the Town* (1949) also directed by Gene Kelly and Stanley Donen and *An American in Paris* (1951) directed by Vincente Minnelli. A triumph in grandeur, originality and technical composition its own right, the sequence encapsulates the sophistication and artistic values of the entire film, a work of art that lives on as a monument to the Hollywood musical's indelible past. LP

4 Three's company: Cosmo Brown (Donald O'Connor), Kathy Selden (Debbie Reynolds) and Don Lockwood transform a wooden talkie into an opulent musical.

5 If the spirit so moves you: Swayed by spectacle, MGM pulled out all the stops for its big-budget musicals.

6 The Doublemint Twins: Hollywood power-players Don and Cosmo recall their humble beginnings on the vaudeville circuit in the number "Fit as a Fiddle."

"The all-singin', all-dancin' Kelly – who also co-directed the film and the musical numbers – is well up to par. But the comic O'Connor, joining him in song and hoofing routines, almost steals the show." *Variety*

GENE KELLY (1912–1996)

Gene Kelly embodied a cross-section of Middle America in nearly 30 movie musicals. Whether as a sailor, football player or returning war veteran, Kelly's screen characters were almost always bursting with optimism and vigor. His career started off on Broadway at the end of the 1930s where his star performance as "Pal Joey" got Hollywood's attention. In 1942, Kelly reprised the role for film and remained under contract with MGM for nearly 15 years. It was during this time that he met up with producer Arthur Freed, who helped Kelly gain more control of his movies as both choreographer and director. Kelly's many-year collaboration with director/performer Stanley Donen was also an instrumental career shaper; the two men joined forces for some of Hollywood's best integrated musicals like *On the Town* (1949), *Singin' in the Rain* (1952) and *It's Always Fair Weather* (1955).

Kelly's sensational dance style was the synthesis of athletic ability and pure charisma. Unlike the debonair Fred Astaire's liquid moves, Kelly was all pizzazz, and many of his characterizations have their roots in vaudeville and Commedia dell'Arte. Indeed the differences of two men are manifold: song and dance were Astaire's means of entering a lady's heart, whereas for Kelly they were, above all else, the expression of camaraderie. Many of Kelly's films and dance numbers were therefore built around three actors rather than two. This, in turn, allowed room for comic sidekicks like Phil Silvers, Jules Munshin or Donald O'Connor to get in on the fun. In addition, it was almost a given that a Kelly musical would contain a more somber solo number: the apparent denial by a female love interest gave his characters a reason to lose themselves in fantasies and daydreams *à la* ballet sequences in *On the Town* and *An American in Paris*. On occasion, Kelly acted in non-musicals, and his performance in George Sidney's film *The Three Musketeers* (1948) shows that he didn't need to sing in order to shine. However, a little music never hurt and musketeer D'Artagnan's sword fights were rhythmically staged. In 1996, Gene Kelly died of complications following a stroke.

IVANHOE

1952 - USA / GREAT BRITAIN - 106 MIN. - COLOR - HISTORICAL EPIC, LITERARY ADAPTATION

DIRECTOR RICHARD THORPE (1896–1991)
SCREENPLAY NOEL LANGLEY, based on the novel of the same name by SIR WALTER SCOTT
DIRECTOR OF PHOTOGRAPHY FREDDIE YOUNG EDITING FRANK CLARKE MUSIC MIKLÓS RÓZSA PRODUCTION PANDRO S. BERMAN
for LOEW'S INC., MGM.

STARRING ROBERT TAYLOR (Ivanhoe), ELIZABETH TAYLOR (Rebecca), JOAN FONTAINE (Rowena),
GEORGE SANDERS (Sir Brian de Bois-Guilbert), EMLYN WILLIAMS (Wamba), ROBERT DOUGLAS (Sir Hugh de Bracy),
FINLAY CURRIE (Cedric), FELIX AYLMER (Isaac), FRANCIS DE WOLFF (Front de Bœuf), GUY ROLFE (Prince John),
NORMAN WOOLAND (King Richard the Lionheart), HAROLD WARRENDER (Locksley a.k.a. Robin Hood).

"My heart was a lion; but now it's in chains ..."

They didn't call it Technicolor for nothing. The brilliant blues and greens of Lady Rowena's (Joan Fontaine) gowns that do such a spectacular job of setting off her blonde tresses; the illustrious azures and white robe of scoundrel Sir Brian de Bois-Guilbert (George Sanders), and the rich reds, spun of fine fabrics, proudly sported by each of the knights attending the tournament at Ashby.

In a matt black armor on a soot-colored steed, Anglo-Saxon nobleman Sir Wilfred of Ivanhoe (Robert Taylor) is the complete antithesis. He challenges the Norman aristocrat to a duel in an effort to champion the lovesick Rebecca (Elizabeth Taylor) in a trial by combat. The black-haired Jewess in white tatters has been condemned to burn at the stake for witchcraft unless her monochrome match Ivanhoe can save her. But even if he succeeds, his heart belongs to another ...

Color quickly became a hot commodity in 1950s Hollywood. In 1951, just under a quarter of all Tinseltown productions were shot in color. The following year, color features accounted for approximately forty percent of total production, and by 1954 they dominated with sixty-odd percent of the big-budget movie market. This whirlwind development represented a concerted attempt to seize the title of king of the entertainment industry for the big screen. The end of the Second World War triggered a crisis in Hollywood as more and more potential audience members were opting against a night out at the movies. The troops had come home from overseas, and young couples were starting families at lightning pace, resulting in the so-called postwar baby boom. Practically overnight, it seemed, the social landscape had changed, and social values with it. Americans were discovering fundamentally new ways of filling their leisure time.

As if that wasn't enough, the advent of television had started taking its toll on the movie industry. In response to the competition brought on by the new medium and an overall lack of audience enthusiasm, Hollywood went to great lengths to come up with technological innovations like CinemaScope, 3-D and Technicolor that the little screen just couldn't match. These new cinematic formats gave way to an increased production of musicals and, above all else, period pieces, in which the visual enhancements could be shown off to greatest advantage. Spectacles set in biblical times, in ancient and historical Europe, replete with warriors, knights and swashbuckling pirates, proved particularly suitable. It ignited a sort of golden age that by the decade's end consisted of little more than the ash of shoddily produced Italian counterparts.

Although financed by Hollywood heavyweight MGM, a chain of events displaced *Ivanhoe's* entire production to British shores. A dispute between the U.K. film industry and the American studios resulted in an ordinance preventing the transfer of all-American production earnings in Britain to the U.S. The American studios therefore made best use of their semi-frozen British profits by diverting numerous projects to English soil and reinvesting their funds in them. MGM promptly sent producer Pandro S. Berman, director Richard Thorpe and actor Robert Taylor on an extended holiday to the British Isles in the hopes of carrying out the plan. From 1952–55, the trio cranked out three big-budget epics about knights in shining armor: the film adaptation of Sir Walter Scott's *Ivanhoe* (1952), *Knights of the Round Table* (1953), and *The Adventures of Quentin Durward* (1955) – also based on a Walter Scott tale.

Ivanhoe was the most dazzlingly extravagant of these foreign projects. It featured world-class actors, a superb supporting cast, hundreds of extras

2

"All the romance, intrigue and excitement of Sir Walter Scott's classic is captured in Noel Langley's screenplay, and the big Anglo-American cast respond to the theme with lively and vigorous performances. Richard Thorpe has directed with imaginative skill, adroitly moulding the various facets of the yarn and handling the big crowds and spectacular sequences with a surefire touch." *Variety*

JOAN FONTAINE
(b. 1917)

Born in Tokyo, Japan to British parents, Joan Fontaine had her first chance at stardom in 1937 and failed miserably. She was supposed to dance at the side of the great Fred Astaire in the RKO musical *A Damsel in Distress*, directed by George Stevens. But Fontaine's dancing ability being what it was, the studio decided that it might be better if Astaire danced around her rather than with her, and the 20-year-old actress became an industry laughing stock. However, Hollywood was forgiving and the actress was granted a second chance. Under the direction of Alfred Hitchcock in the Daphne du Maurier melodrama *Rebecca* (1940), Fontaine won over audiences as a woman who marries into money only to be terrorized by the ghost of her husband's first wife and the estate caretaker.

A world apart from her robust sister Olivia de Havilland, Joan Fontaine often portrayed more demure creatures. Her part shy, part skeptical smile made her perfectly suited for playing victims. This was to become her on-screen image over the following years thanks to pictures like Alfred Hitchcock's *Suspicion* (1941) in which she acts as a military man's homely daughter who falls for a smooth talking con-artist; in Max Ophül's masterpiece, *Letter from an Unknown Woman* (1948), she played an equally naive young woman obsessed with a concert pianist who doesn't even notice she's alive. On occasion Fontaine was cast against type, proving she had a couple tricks up her sleeve as a sinister murderess in *Ivy* (1947, directed by Sam Wood) and a megalomaniac patron of the arts in *Serenade* (1956, directed by Anthony Mann). Her stint as a colorful beauty however was reserved for opulent period pieces like *Ivanhoe* (1952) and *Frenchman's Creek* (1944, directed by Mitchell Leisen). Towards the end of the 1950s, Fontaine's star began to dwindle and she made only limited screen appearances. Her final film role came in 1966 with Cyril Frankel's horror movie *The Witches* a.k.a. *The Devil's Own*.

1   Knights and white satin: Sir Wilfred of Ivanhoe (Robert Taylor) fights to release the Jewish Rebecca (Elizabeth Taylor) from captivity and opens himself up to divine judgment.

2   From the depths of darkness: Whether the Anglo-Saxons will redeem their honor at the Tournament of Ashby all depends on the abilities of this man.

3   Lancelot and his noble steed: To eschew the pigheaded Cedric, Ivanhoe disguises himself at his father's estate.

4   Let the games begin: Ivanhoe must defeat the aristocratic Sir Brian de Bois-Guilbert (George Sanders) to save Rebecca from certain death.

5   Clash of the Titans: The Anglo-Saxon Princess Rowena (Joan Fontaine) and the chosen people's Rebecca both have their eye on Ivanhoe – and neither intends to share.

and stuntmen as well as artistic director Alfred Junge's awe-inspiring set pieces and decor – a craft he learned at Germany's legendary UFA Studios of *Metropolis* (1927) fame during the 1920s. Among his most stunning accomplishments in *Ivanhoe* is his life-size recreation of Torquilstone Castle complete with moat; erected on the London Boreham Wood Studios' lot, the structure is besieged and stormed by Robin Hood's merry men for approximately 30 screen minutes. More than just a cavalcade of glitz and bright colors, the film's overall attention to detail is exhibited in the extensive research that went into the making of the costumes, fighting arms and sets. To bring what he intended to be – for better or for worse – an authentic rendition of 12th-century England to the screen, director Richard Thorpe hired dozens of medieval historian consultants. It all paid off in the end, literally; *Ivanhoe* was applauded with audience cheers and went on to become one of the biggest box-office hits of its day. And despite being placed at the mercy of Hollywood, the film manages to remain somewhat true to Sir Walter Scott's richly written novel. Most of the book's plotlines show up in the movie in one form or another, including the feud between the Norman upper-class and the Anglo-Saxons, subjugated since their defeat at the Battle of Hastings; Cedric's (Finlay Currie) quarrel with his son Ivanhoe, ignited by the latter's decision to

serve King Richard the Lionheart (Norman Wooland) on one of the crusades; Ivanhoe's love for Cedric's ward Rowena, or his noble effort to rescue persecuted Jews Isaac (Felix Aylmer) and his daughter Rebecca, who pines after her cavalier in vain. Notably absent from the film are Rebecca's actual unsavory prosecutors, forcing the accusation of witchcraft to come from Prince John (Guy Rolfe) and his advisors, as well as homeward-bound King Richard's comical exploits with Robin Hood's men while lying low in Sherwood Forest.

Once the conflicts have been carefully established, Thorpe competently packs the second half of the picture with action sequences. With almost no breathers, one spectacle rides on the coattails of another as we behold the tournament at Ashby, the arrest of Cedric and his entourage by the Normans, the storming of Torquilstone Castle and the decisive duel between Ivanhoe and evildoer Bois-Guilbert – so marvelously interpreted by George Sanders that one can't help but feel sorry for his character. Although this on-screen battle ended in the inevitable triumph, Hollywood finally lost the battle for audience favors just a few years later, leaving the old studio system in a shambles. *Ivanhoe* wasn't spared a bit of the humiliation; just six years later it was forced to trot onto the scene again as a short-lived TV series. In black and white.   LP

THE LITTLE WORLD OF DON CAMILLO
Le Petit Monde de Don Camillo / Il piccolo mondo di Don Camillo

1952 - FRANCE / ITALY - 107 MIN. - B & W - COMEDY

DIRECTOR JULIEN DUVIVIER (1896–1967)
SCREENPLAY JULIEN DUVIVIER, RENÉ BARJAVEL, based on the novel of the same name by GIOVANNI GUARESCHI
DIRECTOR OF PHOTOGRAPHY NICOLAS HAYER EDITING MARIA ROSADA MUSIC ALESSANDRO CICOGNINI
PRODUCTION GIUSEPPE AMATO for FRANCINEX, RIZZOLI-AMATO.

STARRING FERNANDEL (Don Camillo), GINO CERVI (Peppone), SYLVIE (Signorina Christina), VERA TALCHI (Gina), FRANCO INTERLENGHI (Mariolino), CHARLES VISSIÈRES (Bishop), LUCIANO MANARA (Filotti), ARMANDO MIGLIARI (Brusco), LEDA GLORIA (Peppone's wife), MARCO TULLI (Smilzo).

"Your hands are there for blessing, not for fighting!"

These two men have the very best intentions, but they just can't agree on the methods: the plain-talking priest Don Camillo (Fernandel) and his eternal adversary, the communist mayor Peppone (Gino Cervi). In an Italian village in the Po river valley that's still recovering from the effects of World War II, their wheelings and dealings constitute a microcosm of world politics. The Reds have won the election, and they intend to celebrate their victory in style with a big parade to the marketplace; but Don Camillo spoils the triumphal march of the proletariat by drowning out the music with his church bells. Peppone plans to build a *casa del popolo* ("House of the People"); but the priest discovers that the financial arrangements are somewhat murky, and the mayor soon thinks it wise to support a Christian kindergarten. And so it goes, with complaints to the bishop, simultaneous inaugural festivities, and (when it just can't be avoided) a good old-fashioned punch-up. Yet we shouldn't take any of this too seriously; for however doggedly they may cling to their personal ideologies, the Bolshevik and the man of the cloth

are really brothers at heart. For didn't they both fight with the partisans? Just like Peppone, Don Camillo supports the struggling tenant farmers in their dispute with the big landowners. And both of these men are quintessentially Italian characters, quite passionately stubborn in their political convictions.

The creator of Don Camillo and Peppone, the writer and journalist Giovanni Guareschi, was in fact a vehement anti-communist, but his popular tales are free from cynical barbs. Guareschi's combative spirit was matched by a warm-hearted sense of humor that's always closer to the people than to any grand political ideas. Director Julien Duvivier finds a cinematic expression for this striving for harmony in a series of tranquil long shots. The landscape of the Emilia Romagna seems as serene and unthreatening as the village itself, where the town hall and the church have stood peacefully side-by-side for centuries. On one occasion, Camillo and Peppone are having a barney under the bell-rope; but the camera tactfully averts its gaze, turning

1 In with the man upstairs: Jesus is the sole authority, who the pious Don Camillo (Fernandel) looks to for counseling. And the man of the cloak keeps the great Almighty's agenda packed.

2 Doing God's dirty work: When it comes down to the nitty-gritty, the Communist Peppone (Gino Cervi) and the Catholic Don can work together. Does it really matter that Peppone was behind the farming strike that brought them together?

3 Sadist cycles: The versed priest loves to get a rise out of the uneducated Peppone. Their next brawl is as inevitable as Don Camillo's divine scolding.

instead towards the peasants in the field, who are nonplussed to hear the bells jangling at this hour of the day.

The battle between Marx and the Bible is ultimately decided by that higher instance to whom Don Camillo constantly appeals. Though it's never quite clear whether the crucified Christ is merely an embodiment of the hot-tempered cleric's guilty conscience, the quiet voice of the Lord certainly has a moderating effect on his behavior. Don Camillo does penance for his failed attempt to bribe the referee at a soccer match between the Communists and the Catholics. Remembering the injunction to love his neighbor as himself, he abandons his plan to thrash Peppone with an oakwood cudgel. And when

he's instructed not to refuse the holy sacrament of baptism to the Red mayor's son, Don Camillo complies; after all, Peppone is actually a good Christian, even if it's a pretty well-kept secret. The child is christened Libero Antonio Camillo Lenin Peppone.

Fernandel combined a gloomy, hangdog facial expression with a tempestuous, wildly-gesturing physicality. It's said that he wore shoes too large for him in order to perfect his peculiar, characteristic gait. He is such an ideal embodiment of Don Camillo that it's hard to imagine anyone else in the role; so it's a shock to realize that the director had originally foreseen Gino Cervi in the role of the priest. This would have been extremely unfortunate casting,

FERNANDEL
(1903–1971)

The famously "horsefaced" Fernandel was one of the greatest comic character actors in the French cinema, easily ranking alongside Bourvil and Louis de Funès. Born in Marseille as Fernand Joseph Désiré Contandin, he made his first stage appearances as a child, performing in local variety shows with his father. Obliged to make his own living from an early age, he worked as a *chansonnier* in various low vaudeville theaters before making his debut in the theater as a comic actor. In 1928, his success brought him to Paris.
Very much a man of the South, Fernandel appeared in innumerable lightweight movies, frequently cast as a stereotypical, grimacing country bumpkin. He first became really popular in a series of touching adaptations of the works of Marcel Pagnol, including *Angèle*, (1934), *Regain* (1937), and *Le Schpountz* (1938). These films demonstrated his qualities as a fine tragicomic actor. He was rarely to be seen in "serious" roles, but he showed the full range of his talents in Henri Verneuil's *The Sheep has Five Legs* (*Le Mouton à cinq pattes*, 1954), in which he played six leading roles (a father and his five sons). A year before his death, he also gained accolades for his performance in the highly-praised drama *Happy He Who Like Ulysses* (*Heureux qui comme Ulysse*, 1969): in this movie, France's most famous horseface was partnered by real horses onscreen. Much loved for his tender smile and his broad grin, Fernandel died on-set while working on the last Don Camillo film. The pugnacious priest will be his most lasting legacy to the world.

"*The Little World of Don Camillo* is a film about the people, about their mentality, their faith and their religiosity. Fernandel and his pugnacious antagonist Gino Cervi are ideally cast. The wily priest has friendly chats with Jesus, is always ready to cut a deal with God, and gets reminded constantly that he can't play tricks on his Creator." *Lexikon des internationalen Films*

3

"In Don Camillo's little war, the emphasis is on the human resemblance between the priest and his Communist adversary. The film panders to our rejection of the drama and tragedy of modern politics." *André Bazin, in: Parisien libéré*

4　Italian Stalin: Peppone and his supporters celebrate his victory in the election.

5　Painting grace: Don Camillo rushes to get the
Nativity scene finished in time for Christmas.

6　Divine hands: Don Camillo and Peppone argue
about more than just the road to salvation.
The irony of Giovanni Guareschi's text was
by no means lost in the screen adaptation.

7　Church and state: Peppone exploits propaganda
for all it's worth and has the bishop (Charles
Vissières) christen the new city hall. Not to worry,
Don Camillo – you'll get to open a preschool.

as the mustachioed Cervi actually bears a pretty strong resemblance to
Stalin, who was still ruling the Soviet Union at the time. Eventually, of course,
Duvivier cast Cervi as Peppone and Fernandel as Don Camillo. Duvivier had
originally offered the role of the priest to Jacques Tati, who quite correctly
pointed out that his highly controlled comic style was hardly right for the character. And although the Italian producers were in fact most reluctant to see any
Frenchman in the role of Don Camillo, Pierre Brasseur and Jean Gabin were
also allegedly approached by Duvivier before he finally settled on Fernandel.

Times were hard in post-war Europe, and this amusing satire was a
welcome distraction. It was a box-office smash all over the continent, and it
signaled the start of one of the most popular film series of the 50s. *The Little
World of Don Camillo* was followed by *Le Retour de Don Camillo / Il ritorno
di Don Camillo* (1953), *Don Camillo e l'onorevole Peppone* (1955), *Don
Camillo … Monsigneur! / Don Camillo monsignore ma non troppo* (1961) and
Don Camillo en Russie / Il compagno Don Camillo (1965). These later films,
however, only occasionally recalled the charm of the original.

LIMELIGHT

1952 - USA - 140 MIN. - B & W - DRAMA

DIRECTOR CHARLES CHAPLIN (1889–1977)
SCREENPLAY CHARLES CHAPLIN **DIRECTOR OF PHOTOGRAPHY** KARL STRUSS **EDITING** JOE INGE **MUSIC** CHARLES CHAPLIN
PRODUCTION CHARLES CHAPLIN for CELEBRATED PRODUCTIONS, UNITED ARTISTS.

STARRING CHARLES CHAPLIN (Calvero), CLAIRE BLOOM (Thereza, "Terry"), BUSTER KEATON (Calvero's partner /
Old Comedian), SYDNEY CHAPLIN (Neville), NORMAN LLOYD (Bodalink), MARJORIE BENNETT (Mrs. Alsop),
WHEELER DRYDEN (Doctor / Clown), NIGEL BRUCE (Mr. Postant), BARRY BERNARD (John Redfern),
LEONARD MUDIE (Doctor).

ACADEMY AWARDS 1972 OSCAR for BEST MUSIC (Charles Chaplin, Ray Rasch, Larry Russell).

"It's the tramp in me."

London, 1914: Calvero (Charles Chaplin) was once a famous clown, a popular star of the music halls, but those days are long gone. Calvero has grown old, and his gags just aren't funny any more, so these days he's spending much more time in pubs than in theaters. Everything changes when he meets Terry (Claire Bloom), a former dancer who is paralyzed. After persuading the girl not to commit suicide, he "adopts" her and helps her to rediscover her love of life. In the process, the comedian seems to rediscover himself. But as Terry recovers from her illness and starts a successful career as a ballerina, Calvero is forced to recognize that his art is now a thing of the past. Terry loves Calvero and wants to marry him, though she's also in love with a composer (Sydney Chaplin) who's more her own age. Calvero leaves her and goes back to his roots as a small-time performer with a bunch of street musicians. Terry finds him and helps him achieve one final triumphant performance. As the audience cheers and applauds, Calvero suffers a heart attack and dies behind the scenes.

Like every late work by a great artist, *Limelight* looks back, takes stock and says farewell. The London depicted in this film was constructed in the studio, and it shows the city as Chaplin must have experienced it in his youth: a Victorian metropolis poised on the edge of the modern era. Calvero can feel the approaching change. According to Chaplin, the character was based on his own father, a popular vaudeville artist who eventually succumbed to the bottle. But in essence, *Limelight* is a melancholy self-portrait. It reflects both the humiliating decline in popularity Chaplin had suffered in America, and his private happiness with a wife almost 40 years his junior. And it's significant that this is the first of Chaplin's films in which he appears without make-up – *Limelight* shows us the man without the mask, so to speak.

The cast list also makes it clear what a personal film this was. Besides his son Sydney, four other Chaplin children – including Geraldine – and a half-brother appeared before the camera; and in one brief shot, even

Chaplin wife Oona can be identified as a double of Claire Bloom. He also persuaded several actors from the silent-film era to take part, and this indicates a further dimension of the movie: Chaplin's coming-to-terms with his status as a white-haired monument of cinematic history.

For while Calvero bears the traits of the aged Chaplin, the clown he plays is clearly based on the figure that made Chaplin world-famous: though the hat and the moustache may be a little different, the baggy pants, the too-tight jacket and the walking stick are trademark attributes of the Little Tramp. So it's no surprise that Calvero's flea-circus number is also borrowed from an earlier Chaplin movie.

In their form, too, Calvero's performances are also reminiscent of Chaplin's silent-era work. The use of a notably static camera reinforces the old-

"In Claire Bloom, Chaplin has found one of his loveliest leading ladies and an actress of lyric grace. Chaplin's own acting now and again glimmers with the poignancy of his beloved little tramp." *Time Magazine*

1   Send in the clowns: Calvero's (Charles Chaplin) glory days may be over, but young Terry's (Claire Bloom) dancing career has only just begun.

2   A May-December romance: *Limelight* is also a personal reflection on Chaplin's much-publicized marriage to Oona, who was 40 years his junior.

3   At home with Mrs. Danvers: The good Mrs. Alsop (Marjorie Bennett) has no intention of cowing down to her new young mistress.

4   Old pros: *Limelight* features slapstick veterans Charles Chaplin and Buster Keaton recreating their silent-era magic. It is the only film in which the actors appear side by side.

fashioned, anachronistic quality of these scenes. There's no doubt that this is a thoroughly intentional ploy, for the "performance" scenes are fully integrated into the rest of the film, and they reflect the state of Calvero's soul. Filled with self-doubt, the clown goes through routines that are quite oppressively unfunny; for the more stubbornly the spectators refuse to applaud, the harder he strains to win their approval. Chaplin's performance makes this horrible tension brilliantly clear.

So the final gala is all the more glorious, featuring Chaplin side-by-side with his great comic antithesis, Buster Keaton. This was the one and only time the two masters of silent comedy appeared on stage together, and it's clearly the highpoint of the film. Their grandiose slapstick number – a

grotesque concert, in which the instruments are smashed up with anarchic glee – is not merely a personal triumph for Calvero, but a celebration of the art of comic mime.

With *Limelight*, Chaplin took a stand against the transience of movie-making fashions and demanded respect for what he and others had achieved for the cinema and cinemagoers in previous years. For four decades, he had been writing film history. In the America of Senator Joseph McCarthy, though, there was little chance for a free spirit like Chaplin: following an unprecedented campaign of persecution by right-wing circles, he left the U.S. immediately after completing the film.

JH

CHARLES CHAPLIN His pants were too baggy, his jacket too tight and his shoes enormous; he sported a battered bowler hat, a strange little moustache, and a walking stick. The Little Tramp waddled his way across the silver screen – and his creator became the most famous man in the world.

Charles Spencer Chaplin (b. 1889 in London, d. 1977 in Corsier-sur-Vevey, Switzerland) grew up in the poorest of circumstances. He gained his earliest stage experience as a child in various London musical halls, and in 1913 he moved to Hollywood. Very quickly, he was on his way to becoming the world's most popular slapstick comedian. Almost from the start, Chaplin directed his own films; and from 1919 onwards, after he had co-founded United Artists, he also became his own producer. As his popularity grew, Chaplin developed the desire to move his audiences rather than merely amusing them. In this respect, *The Kid* (1920) was the first in a series of great silent film comedies, including *The Gold Rush* (1925), *The Circus* (1928) and *City Lights* (1931). In *Modern Times* (1936), Chaplin focused more strongly than hitherto on social issues; this movie shows him as the Tramp for the last time, and marked his farewell to the silent film. After *The Great Dictator* (1940), his daring and delightful Hitler parody, Chaplin's fortunes in America began to decline. A dubious paternity case was brought against him and he was subjected to a massive campaign of harassment because of his allegedly socialist views. In 1952, after completing *Limelight*, Chaplin finally saw no other choice than to leave the United States for Europe, where he made two more films. In 1972, Hollywood made a gesture towards reconciliation by presenting him with an Oscar for his life's work. Three years later, the Queen awarded him a knighthood.

THE CRIMSON PIRATE

1952 - USA - 105 MIN. - COLOR - PIRATE MOVIE, COMEDY

DIRECTOR ROBERT SIODMAK (1900–1973)
SCREENPLAY ROLAND KIBBEE DIRECTOR OF PHOTOGRAPHY OTTO HELLER EDITING JACK HARRIS MUSIC WILLIAM ALWYN
PRODUCTION HAROLD HECHT, BURT LANCASTER for WARNER BROS.

STARRING BURT LANCASTER (Vallo), NICK CRAVAT (Ojo), EVA BARTOK (Consuelo), TORIN THATCHER (Humble Bellows), JAMES HAYTER (Professor Elie Prudence), LESLIE BRADLEY (Baron Don José Gruda), MARGOT GRAHAME (Bianca), NOEL PURCELL (Pablo Murphy), FREDERICK LEISTER (El Libre), ELIOT MAKEHAM (Governor).

"Believe only what you see. No, believe half of what you see."

In grand renegade tradition, Cap'n Vallo (Burt Lancaster), better known as "The Crimson Pirate," takes command of the Caribbean and the screen in this 18th-century period adventure. Facing this maritime Robin Hood is Baron Gruda (Leslie Bradley), a minion of the Spanish king who has been ordered to do whatever it takes to crush the uprisings against the crown in the island colonies. Just as Gruda's warship gains the approach on what seems to be an abandoned vessel, Vallo's crew emerges from the woodwork – literally. A short naval battle ends with the Spanish emissary's defeat, and Vallo assumes command of what proves an imperial treasure barge teeming with weapons and booty. A lucrative day's work, in principle, as Vallo intends to sell the loot to the rebellion commandos for a prince's ransom. The prospective buyers, however, are weary of doing business with an unscrupulous captain and his racketeering sea dogs. Furthermore, Baron Gruda, who hasn't yet breathed his last, thirsts for revenge. The stakes are raised when Vallo falls for Consuelo (Eva Bartok), the daughter of rebel leader El Libre (Frederick Leister), and joins the freedom fighters' cause, and soon finds himself entangled in a full-blown war.

This Technicolor spectacle is packed with daredevil massacres, surly buccaneers, and the romance of the high seas: *The Crimson Pirate* pulls out all the stops and delivers gale-force action from the word go. But best of all is the unbeatable blend of non-stop humor and death-defying stunts supplied by principle pirates Vallo, who never fails to laugh in the face of danger, and

Ojo (Nick Cravat), his mute midget sidekick, a character every bit as sly as the illustrious frontman. If you're guessing Lancaster and Cravat's pairing was the product of fluke Hollywood casting, guess again. Prior to launching their movie career, the two men traveled the circus circuit as an acrobat duo. Although first reunited for the screen in Jacques Tourneur's knights and rogues picture *The Flame and the Arrow* (1950), *The Crimson Pirate* served as the vehicle Lancaster and Cravat needed to show what they were truly capable of – both in terms of acrobatics and comedy. There's simply no mistaking the pair's big-top beginnings as Vallo and Ojo leap in sync atop walls, loop backwards, swing themselves up the sides of walls with carpet poles, use baldachins as trampolines or trap soldiers with fishing nets.

Given these dazzling displays of human fireworks, it is easy to write off *The Crimson Pirate* as pure entertainment. There are, however, deeper readings. Despite the gross revisions Waldo Salt's original screenplay was subjected to (Salt was blacklisted for putative communist activity by McCarthy & Co.), there's still a smidgen of subversive ideology woven into its fabric. While any intended analogies with the imminent people's uprising undoubtedly got lost under all the layers of period garments, the on-screen revolutionaries do clearly engage in a new type of technological warfare. Movie audiences saw the characters wage war with nitroglycerine, the largely untested new wonder weapon of the depicted age, which in the 1950s, was unmistakably a reference to the widely feared Soviet nuclear threat.

"Half, indeed! Any viewer with a drop of red blood in his veins and with fond memories of the Douglas Fairbanks Sr. school of derring-do should be happy to go on this last cruise of the crimson pirate." *The New York Times*

1   Love for sail: Back-dropped by high tides and bright colors, the young Consuelo (Eva Bartok) sparks revolutionary thoughts in Captain Vallos (Burt Lancaster).

2   Bombs away! *The Crimson Pirate* was the last great splash for Hollywood pirate movies. From then on, exorbitant production costs sank almost all proposals in the genre.

3   Yo-ho-ho-ho, a pirate's life for me: Burt Lancaster (right) and Nick Cravat (left) as the Robin Hood and Little John of the Caribbean. The acrobatic duo were a circus act prior to their Hollywood debut.

4 Swashbuckling stud: The handsome Burt Lancaster drew women to the cinema like a magnet, particularly in the early 1950s.

5 A goon of globalization: Opportunists like Baron Gruda (Leslie Bradley), a loyal servant of the Spanish King, served as choice villains in classic pirate movies.

6 Bound and gagged, but not for long: Neither as a movie hero nor in real life did Lancaster let anyone do his talking for him. It's no wonder he decided to found his own production company in 1948.

Citing *The Crimson Pirate* as an example of "leftist" Hollywood film-making would be a bit of a stretch, although the picture does revel in an un-abashed anti-establishment sensibility that always favors chaos over order. Plot points are cut short, battle sequences suddenly become chase scenes, and pathos is sadistically deflated with comedy. Doubly delicious is the scene in which patrolling soldiers, lined up according to rank and file, fall like dominos – for it is a moment that captures both the picture's propensity for chaos and the painstaking precision required to stage the semblance thereof. If *The Crimson Pirate* is an undisputed highpoint in the history of pirate movies,

that honor is at least partially attributable to the picture's underlying spirit of anarchy – a spirit bound up with the utopian notion of freedom that lies at the heart of this genre. This was one of the last hurrahs in big-budget swash-buckler fantasy: with the impending collapse of the old studio system, the financial demands of productions involving ships on the open sea prevented such projects from being filmed at all. European attempts at the genre, which took off in the 1960s, often landlocked the pirates in a handful of on-shore locales and never succeeded in recreating the sense of exhilaration exuded by Hollywood's Golden Age.   UB

ROBERT SIODMAK (1900–1973)

Born in Dresden, Germany, Robert Siodmak came to the United States an exile and instantly flourished as a director of Hollywood mysteries during the 1940s. Breathing life into pictures like *Phantom Lady* (1943/44), *The Spiral Staircase* (1945), *The Killers* (1946) and *Criss Cross* (1948), he proved himself a master of film noir, infusing his work with an expressive visual aesthetic and an air of pessimism widely attributed to his German origins. Siodak first emerged on the directing scene with *People on Sunday* (*Menschen am Sonntag*, 1929), a charming summertime portrait of four young Berliners who spend an ordinary Sunday at the lake. While the film had little in common with Siodak's later work, one could deem it a precursor to contemporary, independent filmmaking methods that rely on amateur actors and existing locations. Among the famous names directly involved on the project were Siodmak's brother Curt, Billy Wilder, Fred Zinnemann, Eugen Schüfftan and Edgar G. Ulmer. Traces of the darker aesthetic Siodmak would one day shape into his Hollywood work can be seen in most of his subsequent films, including those he shot for the German Ufa Studios and, following the Nazi rise to power, those he made in France. However, one need but view the swashbuckling adventure *The Crimson Pirate*, (1952) to realize that Siodmak's talents weren't limited to film noir. After this film's completion, Siodmak returned to Europe, first resettling in France, then later in Germany. Although *The Devil Strikes at Night* (*Nachts, wenn der Teufel kam*, 1957) was nominated for an Oscar, Siodmak's later pictures hardly live up to the excellence of his earlier work. This may well be a reason why it took so long for his oeuvre to gain the critical acclaim

MONSIEUR HULOT'S HOLIDAY
Les Vacances de Monsieur Hulot

1953 - FRANCE - 89 MIN. - B & W - COMEDY

DIRECTOR JACQUES TATI (1908–1982)
SCREENPLAY JACQUES TATI, HENRI MARQUET DIRECTOR OF PHOTOGRAPHY JACQUES MERCANTON, JEAN MOUSSELLE
EDITING SUZANNE BARON, CHARLES BRETONEICHE, JACQUES GRASSI MUSIC ALAIN ROMANS
PRODUCTION FRED ORAIN for CADY FILMS, SPECTA FILMS.

STARRING JACQUES TATI (Monsieur Hulot), NATHALIE PASCAUD (Martine), MICHÈLE ROLLA (The Aunt), VALENTINE CAMAX (Englishwoman), LOUIS PERRAULT (Fred), ANDRÉ DUBOIS (Commandant), LUCIEN FRÉGIS (Hotel Proprietor), RAYMOND CARL (Waiter), RENÉ LACOURT (Strolling Man), MARGUERITE GÉRARD (Strolling Woman).

"Oh, you know him, do you? … He's quite the gentleman!"

It's summer and business is booming at a small beach resort on the French Atlantic coast. The happy vacationers succumb without protest to the usual regimentation: all meals are served strictly according to schedule, and day trips, bridge games and fancy dress parties are rigorously organized. For the hotel proprietor (Lucien Frégis) and his head waiter (Raymond Carl), it's a tough daily routine, but they're determined to ensure that everything goes according to plan. But one day, a guest appears who does not make their lives any easier: a clumsy, gangly pipe-smoker in a ridiculously dilapidated car. It's Monsieur Hulot (Jacques Tati): impeccably polite, interested in canoeing, riding, tennis and ping-pong, and a guarantee of sheer chaos wherever he goes.

Monsieur Hulot's Holiday introduced the character with whom Jacques Tati would forever be identified. In the 20 years that followed, he would go on to make three further Hulot films. Like the mailman in *School for Postmen* (*L'École des facteurs*, 1947) and the main character in *The Big Day* (*Jour de fête*, 1947/49), Monsier Hulot is a typical "little man," the very embodiment of the average petty-bourgeois. This goes a long way towards explaining the figure's popularity, for almost every viewer identifies to some extent with Hulot's clumsy attempts to negotiate the innumerable hurdles of modern life.

In his skeptical attitude towards a society "blessed" by technological progress, Tati has often been compared to Charlie Chaplin. *Monsieur Hulot's Holiday*, however, is much less preoccupied with this topic than the later Hulot movies. Here, Hulot appears without an umbrella or a raincoat, his two indispensable trademark attributes in the subsequent films, and presumably not just because the whole movie is suffused with sunshine. While on vacation at the seaside, Monsieur Hulot simply has less to do with the cold rationalized world of man-made objects than with the bizarre behavior of his fellow human beings.

Monsieur Hulot guides his viewers through a movie that serves up a loose series of independent and disparate scenes rather than telling a clearly structured story. Tati's film is governed by a "dramaturgy of the moment" which finds its material in the grotesque daily rituals of people on vacation. Certainly, it's Hulot who is mainly responsible for most of the film's gags, for it's he who constantly fouls up the aforementioned holiday rites. On one occasion, he opens the door to the hotel lobby, and a strong gust of wind

"*Mr. Hulot's Holiday* appears to be a contemporary French attempt to make silent film in sound."

Time Magazine

1   Jacques in the box: Monsieur Hulot popped onto the scene and turned Tati into an overnight sensation.

2   Where's the ladies room? Monsieur Hulot (left) stumbles upon the uncouth aspects of life at the French seaside …

3   … and makes a total ass of himself in the process.

literally blows the assembled guests off their feet. Yet the film's comic effect is not solely attributable to Tati's slapstick physical humor; it's also a result of his distanced observation of what counts as normalcy. Banal, everyday actions become strangely funny – and sometimes tragic – when repeated incessantly. Take that old couple walking on the beach: the corpulent wife strides ahead, emitting brief exclamations of delight, while her husband follows her silently a few paces behind. As she picks up seashells, she presents them to her man – who simply throws them away. The shells return to the sea with a laconic but resonant plop.

     This scene also demonstrates Tati's extraordinary use of acoustic elements. In his films, noises of all sorts play as much of a role as dialog, and they gradually take on an almost palpable life of their own. Tati uses sound to show that everything has a funny side: he takes scraps of conversation and distorts them so that they sound ludicrous; he exaggerates perfectly harmless noises until they acquire a positively uncanny quality. Thus sound becomes an element that does more than merely underscore the film or accentuate its rhythm; it's also used to strengthen the effect of particular scenes (note the curious noise made by the swinging door in the dining room).

     There's something undeniably touching about Hulot's chronically disharmonious relationship with his surroundings. By the time his vacation draws to a close, most of the other holidaymakers have rejected him. Yet the comedy survives, for although Hulot's situation may be melancholy, there's clearly no reason for despair – next year, they'll all meet again in the same place. At the end of the movie, a vaguely defiant Monsieur Hulot is sitting with the kids at the side of the street. They're busy throwing sand at each other.   UB

4

4   Plastic man: In the grand slapstick tradition of the
     silent-movie era, Tati dazzles audiences with wild
     stunts and acrobatics.

5   A most dignified pipe smoker indeed: Film critic
     Georges Sadoul named Tati the greatest French
     comic next to Max Linder.

SLAPSTICK   The term "slapstick" denotes a kind of rough physical comedy with universal appeal. It was strongly influenced by the popular comic turns in variety and vaudeville theaters, and it enjoyed its golden age in the American cinema of the silent era. Mack Sennett's Keystone Film Company, founded in 1912, had enormous success with its one- and two-act slapstick comedies. Wild chases and custard-pie fights were standard elements in these films, which were notable for their incredibly fast tempo and their frequently negligible storylines. While the anarchic humor of the Keystone comedies knew no bounds and respected no authorities, they strictly observed the convention that every character would survive the movie without serious injury – even those who had been through hell and high water. The masters of slapstick, such as Charlie Chaplin, Buster Keaton and Harold Lloyd, soon developed their own personal styles and proved that slapstick was capable of taking on subtle forms. As the second decade of the 20th century came to a close, longer features were becoming more popular, and the slapstick masters followed this tendency. As a result, plotlines began to acquire more importance, so that slapstick gradually became just one element in a variety of genres. As the era of the "talkies" began, slapstick began to lose ground. Since then, only a few comedians, such as Jerry Lewis and Jacques Tati, have explicitly embraced the slapstick tradition.

TALES OF UGETSU
Ugetsu monogatari

1953 - JAPAN - 96 MIN. - B & W - DRAMA

DIRECTOR KENJI MIZOGUCHI (1898–1956)
SCREENPLAY MATSUTARO KAWAGUCHI, YODA YOSHIKATA, based on the short stories "Jasei no In" and "Asaji ga Yado" by AKINARI UEDA DIRECTOR OF PHOTOGRAPHY KAZUO MIYAGAWA EDITING MITSUZO MIYATA MUSIC FUMIO HAYASAKA, TAMEKICHI MOCHIZUKI PRODUCTION MASAICHI NAGATA for DAIEI STUDIOS.

STARRING MASAYUKI MORI (Genjurô), SAKAE OZAWA (Tôbei), KINUYO TANAKA (Miyagi), MITSUKO MITO (Ohama), MACHIKO KYÔ (Wakasa), ICHISABURO SAWAMURA (Genichi), KIKUE MÔRI (Ukon), EIGORO ONOE (Samurai), SUGISAKU AOYAMA (OLD PRIEST).

IFF VENICE 1953 SILVER LION (Kenji Mizoguchi).

"You want to throw away your family and your life?"

Japan, 1582. Civil war is raging. Yet it's not the conflict itself, but their own greed and hubris that ruins the lives of two brothers – potter Genjurô (Masayuki Mori) and farmer Tôbei (Sakae Ozawa). Genjurô, who lives with his wife Miyagi (Kinuyo Tanaka) and his son Genichi (Ichisaburo Sawamura), has made a lot of money selling his wares at the market in the nearest town. With the soldiers gradually approaching the village, Genjurô carries on working away at his wheel, for the more he sells, the better he will be able to provide for his family. His brother, the peasant farmer Tôbei – who's married to Ohama (Mitsuko Mito) – is driven by the desire to become a samurai. The problem is he's neither of noble blood, nor can he afford to buy himself a lance and a suit of armor. When the troops finally reach the village, the brothers and their families flee across the lake in a boat, taking all the earthenware with them. Their destination is the city of Oziwa, but before long, the men and the women will be separated.

With *Tales of Ugetsu* (literally, *Tales of the Pale and Mysterious Moon after the Rain*) the great Japanese director Kenji Mizoguchi made a complex movie with a simple moral. After a realistic beginning, we find ourselves in the midst of a poetic ghost story. Genjurô, the potter, who had had visions of his wife in fine, expensive clothing, gradually drifts off into a world that's entirely of his own imagining. His yearning for wealth and happiness leads him into the arms of the lonely Princess Wakasa (Machiko Kyô), who seems to have been waiting for him all her life. She's a fragile-looking creature, beautiful and strangely attractive. Wakasa moves like a character from No Theater – a dramatic form in which ghost stories play a major role – and as

"Mizoguchi's background as a paintershows in the lovely and artful compositions he sets before the viewer."
Motion Picture Guide

1 One good turn deserves another: Pursuing his ambitions at all cost Tôbei (Sakae Ozawa) gains samurai status, only to find that his wife has sought out a life of prostitution.

2 Simple tastes: A princess takes a special interest in the modest potter, Genjurô (Masayuki Mori).

3 Shinto Circe: Princess Wakasa (Machiko Kyô) sweeps Genjurô off his feet …

4 … and makes a veritable Ulysses of him as he gradually forgets wife, child and the life he once led.

5 The exorcist: An old sage helps Genjurô (left) recognize that Princess Wakasa died long ago and that the Wasaka he lives with is just a ghost.

it turns out, this princess is indeed a ghost, for the real Wakasa died long ago. When Genjurô finally makes his way home, the irony is bitter indeed: his real wife has died in his absence.

His brother Tôbei is not much luckier. He achieves his ambition of becoming a samurai, but only by means of a trick. And when he and his men stop off for a bit of rest and recreation at a geisha house, he finds that one of the prostitutes is his own wife. After being attacked and raped by marauding soldiers, Ohama has had to sell her body to survive.

Mizoguchi and his scriptwriters combined and adapted two tales: the bittersweet story of Genjurô and the more sober and shocking tale of Tôbei. Both of them are to be found in the collection *Ugetsu monogatari*, by Akinari Ueda (1734–1809), a popular writer of ghost stories. The film is an aesthetic triumph, in which many lengthy sequences were shot without a single cut, and it's magnificently composed in high-contrast black-and-white. The camera always keeps its distance, never zooming in. Transitions are daringly managed by means of skilful cross-fades, and the camera often scans the scene from

KENJI MIZOGUCHI

Together with Akira Kurosawa and Yasujirô Ozu, Kenji Mizoguchi (1898–1956) is regarded as one of the great masters of the Japanese cinema. These were the three filmmakers who first drew the attention of Western moviegoers to the Japanese cinema, and Mizoguchi is seen as the "women's director" among them.

He was born into poverty in Tokyo in 1898, and saw his older sister sold off as a geisha. After the death of his mother, he lived with this sister for some time. It may have been these experiences that sensitized him to the feelings of women. Certainly, female figures are often at the heart of his films, and their plight exemplifies the mechanisms of social oppression. *The Life of Oharu* (*Saikaku ichidai onna*, 1952), for example, depicts the daughter of a Japanese temple official in the 17th century. She falls in love with a house servant, and both are severely punished for crossing the barriers of class. In *The Bailiff* (*Sanshô dayû*, 1954), the woman suffers a similarly grim fate: she and her two children go off in search of her husband; but in the course of her journey, she's captured, her feet are mutilated, and she is forced to become a courtesan. These two films, and *Tales of Ugetsu* (*Ugetsu monogatari*, 1953), are Mizoguchi's greatest works.

Despite suffering from poor health for most of his life, Kenji Mizoguchi made around 80 movies in total. He died of leukemia in 1956.

"At the end of *Ugetsu*, aware we have seen a fable, we also feel curiously as if we have witnessed true lives and fates."

6   The bearer of bad news: Genjurô's wife Miyagi (Kinuyo Tanaka) cherishes his craft but denounces his all-consuming ambition.

7   The spoils of conquest: Miyagi and her son are left to fend for themselves and fall into the clutches of war-faring soldiers.

8   Genjurô (right) learns firsthand that the bigger they are, the harder they fall.

9   Crib notes: The wise man's spells, etched into Genjurô's skin, have saved the samurai from Princess Wakasa's ghostly influence. But the magic characters have little impact on the living.

right to left, like the eyes of a Japanese reader. In the two wonderful tracking shots that open and close the film, the camera moves towards and away from Genjurô's village, as if the filmmaker were opening and closing a book.

These long, unedited shots – so-called "plan sequences" – are the most striking formal characteristic of Mizoguchi's films; his sympathy for women is what impresses us most about their contents. Even if men are the active protagonists of *Tales of Ugetsu*, women are clearly the stronger char-acters. Miyagi and Ohama are the embodiment of reason and good sense, and they suffer the terrible consequences of their husbands' overweening ambition. Even Princess Wakasa is an unhappy woman – so desperately un-happy in her earthly existence that she returns as a ghost to demand the happiness she missed. And in a way, Genjurô's wife Miyagi also manages to overcome mortality: for she remains with her husband as a disembodied voice, reminding him to lead a humble, hard-working life.   HJK

THE NAKED SPUR

1953 - USA - 91 MIN. - COLOR - WESTERN

DIRECTOR ANTHONY MANN (1906–1967)
SCREENPLAY SAM ROLFE, HAROLD JACK BLOOM DIRECTOR OF PHOTOGRAPHY WILLIAM C. MELLOR EDITING GEORGE WHITE
MUSIC BRONISLAU KAPER PRODUCTION WILLIAM H. WRIGHT for LOEW'S INC., MGM.

STARRING JAMES STEWART (Howard Kemp), JANET LEIGH (Lina Patch), ROBERT RYAN (Ben Vandergroat),
RALPH MEEKER (Roy Anderson), MILLARD MITCHELL (Jesse Tate).

"Money. All I care about is the money!"

Revolvers make tight shots that much tighter. Entering the film, we are confronted by the firearm of Civil War veteran and rancher Howard Kemp (James Stewart), who has been tracking cold-blooded killer Ben Vandergroat (Robert Ryan) through the Kansas wilderness for weeks. But when the trail goes cold in the mountains, Kemp calls for backup, and nabs Ben and his girl Lina Patch (Janet Leigh) with the help of old prospector Jesse Tate (Millard Mitchell) and army deserter Roy Anderson (Ralph Meeker). Howard's line of work isn't the law – it's bounty hunting, and Ben's head is sure to fetch a handsome ransom. Obliged to share the loot with a motley crew of men who helped him out, he heads for Abilene to close the deal. Ben might have lost his weapon, but he still manages to undermine the group's fragile sense of trust by promising Jesse a goldmine in exchange for his freedom. A trick, of course, and when Ben rewards him with death instead, the others are back at square one, and the killer has a hilltop advan-

tage. He almost gets away with it, until Lina switches sides, Ben takes a final bullet and falls dead into the river rapids. Roy tries to recover the body, which is the group's only claim to the reward money, and is swept away to his death: Howard, driven by a bitter, almost supernatural strength, single-handedly drags Ben's body from the water and ties it to his horse. But it is Lina who performs the true act of heroism by making a man of Howard. The two of them bury the past and Ben along with it, and set off for California to start a new life as man and wife.

Few Westerns have transformed the North American landscape from a backdrop to a central character as poetically *The Naked Spur*. Anthony Mann's dramatic cinematography is far from standard fare: the protagonists are filmed from both overhead and upward angles, and atmospheric close-ups are as content-laden as the narrative itself. Noticeably absent from this movie are all of the genre's classic devices. Time and again, the camera with-

holds a straight-on view of the actors, with some scenes filmed from behind as concealed players speak amongst themselves – a clue that the psychological make-up of the characters and the greed, envy and thirst for vengeance that have them in their grip are the true focus of the action.

It's a world where no-one is to be trusted. James Stewart plays an anti-hero, who would give anything to win back the farm his backstabbing former fiancée sold while he was in the service. Jesse suffers from gold fever and Roy systematically guns down any Indian he can lure out of hiding. Even the "virtuous" Lina rides with outlaws – not surprising considering her father was one too.

It is a film set apart by its brutal candor. Murder after murder is motivated by petty self-interest, while Howard faces up to inhuman challenges, his integrity increasingly consumed by the mission that obsesses him. By the end of the film he has become such a ruffian that it takes all the willpower he can muster not to sell his arch-enemy's corpse like a piece of meat.

The Naked Spur casts a critical eye on both Manifest Destiny and the Wild West, an era still highly revered in the 1950s. Only Lina's unconditional love is capable of saving the protagonist from the spiral of brutality and despair. In fact, *she* is the one who proposes marriage – thus supplying him with a means of escaping a life of hate, greed and unabashed violence. She is the guiding light of goodness in a film that is otherwise utterly bleak. A woman with a nondescript past, she promises release from his self-obsessed ways and a fresh start in California, a land where history has virtually no meaning. PLB

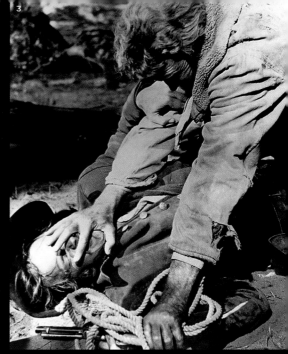

" Choosin' a way to die? What's the difference? Choosin' a way to live – that's the hard part."

Film quote: Ben Vandergroat (Robert Ryan)

1   His main squeeze: Ben Vandergroat (Robert Ryan) doesn't intend to give Lina Patch (Janet Leigh) up for some petty ransom.

2   Don't leave home without it: Howard Kemp (James Stewart) uses his universally recognized credit card whenever he wants to take charge.

3   It's just a matter of time before one of these brutes cries "Careful! You could poke somebody's eye out!"

4   Momentary emasculation: Ben is relieved of his gun …

5   … but not his cunning. And within minutes, he's the one carrying the biggest piece again.

6　Basic equipment: It's best to let your rifle do the
talking.

7　All wet or just treading water? Either way, Howard
is at the mercy of Mother Nature.

"What is the price of blood? The answer to that question only becomes clear after a gruelling psychological journey." *Les lettres françaises*

**ANTHONY MANN
(1906–1967)**

Native Californian filmmaker Anthony Mann shot a slew of film noir thrillers prior to devoting himself to the Hollywood Western renaissance of the 1950s. James Stewart, who before his collaboration with Mann was generally known for his work in light comedies, played the anti-hero on the verge of collapse in the director's *The Naked Spur* (1953) as well as in darker pieces like *Winchester '73* (1950), *Bend of the River* (1951), *The Far Country* (1954) and *The Man from Laramie* (1955). Mann's cinematic work was also characterized by elaborate on-screen acting constellations underscored by the bold visual execution of his subject matter. Shortly after Mann started work on *Spartacus* (1960), producer Kirk Douglas replaced the director with Stanley Kubrick; nonetheless, Mann got his chance at staging wide-screen ancient epics for the American cinema with smash hits

GENTLEMEN PREFER BLONDES

1953 - USA - 91 MIN. - COLOR - COMEDY

DIRECTOR HOWARD HAWKS (1896–1977)
SCREENPLAY CHARLES LEDERER, based on the stage play of the same name by JOSEPH FIELDS and ANITA LOOS
as well as the latter's novel of the same name DIRECTOR OF PHOTOGRAPHY HARRY J. WILD EDITING HUGH S. FOWLER
MUSIC LEO ROBIN, JULE STYNE, HAROLD ADAMSON, HOAGY CARMICHAEL
PRODUCTION SOL C. SIEGEL for 20TH CENTURY FOX.

STARRING JANE RUSSELL (Dorothy Shaw), MARILYN MONROE (Lorelei Lee),
CHARLES COBURN (Sir Francis "Piggy" Beekman), ELLIOTT REID (Ernie Malone), TOMMY NOONAN (Gus Esmond),
TAYLOR HOLMES (Mr. Esmond Sr.), GEORGE WINSLOW (Henry Spofford III), NORMA VARDEN (Lady Beekman),
MARCEL DALIO (Magistrate), HOWARD WENDELL (Watson).

"Don't you know that a man being rich is like a girl being pretty?"

In flashy red gowns, material girls Marilyn Monroe and Jane Russell descend an opulent staircase that just screams "showstopper." All smiles and practically bursting at the seams, the starlets sing of their modest beginnings, claiming to be "just two little girls from Little Rock."

Yeah, right. You'd have to have spent your entire life in solitary to believe that a movie starring these two Hollywood bombshells could seriously be a tale of inexperienced young innocents with wide-eyed ambitions. Then again, maybe Little Rock has a knack for producing all-American knockouts …

Howard Hawk's musical comedy *Gentlemen Prefer Blondes* is all fluff and crayola colors, set in a dimension outside of reality as we know it. This is, in fact, its great asset; for it leaves the picture a free hand in flaunting its buxom collateral. They're vamps one moment and dumb blondes the next, either dangerously close to spilling out of their frocks, or ravishingly poised and statuesque. Still, there's more to this picture than meets the eye. Beyond serving as a star vehicle for Russell and Monroe, the script, based on Anita Loos' 1925 novel of the same name, has its roots in literary satire, cleverly examining the ties between sex and money, while managing to avoid trite gender-biased pitfalls.

With a moral stance that transcends her blondeness, Lorelei Lee (Marilyn Monroe) isn't the kind of girl to go racing after her fiancé's fortune. No, she'd much rather go straight to the source and lay claim to her future father-in-law's more considerable mound of greenbacks. And the aging millionaire in question, Gus Esmond Sr. (Taylor Holmes), is left at such a loss by Lorelei's brazen overtures that he bypasses any chance he might have of throwing a monkey wrench into his gawky son's plans to marry her. Truly, when it comes down to it, the elderly tycoon shares the young vixen's shrewd worldview that beauty can be purchased with money and vice-versa – a fact of life that is neither new to the public nor to film narrative. What does, however, make for an enticing watch is the means by which the movie gives the classic gender delineation of this debate a run for its money. Lorelei exudes that patented brand of blonde naiveté that men just can't say no to, knocking them dead with the flutter of an eye or a lascivious swing of her hips. However, her premeditated manner wipes all traces of airhead from her lively laugh, her way of speaking and her body language – and the product is a tongue-in-cheek self-portrait of what would become the actress' immortal Hollywood persona. She knows just what men want, and reveals herself to them as the ultimate vision of womanliness, blonde and crisp as dawn. Indeed, her character's namesake intentionally references the Romantic Loreley character, a river mermaid who lured sailors to their death, immortalized in a poem by the German writer Heinrich Heine. Only here, instead of having the men vainly attempt to resist Lorelei's charms, they give into them wholeheartedly. While *Gentlemen Prefer Blondes* may have given Marilyn's image as a sex goddess its lasting contours, there was still something undeniably glossy and artificial about the actress at this point in her career. Monroe is as

illustrious as a storefront mannequin when she sings "Diamonds Are A Girl's Best Friend," expertly choreographed by Jack Cole – who Howard Hawks, incidentally, had direct all the musical numbers. Her feminine spin on materialism crescendos in a full-on stage show that celebrates the happy marriage of sex and money, a symbiosis in which the eternal appeal of the rocks that "don't lose their shape" is exchanged for the ephemeral charms of the female body. For while love's flame may dwindle, values measured in carats are sure to last forever.

While Lorelei relies on her feminine charms to gain access to men's checkbooks, her brunette – and more carnal – counterpart Dorothy (Jane Russell) sets her sights on the men themselves. As the two friends board the ship to Paris – the city of love – America's entire Olympic team jumps aboard

"*Gentlemen Prefer Blondes* is just pure unadulterated glamorous fun with a pair of very sexy leads and some extremely catchy tunes." Edinburgh University Film Society

1 Razzle dazzle: Dorothy (Jane Russell) and Lorelei (Marilyn Monroe), two little girls from Little Rock, are music to men's ears.

2 The love boat: Dorothy Shaw is looking for Mr. Right aboard the Good Ship Lollypop.

3 Can I borrow that? Dorothy tries on the judge's wig to see if gentlemen really do prefer blondes.

4 Tricks of the trade: Dorothy and Lorelei see through Ernie (Elliott Reid) the moment he hits the scene.

5 The French connection: Dorothy and Lorelei rekindle old ties between Little Rock and Paris.

6 Booster seat: Lorelei rethinks whether she's up for life with a young millionaire.

too, providing the film with a golden opportunity to capture muscular male bodies on camera and Jane Russell's Dorothy character to sing of her love for them. Too bad that the striking male specimens have to be in bed with lights out by 9pm. Not that this presents a real deterrent for a resourceful broad who's tough as nails. She simply goes off on the prowl when no-one's looking, unexpectedly crossing paths with private eye Ernie Malone (Elliott Reid), a man who not only has been commissioned to trail Lorelei and gather whatever dirt he can on her that could point to her infidelity, but also proves to be Dorothy's kindred spirit. Not too long thereafter, and several entanglements

later, both women have the men of their dreams eating out of the palms of their hands: Lorelei ends up with the millionaire and Dorothy gets her man. A double wedding finale serves as the perfect means to muddle Lorelei and Dorothy's individual reasons for wanting to get married, for it's a scene in which the women are dressed like twins. Even the gestures used to place the ring on the brides' fingers – synchronized to the wedding bell tune of "Diamonds Are A Girl's Best Friend" – do not differ in the least. The concluding statement simply couldn't be clearer – money and sex are two ends of the same stick.

7   Gold diggers hitting the mother load.

8   All decked out: Marilyn Monroe's ship officially
     came in with *Gentlemen Prefer Blondes*.

"*Gentlemen Prefer Blondes* is apparently predicated on the theory that if half the moviegoing population prefers Marilyn Monroe and half prefers Jane Russell, then just about everybody will be devastated by a picture that features both."

Time Magazine

**MARILYN MONROE
(1926–1962)**

She was not just one of the greatest stars to ever grace the screen, she was and is a legend in her own right. With the possible exception of Elvis Presley, no celebrity has ever come close to matching Marilyn Monroe's status as a pop icon. The magic allure she possessed pulses as much now as it did forty years ago. Her face, highlighted by a slightly opened mouth, joined the ranks of high art when Andy Warhol preserved it in silk screen, capturing the common man's imagination for all time to come.

Born Norma Jean Mortenson in 1926, she started off as a photo model before making her way to the big screen. 20th Century Fox recreated her as a naive blonde beauty they christened Marilyn Monroe. She broke through to the Hollywood A-list in 1953 with filmmaker Henry Hathaway's *Niagara*, one of the few examples of film noir shot in color. Classics like Howard Hawks' *Gentlemen Prefer Blondes* (1953) and Billy Wilder's *The Seven Year Itch* (1955) and *Some Like It Hot* (1959) consecrated her sex-goddess image. "You could earn a fortune simply by standing in front of the camera, or walking from side to side without ever needing to act," personal acting coach Michael Tschechow once told her. But a fortune wasn't what the real life Marilyn was after. Right up until the end of her life, she tried to rid herself of her vixen image and land serious roles. In 1955, she went to New York, where she met writer Arthur Miller, marrying him there the following year. It was at around this time that Monroe enrolled in an acting class with Lee Strasberg at his world famous Actors' Studio, where she studied the Stanislavski method. Her acting style had changed dramatically by the time she shot *Bus Stop* with Joshua Logan in 1956. Nonetheless, her established Hollywood image continued to persecute her. Monroe's off-screen life was as much of a nightmare as her on-screen life was glamorous. She suffered from depression and was addicted to prescription drugs. In the early morning hours of August 4th, 1962, she fatally overdosed on sleeping pills before shooting wrapped up on her final picture, George Cukor's *Something's Got to Give*. The exact circumstances of Monroe's death remain unexplained to this day.

ROMAN HOLIDAY

953 - USA - 118 MIN. - B & W - ROMANTIC COMEDY

DIRECTOR William Wyler (1902–1981)
SCREENPLAY IAN MCLELLAN HUNTER, JOHN DIGHTON, DALTON TRUMBO DIRECTOR OF PHOTOGRAPHY FRANK F. PLANER, HENRI ALEKAN EDITING ROBERT SWINK MUSIC GEORGES AURIC PRODUCTION WILLIAM WYLER for PARAMOUNT PICTURES.

STARRING GREGORY PECK (Joe Bradley), AUDREY HEPBURN (Princess Ann), EDDIE ALBERT (Irving Radovich), HARTLEY POWER (Mr. Hennessy), HARCOURT WILLIAMS (Ambassodor), MARGARET RAWLINGS (Countess Vereberg), TULLIO CARMINATI (General Provno), PAOLO CARLINI (Mario Delani), CLAUDIO ERMELLI (Giovanni), PAOLA BORBONI (Charwoman).

ACADEMY AWARDS 1953 OSCARS for BEST ACTRESS (Audrey Hepburn), BEST SCREENPLAY (Ian McLellan Hunter, Dalton Trumbo [acknowledged posthumously in 1993]), BEST COSTUMES (Edith Head).

"It's always open season on princesses."

Rome if you want to! But alas, dutiful Princess Ann's (Audrey Hepburn) good-will visit to the Italian capital is scheduled full of press conferences, endless commitments – and little sightseeing. However, there's nothing that the youthful crown princess of an unmentioned European country would like better than a day away from the burdens of royalty. And so she runs off, if only for twenty-four hours, seizing what is in all probability her only chance to do whatever her heart desires. The irony is, of course, that her Royal High-ness dreams of experiencing life as we know it, hoping to inconspicuously blend in with the commoners as she ventures out on a *Roman Holiday*.

Even half a century later, there's nothing quite like rediscovering the magic of everyday life at Audrey Hepburn's side. We dive into a pool of nos-talgia as the ingenue saunters into street cafés and down crowded boule-vards, eats *gelato* and motors through the city on a scooter; she hits the sights, slums it in pajamas, has her hair cut short and chic, and sweeps us off our feet while dancing her worries away.

For the cinema's favorite princess, it is a day of absolute liberation and first love. She crosses paths with Joe Bradley (Gregory Peck), an American journalist initially keen on writing an exclusive feature about her. And so it happens that Bradley escorts her through the city, giving the privileged young woman something her pampering advisors have continually denied her – a taste of adulthood.

Roman Holiday represented a landmark in the career of leading actress Audrey Hepburn. Prior to her breakout performance here, Hepburn's roles had consisted of bit parts in low-budget British films and, more notably, creating the title role in Colette's "Gigi" for the Broadway stage. With a little help from director William Wyler, the twenty-four-year old managed to win an Oscar for her first Hollywood engagement.

She was the talk of town practically overnight. Filmmaker Billy Wilder jok-ingly declared that Hepburn's appearance on the scene would make bosoms a thing of the past, while others declared that those blonde bombshells would soon be lining up for unemployment benefit. But closer observation of the era's cinematic trends tells a different story; Howard Hawks' *Gentlemen Prefer Blondes*, the film that launched Marilyn Monroe to the stars, premiered in the U.S. at roughly the same time as *Roman Holiday* – so much for unemployment. On the other hand, Hepburn and the somewhat similar-looking Leslie Caron got their foothold in Hollywood through romantic charm rather than erotic charge. They were pioneers who helped the girlish waif find her niche in the hearts of audiences who, until the 1950s, had really not known her at all.

Hepburn's great strength was her uncompromising naturalism in front of the camera. Combined with her style, cultivated wit and background as a trained dancer, it made her a screen sensation. When William Wyler had Briton Thorold Dickinson film Hepburn for a screen test required by Para-mount, he asked for the camera to continue shooting after the actress had finished her scene so that he could get a feel for the real Audrey. Wyler would fondly recall how utterly charming he had found her, knowing instantly that she would make a perfect princess.

There were those, however, for whom *Roman Holiday* was by no means a fairy tale. Dalton Trumbo had drafted the original treatment during the late 1940s. It was the time of the communist scare, and the House un-American Activities Committee had placed the screenwriter on their infamous blacklist. Trumbo therefore had to rely on the help of others in order to continue work-ing, having friend and fellow screenwriter Ian McLellan Hunter act as his front man. The latter then managed to sell the script to director Frank Capra, who had originally hoped to shoot the picture in 1948 with actors Elizabeth

Taylor and Cary Grant. However, this was also the year in which Capra's production company Liberty Films was bought up by Paramount; they allocated him a meager 1.5 million dollar budget for the picture which he turned down, as he revealed in his autobiography.

William Wyler was therefore called in to replace him. Principally known for directing opulent studio melodramas, he seemed a rather unlikely choice to orchestrate an on-location romantic comedy; and it had been years since he'd dabbled in the genre. Still, what Wyler did have going for him was not only an excellent rapport with the actors – Gregory Peck and Eddie Albert shine in their roles as the amiable, sloppy and at best semi-reputable reporter photographer duo – but also that certain brand of cultivation, tact and levity a European upbringing had afforded him.

"This is Wyler's first venture into comedy in many years and the switch from the heavy dramas he has been associated with since 1935 is all to the good. He times the chuckles with a never-flagging pace, puts heart into the laughs, and points up some tender, poignant scenes in using the smart script and the cast to utmost advantage." *Variety*

Wyler's classy touch is particularly evident in the artful adaptation of the picture's love story, a tale that inevitably ends in a parting of ways. The film never seduces its audience into believing that Ann and Joe's romance has any sort of long-term prospects, for there are simply too many "white lies" between them. It is the "Mouth of Truth" scene, centering on a face-shaped fountain said to bite off the hand of fibbers which best captures this central motif. Ill at ease, the princess cautiously inserts her hand into the stony mouth, but quickly withdraws it before it's too late. Equally disconcerted by the legend, Joe Bradley reaches inside the orifice and suddenly acts as if his entire arm has been swallowed by the rock spirit. At the height of the hulla-baloo, screams fade into giggles, and the couple exchange a knowing glance that confesses their mutual affection and conspiratorial bond.

Nonetheless, *Roman Holiday* saves its first moment of "consummated" intimacy for sunset. It is when Joe and Ann bid each other farewell that they are physically closest, joining in polite kisses and a friendly embrace as they thank each other for what has proved to be a perfect day.

Yet not everyone sees this moment as the height of their romance. French film critic and filmmaker Jacques Doniol-Valcroze contends that it is the press conference at the picture's conclusion that serves as *Roman Holiday's* true love scene. Here, the couple's interactions, i. e. their manner of speaking and body language are predicated by the formalities of the forum they find themselves in. Conversely, they are also free of the façades of yes-terday, meeting for the first time as what they actually are – as princess and journalist. Speaking in a language he knows she will understand, Joe assures

1   Live like common people: Audrey Hepburn says *arrivederci* to the monotony of royal life and goes on a *Roman Holiday*.

2   Who's that sleeping in my bed? It doesn't take long for journalist Joe Bradley (Gregory Peck) to figure out that it ain't Goldilocks.

3   An itch to scratch: Photographer Irving Radovich (Eddie Albert) gets nervous just being this close to a front page story. But need he remind Joe that his loyalties lie with his career first and the crown second?

4   The eleventh hour: And when the clock strikes twelve, the spell will break …

5   The perfect end to a perfect day: No passion, tears, or sorrow. Just the certainty of tomorrow.

6   When in Rome: Do as Hepburn and Peck. Get a pixie cut and zip around town on motorbike.

nn that she will not be let down by her faith in the world, thus communicat-
g that he will not turn their excursion together into a front page exclusive.
response, Princess Ann oversteps the bounds of the mass interview and, in a rather out of character gesture, shakes the hand of her journalist friend With this gentle adieu, a film marked by a grand air of whimsy ends on melancholy note with an honesty that fuels the embers of our heart.

WILLIAM WYLER
(1902–1981)

William Wyler was among the most prominent American filmmakers of his time. It was the hope of every Hollywood actor to be cast in a production by this diehard perfectionist; those graced with the honor were assured a high-profile engagement at the side of someone who knew how to make thespians shine. Indeed, more actors have won Oscars under his direction than that of any other filmmaker; and the number of those he helped get nominated is practically uncountable. Wyler himself captured a total of three golden statuettes over the course of his directing career. Born in Mulhouse, Alsace, when it was still a part of Germany, Wyler got his start in filmmaking with the help of Carl Laemmle, a cousin of his mother's. The founder of Universal Studios, Laemmle employed Willy as a clerk at the studio's New York offices. It wasn't long before the bright young man made his way to Hollywood where he would climb the rungs of the hierarchical ladder, quickly advancing from assistant-to-the-assistant all the way to the helm. His first stint as director was a two-reel Western entitled *Crook Buster* (1925). However his official breakthrough came in 1929 with *Hell's Heroes*, one of Universal's first "all-talking" outdoor productions. In 1935, Wyler signed a generous contract with Samuel Goldwyn, which gave him much creative freedom and ushered in one of the most successful periods of his career. It was during this time, which lasted up until the late 1940s, that Wyler teamed up with cinematographer Gregg Toland for dramas like *The Little Foxes* (1941) and *The Best Years of Our Lives* (1946), a picture still known for its innovative spatial staging and deep-focus photography. In 1944, Wyler shot a noteworthy documentary about a B17's last battle flight entitled *The Memphis Belle – A Story of a Flying Fortress*.
When the auteur theory took the film world by storm in the 1950s, Wyler's work began to be viewed more skeptically. Critics claimed his literary and stage cinematizations were too impersonal. French film theorist André Bazin attributed Wyler with a pretentious predilection for "psychological dramas with a socially critical undertone." Things turned around for Wyler by the end of the 1950s with more roses awaiting him at the winner's circle than ever before; the biblical epic *Ben Hur* (1959) was a phenomenal audience and critical success, distinguished with a total of 1 Academy Awards including that of Best Picture and Best Director. Wyler's career came to an end at the beginning of the 1970s. His last major hi

THE WAGES OF FEAR
Le Salaire de la peur

1953 - FRANCE / ITALY - 156 MIN. – B & W - THRILLER

DIRECTOR HENRI-GEORGES CLOUZOT (1907–1977)
SCREENPLAY HENRI-GEORGES CLOUZOT, JÉRÔME GÉRONIMI, based on the novel of the same name by
GEORGES ARNAUD DIRECTOR OF PHOTOGRAPHY ARMAND THIRARD EDITING HENRI RUST, MADELEINE GUG, ETIENNETTE MUSE
MUSIC GEORGES AURIC PRODUCTION RAYMOND BORDERIE, HENRI-GEORGES CLOUZOT for CICC,
FILMSONOR S.A., FONO ROMA, VERA FILMS.

STARRING YVES MONTAND (Mario), CHARLES VANEL (Jo), PETER VAN EYCK (Bimba),
FOLCO LULLI (Luigi), VÉRA CLOUZOT (Linda), WILLIAM TUBBS (O'Brien), DARIO MORENO (Hernandez),
JO DEST (Smerloff), LUIS DE LIMA (Bernardo), ANTONIO CENTA (Camp Chief).

IFF CANNES 1953 GRAND PRIZE (Henri-Georges Clouzot).

IFF BERLIN 1953 GOLDEN BEAR (Henri-Georges Clouzot).

"Life is like a prison."

In the dusty heat of Las Piedras, a godforsaken hole in Venezuela, life has ground to a halt. Funerals are the liveliest things that ever happen here. While the U.S.-owned Southern Oil Company exploits the country's only real resource, lost souls from every country on earth wait in Las Piedras for a chance to escape their misery. The men are like caged animals dozing in the heat; the sun glows through Venetian blinds, casting barred shadows on faces and lives ravaged by hopelessness. For 30 merciless minutes, the film shows us images of failure, ennui, emptiness, "tristesse:" in San Piedro, *rien ne va plus*. These men are shadows, living out the remainder of their time on earth.

And then one day, a glimmer of hope: an oil well has exploded, and only a second and even bigger explosion can quench the raging fires. Suddenly there's a job opportunity for men with nothing left to lose: candidates are being offered 2000 dollars a head to drive two truckloads of highly explosive nitroglycerine across nearly 200 miles of bad roads and rocky terrain to the scene of the fire. Hundreds apply for the job.

The four lucky winners are a Corsican named Mario (Yves Montand), Jo, a Parisian gangster (Charles Vanel), Luigi, an Italian bricklayer (Folco Lulli) and a German called Bimba (Peter van Eyck). What follows is a cinematic *tour de force* as the men face death at every turn, surviving narrow mountain paths, hairpin bends, potholes, falling rocks and internal conflicts, until finally one of the trucks explodes. Only Mario and Jo are left, and time has altered the balance of power: the swaggering blowhard Jo is now a miserable wreck,

while the greenhorn Mario is a man obsessed. He leaves Jo to perish, and arrives at his destination alone: but after all that, will he make it home?

Clouzot's dramaturgy is highly sophisticated, with the tension cleverly built up and characters who are precisely drawn and credibly developed. It's still miles ahead of most action movies, including William Friedkin's remake, *Sorcerer* (1977). Shot in cool black-and-white, *The Wages of Fear* avoids all sentimentality and thereby achieves a powerful emotional charge. While the early scenes are a compelling evocation of terminal stagnation, the rest of the film develops with the terrible precision and inevitability of death itself.

Filmed in the south of France (because it was cheaper), *The Wages of Fear* marks an early highpoint in a genre that didn't even exist until then: the road movie. Yet it's not a melancholy film, like many later examples of the genre, but a radically existentialist work. Disillusioned and defiant, lacking all hope and therefore ready to risk everything, these four men never stand a chance; but they use that non-existent chance for all that it's worth. Mario has saved a Metro ticket for better days; when he dies, he'll be holding it in

"An existentialist road-movie avant la lettre." *The New York Times*

1   Hotter than hell: The German Bimba (Peter van Eyck) enjoys one last cigarette before crossing the River Styx.

2   Next time, read the map more carefully.

3   Playing God: The Southern Oil Company claims any lives it wants.

4   Heat stroke: In the face of such unprecedented danger, even the level-headed Jo (Charles Vanel) can't keep his cool.

5   Running on empty: Technology is always one step ahead of the common man.

6   A laugh among friends: Folco Lulli as the terminally ill Luigi.

his hand. Jo has always wanted to know what's behind a certain fence in his corner of Paris; and he ultimately finds out: "There's nothing." Luigi has to change his life, or the dust in his lungs will kill him; his last job provides a quicker way out. Bimba (an officer in World War II, like his father) insists on shaving, even in the face of death; in the end, he's blown to smithereens. Mario is the only one who makes it through; and just as he celebrates his improbable triumph, Death comes calling, to claim his dues. To the accompaniment of Strauss' "Blue Danube," we see images of the terrible journey cross-cut with the victory celebrations in Las Piedras. The trucks and the dancers are spinning to the rhythm of a Viennese waltz, and every single one of them is heading for the same final destination.

RV

"The excitement derives entirely from the awareness of nitroglycerine and the gingerly, breathless handling of it. You sit there waiting for the theater to explode." *The New York Times*

7 Dropping like flies: With death at the door, it's hard for the men to show any humanity.

8 False idyll: Life in Las Piedras ain't all it's cracked up to be. Anyone who gets his hands on cash ships out before he's through counting it.

9 Take these broken wings: Local hussy Linda (Véra Clouzot) sets her sights on Mario (Yves Montand), the only man who doesn't treat her like the plague. In truth, she is the only person left who is capable of demonstrating genuine emotion.

CHARLES VANEL
(1892–1989)

By the 1950s, Charles Vanel was already a Grand Old Man of the French cinema. Born in Brittany, his original plans for a career at sea were dashed by his near-sightedness. So he became an actor, arriving at the movies via Sacha Guitry's traveling theater. In the 20s, he was a popular Romantic leading man, as in René Clair's *La Proie du vent* (1926). In 1928, he played Napoleon in the German production *Waterloo*. In the 50s, he appeared in a number of socially critical thrillers, in which he embodied a range of shady, taciturn characters. For these compellingly understated performances, he received several acting awards. Towards the end of his working life, he delighted moviegoers and critics as the state prosecutor Varga in the silent sequences of the Mafia film, *Illustrious Corpses*, a.k.a *The Context* (*Cadaveri eccellenti / Cadavres exquis*, 1976). It was a return to the roots of the cinema. With over 100 films in a career spanning 70 years, Charles Vanel had stamped his name indelibly on the history of the movies.

FROM HERE TO ETERNITY

⬆︎⬆︎⬆︎⬆︎⬆︎⬆︎⬆︎⬆︎⬆︎

1953 - USA - 118 MIN. - B & W - DRAMA, WAR FILM

DIRECTOR FRED ZINNEMANN (1907–1997)
SCREENPLAY DANIEL TARADASH, based on the novel of the same name by JAMES JONES
DIRECTOR OF PHOTOGRAPHY BURNETT GUFFEY EDITING WILLIAM A. LYON MUSIC GEORGE DUNING (background music),
JAMES JONES, FRED KARGER, ROBERT WELLS (Song: "Re-Enlistment Blues")
PRODUCTION BUDDY ADLER for COLUMBIA PICTURES CORPORATION.

STARRING BURT LANCASTER (Sergeant Milton Warden), MONTGOMERY CLIFT (Private Robert E. Lee Prewitt),
DEBORAH KERR (Karen Holmes), DONNA REED (Alma Burke), FRANK SINATRA (Private Angelo Maggio),
PHILIP OBER (Captain Dana Holmes), MICKEY SHAUGHNESSY (Sergeant Leva), ERNEST BORGNINE
(Sergeant James R. "Fatso" Judson), JACK WARDEN (Corporal Buckley), JOHN DENNIS (Sergeant Ike Galovitch),
BARBARA MORRISON (Mrs. Kipfer).

ACADEMY AWARDS 1953 OSCARS for BEST FILM (Buddy Adler), BEST DIRECTOR (Fred Zinnemann),
BEST SUPPORTING ACTOR (Frank Sinatra), BEST SUPPORTING ACTRESS (Donna Reed),
BEST ADAPTED SCREENPLAY (Daniel Taradash), BEST CINEMATOGRAPHY (Burnett Guffey),
BEST EDITING (William A. Lyon), and BEST SOUND (John P. Livadary).

"If a man don't go his own way, he's nothin'."

They said it couldn't be done. To adapt James Jones' controversial bestseller for the screen was such a risky undertaking that many dubbed it "Cohn's Folly," after the legendary chief of Columbia Pictures, Harry Cohn. The problem was simple: the book dealt with adultery, prostitution and alcoholism, and thus broke practically every taboo in the Production Code. To add insult to injury, it cast a very cold eye on the Army, which it depicted as riddled with corruption, brutality and the routine misuse of power. Director Fred Zinnemann solved the problem partly by watering down the plot; but much more importantly, he trumped his opponents with an unbeatable all-star cast. Featuring a host of fine character actors including Burt Lancaster, Montgomery Clift, Frank Sinatra, Deborah Kerr and Donna Reed, *From Here to Eternity* became a classic American melodrama.

A U.S. Army base on Hawaii in 1941, just before the Japanese attack on Pearl Harbor: Private Robert E. Lee Prewitt (Montgomery Clift) has had himself transferred from the Music Corps to the infantry. After he refuses to join the boxing team, Captain Holmes (Philip Ober) makes his life hell. Only the "perfect soldier" Sergeant Warden (Burt Lancaster) and the joker Angelo Maggio (Frank Sinatra) have any sympathy for the stubborn, tight-lipped Prewitt. But Warden is reluctant to step out of line, for he's having an affair with Holmes' frustrated wife Karen (Deborah Kerr); and when Angelo courageously takes Prewitt's side in a fight, he just ends up sharing the guy's punishment.

Even outside the barracks, egos are rampant. In a nightclub (a brothel in the original novel, of course), the military males jostle and fight for alpha

1   The riptides of love: Sergeant Warden (Burt
    Lancaster) and Karen Holmes (Deborah Kerr),
    the wife of his commander.

2   Lost horizons: Karen's cool façade conceals her
    thirst for a life of unabated passion and discovery.
    Her only shot at it lies in Warden's hands.

3   Take it like a man: All the discipline and
    military drills in the world can't break Prewitt
    (Montgomery Clift).

status. Here, the uniform is replaced by a Hawaii shirt, rank counts for noth-ing and alcohol takes care of the rest. This is where Prewitt falls for the "cocktail hostess" Alma (Donna Reed). But their love affair is doomed to fail: Prewitt is already married to the Army, though it's very much a love-hate relationship. Warden, too, can't bring himself to sacrifice his soldier's loyalty for the sake of an uncertain future with Karen, though passions run high; their unforgettable kiss on the beach marked the outer limits of the permissible in 1950s Hollywood. Even before the Japanese launch their attack, this minia-ture American society is already a blood-soaked battlefield.

From Here to Eternity has everything an epic movie needs: men strug-gling against the institutions that define them, women hungry for life, and a catastrophe that breaks the links they've worked so hard to forge. Yet the movie is also impressive in the way it links and balances a series of quiet dramas. Insoluble conflicts explode into violent outbursts and moments of bitter truth, yet ultimately nothing has been gained. Angelo dies of the injuries he receives at the hands of the sadistic Sergeant "Fatso" Judson (Ernest Borgnine). Prewitt himself is shot by his own comrades while attempting to aid them in battle. His tormentor Holmes is found guilty of unnecessary

"Almost a disaster film, *From Here to Eternity* juggles a large cast, multiple romances, and a sense of impending doom all the way to the big Pearl Harbor blowout."

The Village Voice

4 Fraternizing with the enemy: Prewitt and Warden get along famously outside the military arena.

5 Beyond rank and file: With the barracks behind him, the Italian-American Angelo (Frank Sinatra) knocks some sense into the smarmy Fatso (Ernest Borgnine). It's a fight with a doubly fatal outcome.

6 The third trumpet: The sounds of jazz will be long forgotten, when 'Prew' plays the Tattoo in acknowledgment of Angelo's death.

cruelty by a military tribunal, in Jones' novel, by contrast, he was actually promoted for his sins.

Some bold casting decisions breathed life into these rather rigidly defined roles. Lanky Montgomery Clift plays the lone wolf Prewitt with such conviction that it's even possible to believe he's a boxer. Elegant Deborah Kerr gives a convincing performance as a notorious adulteress. Frank Sinatra, at the nadir of his career, won an Oscar as Best Supporting Actor – without singing a note. At the time, rumors circulated that he'd gotten the role thanks to his Mafia connections, a topic dealt with in *The Godfather* (1972) nearly two decades later.

PB

7   Fireworks on the sand: The kiss that crossed all lines of Hollywood decency. At least they kept their swimsuits on.

8   Drown your sorrows: Wanted for Fatso's murder, Prewitt finds sanctuary with Alma Burke (Donna Reed). Escape, however, isn't to be theirs.

"Eyes will moisten and throats will choke when Clift plays taps on an Army bugle for his friend Sinatra after the latter dies at the hands of Ernest Borgnine, the sadist Sergeant in charge of the prison stockade. There will be cheers for Borgnine's death when Clift seeks out the killer and stabs him to death, and then sorrow when Clift goes to his own death while trying to rejoin his company when the Japs strike." *Variety*

7

FRED ZINNEMANN
(1907–1997)

Fred Zinnemann was born in Vienna, Austria, and emigrated to the U.S. in 1929. A four-time Oscar winner, he was one of Hollywood's great European filmmakers. Zinnemann, a trained cameraman, had already worked with Billy Wilder and Robert Siodmak in Berlin; but unlike them, he had the reputation of being a solid, craftsman-like director. This may derive from his decisive encounter with the documentary filmmaker Robert Flaherty, who had a lasting influence on his style. Zinnemann chose to observe people in difficult situations. In 1944, he directed his first major feature, *The Seventh Cross*, based on the novel by Anna Seghers. The film depicts the fate of a fugitive from a concentration camp, and it garnered much acclaim. It was followed by *The Search* (1948), starring the exciting new discovery Montgomery Clift. Zinnemann and his cast and crew worked among the bombed-out ruins of post-war Germany.

A thread that runs through all his films is the moral dilemma faced by a protagonist who's forced to act. The best example of this motif is Gary Cooper's lonely struggle as the sheriff of a frightened small town community in *High Noon* (1952). Along with *From Here to Eternity* (1953), this atypical Western is regarded as one of his most successful films. Zinnemann examined similar conflicts in *The Men* (1950), with Marlon Brando as a wounded war veteran, and *The Nun's Story* (1959), starring Audrey Hepburn as the doubt-plagued Sister Luke. He crowned his career with two literary adaptations that were showered with prizes and accolades: *A Man for All Seasons* (1966) and *Julia* (1977).

REAR WINDOW

954 - USA - 112 MIN. - COLOR - THRILLER

DIRECTOR ALFRED HITCHCOCK (1899–1980)
SCREENPLAY JOHN MICHAEL HAYES, based on the short story *IT HAD TO BE MURDER* by CORNELL WOOLRICH
DIRECTOR OF PHOTOGRAPHY ROBERT BURKS EDITING GEORGE TOMASINI MUSIC FRANZ WAXMAN PRODUCTION ALFRED HITCHCOCK
for PATRON INC., PARAMOUNT PICTURES.

STARRING JAMES STEWART (L. B. Jeffries), GRACE KELLY (Lisa Carol Fremont),
WENDELL COREY (Lieutenant Tom Doyle), THELMA RITTER (Stella), RAYMOND BURR (Lars Thorwald),
JUDITH EVELYN (Miss Lonelyheart), ROSS BAGDASARIAN (Songwriter), GEORGINE DARCY (Miss Torso),
IRENE WINSTON (Mrs. Thorwald), SARA BERNER (Woman on the fire escape),
FRANK CADY (Man on the fire escape).

"We've become a race of Peeping Toms."

A heat so thick you could cut it with a knife has taken hold of New York and claimed it as its own. Among those feeling the burn is L. B. Jeffries (James Stewart), a temporarily wheelchair-bound photographer cooped up in his apartment after a spot of bad luck. The shot pans over his right leg, locked in place from hip to toe by a cast, past a broken camera, until finally arriving at a photograph of the disabling incident – a car race that ended in a wreck. Hitchcock's careful arrangement of objects breathes life into the frames of *Rear Window*. Here, shots read like still-life paintings, with another showing a sandwich and an ordinary glass of milk positioned near a large pair of binoculars on top of a table. These are the articles that help Jeffries pass the time now. For in his immobilized state, the photographer keeps his eagle eye in form by indulging in a rather deviant pastime – peering into his neighbors' apartments and their private lives.

The bits of business he observes in his own backyard keep Jeffries' mind occupied and far away from the issue plaguing his soul – namely the question of marriage. Lisa Carol Fremont (Grace Kelly), a fashion designer as affluent as she is attractive, has her sights set on marching him to the altar.

Jeffries, however, has his doubts. He tells himself that she's just too good for him, and doubts whether she can adapt to his lifestyle as a globetrotting photographer? But before long, convalescent Jeffries begins to take a particular interest in an apartment opposite his, and a chain of mysterious events from within distract him and Lisa from the problem at hand.

Just a few windows away, salesman Lars Thorwald (Raymond Burr) and his crabby, bedridden wife (Irene Winston) maintain an unhappy marriage marked by constant bickering. Then one day Mrs. Thorwald isn't there anymore, and hubby starts behaving strangely, sporadically leaving and reentering the apartment one stormy night with an unwieldy looking suitcase. On account of the facts, one can't help but wonder whether Thorwald has conveniently disposed of his wife.

Hitchcock once said that he would have liked to stage one of his movies in a phone booth. Although he personally never followed through on the idea, it has since been adapted for the screen by filmmaker Joel Schumacher (*Phone Booth*, 2002). Hitchcock did, however, direct two pieces that unfold within claustrophobic spaces. *Rope* (1948) plays out entirely within a New

GRACE KELLY
(1929–1982)

An actress falls in love with an aristocrat, marries him and becomes the regent of a small European principality. It may sound like something only Hollywood could dream up, but it was a real chapter in Grace Kelly's life. While filming Hitchcock's *To Catch a Thief* (1955) on the French Riviera, the young actress met Prince Rainier of Monaco and within a year she was Princess Gracia Patricia. It seemed the fairy-tale ending to a bright albeit short film career. The runway model got her start in Hollywood with a minor role in the drama *Fourteen Hours*. In her second film, the Western classic *High Noon* (1952), Grace played opposite former silver-screen great Gary Cooper. He was to be the first in a series of Hollywood legends she would play opposite – names like Clark Gable, Bing Crosby, Ray Milland, Cary Grant and James Stewart. *Rear Window* (1954), starring Jimmy Stewart, washed away any doubt as to whether the young beauty was just a passing fancy. Kelly was as much an actress as she was a ravishing superstar, and she proved it that same year as *The Country Girl* in which she plays wife to Bing Crosby's suffering alcoholic character. It was a performance that won Kelly her sole Oscar. The list of prominent directors she collaborated with includes Fred Zinnemann (*High Noon*) and John Ford (*Mogambo* (1953). However it was Alfred Hitchcock who loved her most. On three occasions the British filmmaker elevated her ice-cold allure to heights no other actress ever managed to attain. In her final Hitchcock film, *To Catch a Thief*, she played an elegant society woman with a flair for adventure and a sizzling erotic charge. After making Prince Rainier's acquaintance she appeared in *High Society* and *The Swan*, her two final Hollywood pictures; fittingly, she assumes the part of a princess in the latter. Her glamorous 1956 marriage to Prince Rainier was like a fairy tale come true. The news that buzzed through the world on September 14th, 1982 announcing that Grace Kelly had lost her life in a freak car accident at the age of fifty-two was equally unreal. Several details of the tragedy remain unexplained to this day.

picture never ventures beyond the housing complex where Jeffries resides, with most of the shots constrained to his interior living space, and only a handful reaching past to the outside world "confronting" him, i.e. the apartments of the tenants across the way.

Hitchcock turns this seemingly straightforward set-up into a rich, cinematic investigation that operates on multiple levels at once. Brilliantly acted and deliciously scripted, *Rear Window* emerges as the suspense-filled story of a photographer – a career voyeur if you will – for whom mere observation becomes a life-threatening pastime.

A closer reading of the film reveals clear parallels between the things Jeffries observes and his own life. Indeed, the episodes Jeffries witnesses in

"The hero is trapped in a wheelchair, and we're trapped too — trapped inside his point of view, inside his lack of freedom and his limited options." *Chicago Sun-Times*

1   Material witnesses: She's in textiles and he's in traction. James Stewart and Grace Kelly make quite the couple in *Rear Window*.

2   Right in their own backyard: Lisa (Grace Kelly) can't decide whether the wheelchair bound

L.B. Jeffries (James Stewart) is really on to something or just stir crazy.

3   Sticking his foot out: Heat, boredom and incapacitation have turned photographer Jeffries into a regular Peeping Tom and professional busybody.

4   A spotless case: If Jeffries can't convince Lisa and his maid Stella (Thelma Ritter, left) of what he's seen, his neighbor across the way might make a clean sweep of things.

5 Chutes and ladders: From togetherness and isolation, to newlyweds and broken families, Jeffries witnesses all of life's highs and lows from the comfort of his own home.

6 Viewfinders: "I just wonder whether it's really all that moral to spy on a guy with a telescope and a pair of binoculars," says Stella the maid, housekeeper & voice of reason.

"Hitchcock often oversold *Rear Window* as an experience of 'delicious terror,' but it's also a subtle romantic comedy. The terror comes as much from the film's claustrophobia ... as its suggestion of the inevitability of incidental invasions of privacy." *San Francisco Examiner*

his courtyard are unique vignettes on love which comment on his personal fear of commitment. We see the newlyweds who while away the hours in bed; the scantily clad dancer who receives numerous gentleman callers; and Miss Lonelyheart, who in her eternal solitude sets the table for company she knows isn't coming. And then there are the Thorwalds – at each other's throats often enough to almost warrant Mr. Thorwald doing in the little Mrs.

These manifold tales of loneliness and togetherness, of sharing a life as opposed to merely sharing a living space, are the physical manifestation of the fears racing through Jeffries' mind. And he feels a particular bond to Mrs.

Thorwald, who is confined to her bed much in the same way as the photographer is to his wheelchair.

There is also a third storyline woven into the movie's fabric that one could describe as a litmus test. By acting as her invalid boyfriend's spy and snooping through the Thorwalds' apartment, Lisa demonstrates just how adventurous she can be. The sophisticated blonde beauty thus proves herself well-suited for a life at go-getter Jeffries' side. It's no fluke that by the end of the picture the one-time proponent of dresses and high heels is seen sporting jeans and sneakers.

HJK

CREATURE FROM THE BLACK LAGOON

1954 - USA - 79 MIN. - B & W - HORROR FILM

DIRECTOR JACK ARNOLD (1916–1992)
SCREENPLAY HARRY ESSEX, ARTHUR A. ROSS, MAURICE ZIMM DIRECTOR OF PHOTOGRAPHY WILLIAM E. SNYDER
EDITING TED J. KENT MUSIC HENRY MANCINI, ROBERT EMMETT DOLAN, MILTON ROSEN, HANS J. SALTER,
HERMAN STEIN PRODUCTION WILLIAM ALLAND for UNIVERSAL INTERNATIONAL PICTURES.

STARRING RICHARD CARLSON (David Reed), JULIE ADAMS (Kay), RICHARD DENNING (Mark Williams),
ANTONIO MORENO (Carl Maia), NESTOR PAIVA (Lucas), WHIT BISSELL (Thompson), BERNIE GOZIER (Zee),
HENRY A. ESCALANTE (Chico), RICOU BROWNING (Creature in the water), BEN CHAPMAN (Creature on land).

"It sounds incredible, but it appeared to be human!"

In the uncharted regions of the Amazon, a research team makes a startling discovery. For millions of years, an anomaly – part man, part sea creature – has been nesting in the tropic waters. Now, at long last, scientists have stumbled upon what they believe to be the missing link between humanity and fish-kind! Efforts to trap it are foiled, not by the beast, but by conflicting human interests. David (Richard Carlson) is concerned about the ramifications of removing the amphibian from its natural habitat. But recognition-hungry Mark (Richard Denning) wants to unveil it – dead or alive – for all mankind to behold. Oblivious to the internal squabbles, the creature from the black lagoon has taken a fancy to David's fiancée, Kay (Julie Adams). It climbs aboard the research boat every chance it gets in the hopes of sweeping the beautiful woman off her feet with its slippery fins. Each time, it leaves the vessel empty-handed, but not before killing a member of the crew out of sexual frustration.

Creature from the Black Lagoon has all the ideal B-movie ingredients: barely passable acting, wooden dialog about human nature, and, above all else, a factory-assembled icky goon. Teenagers everywhere raced to the drive-in to see Universal's latest contribution to the hall of monster classics. The star, a top-heavy oaf with lobster claws on land, yet a regular ballerina underwater, proved immensely popular with audiences, supplying the studio with a generation successor to hits like Frankenstein (1931) and The Mummy (1933). The stuntman in the ever-so-imaginative black rubber and latex wetsuit saved the company a bundle on special effects expenditures. After all, who needs stop-motion photography when you can see scaly flippers flop-ping through the Amazon? And who needs the Amazon when you can shoot the picture in a Florida swamp for less than half the price?

A cut and paste plot ensured that the film wouldn't create any other sort of industry upsets. There isn't a trace of any globally dire issue akin to a nuclear threat, something that later inspired numerous other works of B-movie movie aficionado Jack Arnold, such as Tarantula (1955) and The Incredible Shrinking Man (1957). Instead, the picture follows in the formulaic footsteps of great horror flicks like King Kong, and is nothing more than a rehashed telling of "Beauty and the Beast." The scantily clad Kay plays the pivotal role of flaunting her figure and screaming at the top of her lungs whenever the creature surfaces – and rest assured she's always the first to spot him. Meanwhile, the men are busy at work, trying to one up each other as hunters: Mark develops a newfangled water harpoon, and David, in a stroke of genius, comes up with a method of anesthetizing all the river's plant life (whatever that's supposed to accomplish). Four indigenous men lose their lives helping them, and the fifth, a Caucasian, finally moves the research team to emotion.

This enduring vision of all things trashy exhibits an ounce of taste in the staging of a few select scenes. Kay's bathing excursions, accompanied by the occasional crocodile and lovesick monstrosity, are filmed from below with an underwater lens. It makes for the same winning suspense that Jaws (1975) would capitalize on twenty years later. Taken by her swimming technique, the creature shadows Kay in what looks like an erotically charged, synchronized Olympic routine. But minutes later, it is disgusted after she shamelessly contaminates its beautiful abode with a cigarette butt.

1 Leapin' latex: No-one can make the crowd go wild like this grandaddy of horror.

2 Missing link or science project gone awry? And why do its fingers seem to twitch whenever the lovely Kay (Julie Adams) is around?

3 Finger-lickin' good: Why should the scientists fear the creature when it only seems to eat dark meat?

"The underwater scraps between skin divers and the pre-historic thing are sure to pop goose pimples on the susceptible fan, as will the close-up scenes of the scaly, gilled creature." *Variety*

Like some sixty-odd movies filmed in 1953 and 1954, including Arnold's debut feature *It Came from Outer Space* (1953), *Creature from the Black Lagoon* was shot in 3-D, a nifty trend that ended with the advent of the CinemaScope format. Here, however, it proves especially impressive during the graceful underwater sequences. Furthermore, it stunningly enhances the faux Amazon jungle as it brings the viewer into close contact with the gruesome beast lurking in these shimmering black streams. What Jack Arnold can really take pride in is that despite being hokier than hokey this classic B-movie is expertly edited to a suspense-packed seventy-nine minutes, entirely free of drag time. The much beloved badman of the Southern swamplands resurfaced in two sequel projects, *Revenge of the Creature* (1955) and *The Creature Walks Among Us* (1956).   PB

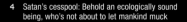

4 Satan's cesspool: Behold an ecologically sound being, who's not about to let mankind muck up his lagoon. Lady-kind is another matter altogether …

**RICOU BROWNING
(b. 1930)**

Will the real creature from the black lagoon please stand up? Difficult, as horror fans all over the world continue to argue over who holds the title. Ben Chapman wore the scaled rubber-suit on land, and Ricou Browning sported it in the water. The creature itself remains one of the cinema's all-time most popular monsters. The role demanded that Browning hold his breath for up to four minutes at a time. In 2003, the two men saw each again for the first time since the shoot at the Creaturefest in Wakulla Springs, Florida: Chapman resurfaced a party animal, whereas Browning had clearly devoted his life to other interests. Born in Florida in 1930, Browning entered the work force as a rescue diver and aquatic show producer. His film career began with *Creature from the Black Lagoon* (1954) and continued to flourish well after the picture's spawn had come and gone. Browning is the creator of the hit TV series *Flipper* (1964–68), for which he also served as director, writer and producer. He tried his hand at children's films time and again, active on projects like *Salty* (1975) – the tale of a sea lion. Browning kept to the water throughout his professional life in Hollywood, whether as a stuntman, stunt coordinator or, most often, as an underwater cameraman. He showed his gusto in the field as the director of the underwater sequences in the James Bond film *Thunderball* (1965), and recreated the magic 20 years later for the remake *Never Say Never Again* (1982/83).

THE SEVEN SAMURAI
Shichinin no samurai

954 - JAPAN - 206 MIN. - B & W - DRAMA

DIRECTOR AKIRA KUROSAWA (1910–1998)
SCREENPLAY SHINOBU HASHIMOTO, HIDEO OGUNI, AKIRA KUROSAWA DIRECTOR OF PHOTOGRAPHY ASAKAZU NAKAI
EDITING AKIRA KUROSAWA MUSIC FUMIO HAYASAKA PRODUCTION SOJIRO MOTOKI for TOHO COMPANY LTD.

STARRING TAKASHI SHIMURA (Kambei Shimada), TOSHIRÔ MIFUNE (Kikuchiyo), YOSHIO INABA (Gorobei Katayama),
SEIJI MIYAGUCHI (Kyuzo), MINORU CHIAKI (Heihachi Hayashida), DAISUKE KATÔ (Shichiroji),
ISAO KIMURA (Katsushiro Okamoto), KEIKO TSUSHIMA (Shino), KAMATARI FUJIWARA (Manzo),
YOSHIO TSUCHIYA (Rikichi), BOKUZEN HIDARI (Yohei).

IFF VENICE 1954 SILVER LION (Akira Kurosawa).

"We won, and yet we lost."

The most celebrated of all samurai films is an epoch-making masterpiece, yet it's also a highly untypical example of this most Japanese of genres. Never before had a camera got so close to these proud warriors, and no previous filmmaker had burdened them with such a menial task as the defense of an impoverished village. So it's little wonder that Akira Kurosawa was decried in his homeland as a "Westernized" director. Such suspicions were apparently confirmed when John Sturges produced his celebrated Western remake, *The Magnificent Seven* (1960). For his own movies, Kurosawa himself had in fact borrowed from John Huston, a director he revered; and in using a modern film language understandable anywhere in the world, he had made a clean break with the strict formalism of Japanese cinema. The result, despite its enormous length, is an enthralling drama. The film builds up slowly, closely observing the complex society it depicts before climaxing in a thrilling extended battle scene. Almost in passing, Kurosawa invented the modern action movie.

This may also be the first film to show how a team of men is assembled in order to carry out a perilous mission. The poverty-stricken inhabitants of a rural village are being ruthlessly exploited by a gang of brutal bandits: year in, year out, they are robbed of the fruits of their labor as soon as the harvest is in. Clearly, they need help; but what could possibly motivate a proud samurai to risk his life for three bowls of rice a day? The village elder has a piece of advice for the desperate peasants: "Find some hungry samurai!" And here it becomes apparent that Kurosawa will submit the classical image of the samurai to a rigorous historical revision; for indeed, by the end of the 16th century, after a serious of grueling civil wars, the Japanese warrior class was clearly on its way out.

The villagers take enormous pains to find the right man, and eventually come up with Kambei (Takashi Shimura), an old warrior who has lost more battles than he's won. Five further samurai follow in their turn, each of whom has different abilities and different motivations for taking on the job. The last

1   Simply dashing: Takashi Shimura as the wise Kambei in one of the best action films of all time.

2   Crazy for you: Kurosawa favorite Toshirô Mifune as fearless funny-face Kikuchiyo.

3   The Lord is my shepherd: Country bumpkin Kikuchiyo is sly when it comes to getting a rise out of others, but he doesn't know how to gain recognition as a samurai for the life of him.

man to come on board is Kikuchiyo (Toshirô Mifune), a boastful drunk who joins the team without even being asked to do so.

As they prepare for battle, the tension grows inexorably. The director's modus operandi resembles that of the wise old warrior Kambei, who draws a map of the territory and starts to keep a tally sheet of the enemy's losses. In a series of calm, unhurried long shots, Kurosawa's camera measures out the village and the paths leading in and out of it. These sequences are complemented by some unforgettable close-ups – portraits of people determined to face the inevitable. As the samurai and the villagers interact and quarrel, Kurosawa shows them in all their human strength and weakness. Here too,

the film is wonderfully intelligent in the way it follows this complex, developing relationship. In the eyes of the warriors, the villagers are mean, cowardly and distrustful; to them, in their turn, the samurai seem arrogant and capricious. The gulf between them has an almost tragic quality, and only Kikuchiyo is capable of bridging it occasionally: with his mad jokes, this trickster figure soon has the village youngsters on his side. Kikuchiyo is himself the son of a peasant, and only this enables any kind of interaction between the two castes. Yet although his humble origins make him the best man to train the villagers – who have no experience of fighting whatsoever – his lack of blue blood also means he can never become a real samurai. The role of

THE WAY OF THE SAMURAI   The samurai were members of a medieval warrior caste who gained enormous repute in the service of powerful warlords. Their code of honor, Bushido (The Way of the Warrior), demanded they show absolute loyalty and unshakeable resolve. In the 1930s, the samurai were first depicted in the Japanese cinema. After World War II, however, Bushido came to be associated with Kamikaze pilots and Japanese nationalism, and the American occupying forces instituted a temporary reduction in the number of historical dramas ("jidai-geki") produced there. With *Rashomon* (1950) and *The Seven Samurai* (*Shichinin no samurai*, 1954), Akira Kurosawa became a master of the genre, although his mythical dramas focused mainly on the "ronin," those vagabond samurai without a master who became such a social problem in 17th-century Japan. Kurosawa's international success led to a lively cross-pollination between the Japanese cinema and the American and European Western. Traces of the samurai can be found in *The Magnificent Seven* (1960) and *A Fistful of Dollars* (*Per un pugno di dollari*, 1964). Their technique of sword fighting also had a clear effect on George Lucas' *Star Wars* trilogy (1977, 1980, 1983); indeed, the very name of the Jedi Knights is derived from the word "jidai-geki". In the 70s, the samurai warrior transmogrified into the Yakuza, the Japanese gangster. Both figures were immortalized in countless B-movies, and these had a huge influence on Western directors. The most original appropriations of the samurai / yakuza motif are to be found in Jean-Pierre Melville's *Le Samouraï* (1967), Jim Jarmusch's *Ghost Dog: The Way of the Samurai* (1999) and Quentin Tarantino's *Kill Bill: Vol. 1* and *Vol. 2* (2003, 2004).

Many characters die in *The Seven Samurai*, but violence and action are not the point of the movie. It is more about duty and social roles. The samurai at the end have lost four of their seven, yet there are no complaints, because that is the samurai's lot. The villagers do not want the samurai around once the bandits are gone, because armed men are a threat to order. That is the nature of society."

Chicago Sun-Times

Kikuchiyo is performed wonderfully by Toshirô Mifune, Kurosawa's favourite actor.

The battle is won, at enormous cost. Four samurai, men of the sword, have suffered the terrible indignity of being killed by guns. Kurosawa however – who was himself the scion of a renowned samurai family – achieves an unparalleled creative synthesis of the traditional and the modern. It's not just the exactness of the characterization that makes this film so memorable, but its sheer visual brilliance. The expressive power of the high-contrast black-and-white photography is amplified by its exceptional depth of focus; phases of quiet contemplativeness are perfectly balanced by dynamic, fast-cut scenes of wild squabbling and bloody battle. Kurosawa also filmed some particularly dramatic death scenes in slow motion, a technique that had a noticeable influence on Sam Peckinpah's seminal Western *The Wild Bunch* (1969).

Incidentally, Akira Kurosawa thanked John Sturges for *The Magnificent Seven* – by presenting him with a samurai sword. PB

4   Follow my leader: Many directors picked up on Kurosawa's astonishing use of slow motion for battle and action scenes.

5   Seven brides for seven samurai: Kikuchiyo relies on hair-brained antics to transcend caste parameters – with marked success.

6   Sticks and stones may break me bones: Kambei's strategy works like a charm and causes the bandits to ride straight into a trap.

JOHNNY GUITAR

1954 - USA - 110 MIN. - COLOR - WESTERN

DIRECTOR NICHOLAS RAY (1911–1979)
SCREENPLAY PHILIP YORDAN, based on the novel of same name by ROY CHANSLOR
DIRECTOR OF PHOTOGRAPHY HARRY STRADLING SR. EDITING RICHARD L. VAN ENGER MUSIC VICTOR YOUNG
PRODUCTION HERBERT J. YATES for REPUBLIC PICTURES CORPORATION.

STARRING JOAN CRAWFORD (Vienna), STERLING HAYDEN (Johnny "Guitar" Logan),
MERCEDES McCAMBRIDGE (Emma Small), SCOTT BRADY (Dancin' Kid), WARD BOND (John McIvers),
BEN COOPER (Turkey Ralston), ERNEST BORGNINE (Bart Lonergan), JOHN CARRADINE (Old Tom),
ROYAL DANO (Corey), FRANK FERGUSON (Marshal Williams).

"I've never seen a woman who was more a man."

Dressed up to the nines in black pants and leather boots, a bitchin' bad ass of the West points her gun at an assembly of human hypocrisy. Prepared to defend herself at all cost, Vienna (Joan Crawford) scans this group of "respectable citizens" from atop a staircase, narrowing her gaze on its ringleader, the wrathful Emma (Mercedes McCambridge). For it was she who gathered the town together to drive the saloon proprietress into the wilderness for subverting local will. While the collective uproar stems from Vienna's efforts to commission a controversial railroad project, Emma's resentment has a more personal root – jealousy. She's been seething on the sidelines whilst sparks fly between the man of her dreams, outlaw Dancin' Kid (Scott Brady), and Vienna. Now the two women stand face to face, nemeses in game of do-or-die. "I'm going to kill you," Emma says. "I know," answers Vienna, "If I don't kill you first."

Nicholas Ray's *Johnny Guitar* is one of the most bizarre Westerns ever filmed. It breaks down the genre's traditional barriers, not just in its extreme stylization (the film has an almost baroque veneer), but also in its reversal of gender archetypes. Women assume roles previously deemed exclusively male, while the men are little more than the objects of female desire. Despite their common ground, the two leads are wonder women determined to gain sole control of the screen: both are born heroines who are getting on in years, and both are fueled by an inexhaustible mutual hate (a constellation later emulated by Henry Terrill and Rufus Hannassey in William Wyler's *The Big Country*, 1958).

Nearing 50 at the time of the shoot, Joan Crawford plays Vienna, a woman with a brass-balls constitution and a drag queen demeanor to match. When it comes to men, she knows what she wants and just how to get it. Her saloon may be a public watering hole, but it's the place where she calls the shots, and so it's depicted as her private sphere throughout the picture. This is made strikingly clear when an unfamiliar face appears on the scene, who, although a foreign presence, isn't exactly a stranger: after a five-year

absence, Johnny Guitar (Sterling ~~ ...

enters it just as nonchalantly as he exited. The film is named after
because of the central role he plays in Vienna's heart rather than for one
see him enact in the present story. Indeed, no-one can pull at her heartstr
like Johnny. A wanted man and legendary sharpshooter, these days his h
reaches more readily for a guitar than it does for a gun, though he still k
one tucked in his saddlebag for peace of mind. There's no mistaking
Vienna views him as the proverbial "right man at the right time," some
that blinds her to the critical danger he presents. A slave to her wh
she's ready to ignore the ultimatum the town denizens have imposed
her, and chooses to stay put rather than pack up by dawn. At once, Jo
and Vienna's past has an inordinate impact on the present predicament.
rekindled love inadvertently drives the lovelorn Dancin' Kid to parta
a bank heist before skipping town. Kid's plan, however, has unantici
repercussions. Vienna just so happens to be at the bank while the ro
takes place, and the townspeople pin her with involvement in the o
A witch-hunt ensues.

While similarities abound between *Johnny Guitar* and director Nic
Ray's subsequent film, *Rebel Without a Cause* (1955), the former c
readily understood as a parable for the McCarthyism of the time. The
in which Emma and townsfolk storm Vienna's house to interrogate
without doubt one of the most riveting sequences the movie has tc
Turkey (Ben Cooper), a member of Dancin' Kid's gang and still very r
kid himself, seeks out Vienna's maternal guidance after being woun
the crime scene. But Emma's lynch mob finds him at the saloon anc

Heartstrings: Vienna (Joan Crawford) and Johnny
(Sterling Hayden) are in tune with one another.

2 Going out with a bang: During a bank heist,
Dancin' Kid shoots at chickens who dare cross
the road and emerges from the scene as the
town scapegoat.

3 How about a quick spin? Vienna would rathe
be luckier in love than games of chance.

"There's only two things in this world that a 'rea
man' needs: a cup of coffee and a good smoke."

m quote: Johnny "Guitar" Logan (Sterling Hayden)

**JOAN CRAWFORD
1904–1977**

Unlike her contemporaries Greta Garbo and Marlene Dietrich, actress Joan Crawford had no interest in preserving the youthful image that ha
her a Hollywood icon. Time and again, she exposed all the battle scars of aging to the camera and turned "revolting" into a mark of style.
her most poignant later performances – and of her entire career for that matter – was Robert Aldrich's *What Ever Happened to Baby Jane?*
a brutal satire on the flipside of stardom co-starring Bette Davis. Crawford entered show business as a dancing ingenue and exited a strik
diva. All her physical features seemed larger than life – her eyebrows, mouth, shoulders and even her gestures. It was as if she had be
destined to play self-confident, driven types – like the title role in Michael Curtiz's *Mildred Pierce* (1945), for which she won an Oscar. Borl
Fay Le Sueur, Joan Crawford stood before the camera more than 80 times during her 50 years in Hollywood. She made her screen debu
silent era, before appearing in director Harry Beaumont's *Our Dancing Daughters* (1928) and emerging as a Jazz Age icon. Under contract wi
Studios, she acted in some of the 1930s' most prominent films such as Edmund Goulding's *Grand Hotel* (1932) opposite Greta Garbo
Milestone's *Rain* (1932) as prostitute Sadie Thompson; and George Cukor's *The Women* (1939). After MGM decided Crawford was bo
poison, she found a new home at Warner Bros, where her star continued to burn up the sky throughout the 1940s. Among her most nota
formances of this era was her portrayal of the schizophrenic Louise Howell in Curtis Bernhardt's *Possessed* (1947), for which she received
nomination. Although she made fewer pictures in the 1950s, they were by no means second-rate. Nicholas Ray's *Johnny Guitar* (1954),
Crawford as a tough-as-nails saloon owner, was one of her more ambitious projects of the decade. After her death in 1977, her adopted d
Christina published *Mommie Dearest: Joan Crawford* (1979), a shockingly candid biography that transformed her public image. In 1981, Fra
adapted *Mommie Dearest* for the screen starring Faye Dunaway as a sadistic, megalomaniac Crawford. Crawford was quoted as saying

4 Throw him out with the trash! Mob cries leave Vienna powerless to help her surrogate son, Turkey (Ben Cooper).

5 Occupying Vienna: Johnny prances back into town and makes Dancin' Kid (Scott Brady) hit the road.

6 Tough Turkey: And now that he's dead, Vienna only has Tom (John Carradine) at her side.

7 Follow the bouncing bullet: "Kiss me once and kiss me twice and kiss me once again, it's been a long long time ..."

"Johnny Guitar is one of those curious composite animals, like the tiglon, the hippolope and the peccadillo, that most people would rather talk about than see. This is a crossbreed of the Western with a psychoanalytic case history. Somehow, German grand opera and just plain better-class suburbia have also slipped into the mixture." *Time Magazine*

advantage of a golden opportunity in their mission to crush Vienna. A woman on the warpath, the raven-clad mistress puts the fear of God into Turkey and forces him to testify against Vienna. The episode reaches its climax when Emma sets fire to the house, and the pathological hatred inscribed on her face takes on cataclysmic physical dimensions. There is no mistaking the fireball's Freudian correlation to Emma's repressed sexual desire. Prior to the showdown in which Vienna puts an end to her enemy's rampage – a scene thoroughly Western in its depiction – we see Emma fatally shoot the Dancin' Kid, and thus extinguish the candle on her own life's dreams. Viewed in this context, *Johnny Guitar* can be interpreted as a cinematic discourse against Puritanism. Much in the same vein as Fritz Lang's *Rancho Notorious* (1952) and Raoul Walsh's *Pursued* (1947), *Johnny Guitar* fuses elements of psycho-analysis with politics, creating what François Truffaut called a "hypnotic Western," further electrified by its dazzling use of color. Shot in Trucolor – a process that gives colors a stunningly plastic look – the film is dominated by reds and greens, with almost no trace of blue. Ray stages the picture so as to play up the colors' narrative potential, carefully assigning tones and shades to his characters while avoiding obvious leitmotifs. Just before the interrogation scene, we see Joan Crawford seated at the piano in a white dress against a glowing-orange saloon wall, and we sense the mayhem that is in store – a brilliant example of emotional anticipation and crisp visual composition. One of the most off-beat Westerns ever made, *Johnny Guitar* is also one of the genre's most sophisticated achievements in color-coding.

KK

GODZILLA
Gojira

954 - JAPAN - 98 MIN. - B & W - SCIENCE FICTION

DIRECTOR ISHIRÔ HONDA (1911–1993)
SCREENPLAY ISHIRÔ HONDA, SHIGERU KAYAMA, TAKEO MURATA **DIRECTOR OF PHOTOGRAPHY** MASAO TAMAI
EDITING KAZUJI TAIRA **MUSIC** AKIRA IFUKUBE **PRODUCTION** TOMOYUKI TANAKA for TOHO FILM.

STARRING AKIRA TAKARADA (Hideto Ogata), MOMOKO KOCHI (Emiko Yamane),
AKIHIKO HIRATA (Dr. Daisuke Serizawa), TAKASHI SHIMURA (Prof. Kyohei Yamane),
FUYUKI MURAKAMI (Tabata), SACHIO SAKAI (Reporter Hagiwara), REN YAMAMOTO (Masaji the Fisherman),
KATSUMI TEZUKA (Reporter / Godzilla), RYOSAKU TAKASUGI (Godzilla),
HARUO NAKAJIMA (Godzilla).

"The century's most frightening monstrosity."

Crushing the maxims of 1950s science fiction, *Godzilla*'s horrors are firmly rooted in contemporary historical and scientific fact. Underwater volcanic eruptions or mines are thought to be steadily sinking fishing boats off the Japanese coast. Then a prehistoric monster sighting on the island of Odo gets paleontologist Kyohei Yamane (Takashi Shimura) and his daughter Emiko (Momoko Kochi) wondering whether something else could lie at the heart of the mystery. Their suspicions are confirmed when they arrive on Odo and are confronted by a one-hundred-foot tall radioactive reptile known as Godzilla (Katsumi Tezuka, Ryosaku Takasugi, Haruo Nakajima).

It seems that nuclear testing in the Pacific has coaxed the beast out of its submarine cavern and into the world of man, leaving Japan is at its mercy. Electric fences, bombs, machine guns and all other forms of defense are no match for Godzilla, and the island nation suddenly becomes a war zone. Those who can flee the cities in a panic, others pray they'll be evacuated. But

nuclear spitfire Godzilla can tear through even the heftiest of barriers. Tokyo is burned to a crisp, and the monster threatens to vent its fury on the rest of the world.

Volunteering at a hospital, Emiko comes face to face with Godzilla's path of mass destruction. Unable to bear the plight of her people any longer, she entrusts her lover, a member of the coastguard, with top secret information: her fiancé Dr. Daisuke Serizawa (Akihiko Hirata) has developed a deadly oxygen blaster, capable of wiping out any conceivable living organism. Despite feeling torn by the great moral obligation of implementing such a weapon, Serizawa is prepared to construct a single bomb to save the planet. He ends up sacrificing himself to kill the monster, annihilating all but a mammoth skeletal silhouette that sinks to the bottom of the ocean.

Unlike the numerous follow-ons it inspired, the original *Godzilla* has a documentary feel to it. By 1954, the United States, Great Britain and France

1   Hold on to your headbands, here comes Godzilla!   2   Lunch.   3   Kamikaze pilots: War planes are like wind-up toys in the claws of the monster.

GODZILLA MOVIES   Movie monsters, along with mythological creatures and dinosaurs, enjoyed overwhelming popularity in the 50s. Combining animation with live action, filmmakers like Ray Harryhausen shot their larger-than-life beings, which were actually model miniatures, with stop-motion photography, painstakingly integrating the beasts into the story one frame at a time. Not so *Godzilla* (*Gojira*, 1954), where an actor squeezed himself into a 100 lb. rubber monster suit. The film was such an astounding success that, to date, 24 further installments have made it to the screen. Highlights include: *King Kong vs. Godzilla* (*Kingukongu tai Gojira*, 1962), *Son of Godzilla* (*Kaijûtô no kessen: Gojira no musuko*, 1967), *All Monsters Attack / Destroy All Monsters* (*Kaijû sôshingeki*, 1968), *King Kong vs. The Bionic Monster* (*Gojira tai Mekagojira*, 1974), *GK2: Godzilla 2000* (*Gojira ni-sen mireniamu*, 1999) and most recently *Godzilla vs. Megaguirus* (*Gojira tai Megagirasu: Jii Shômetsu Sakusen*, 2000). In contrast to the original picture, subsequent adaptations were made as tongue-in-cheek B-movies. Unlike in Western monster flicks, where beasts like King Kong are meant to represent subconscious desires, the Japanese angle on the genre often depicts them as caricatures of current politicians. In later installments, Godzilla, assisted by other imaginary creatures, not only defends Japan against the sea monster Ebirah, but also against alien invaders.

Godzilla is a collective metaphor and a collective nightmare, a message film that says more than its message, that captures, with a horrified poetry, the terrors that stomped through the minds of people 50 years ago." *San Francisco Chronicle*

4   Death star: Hideto Ogata (Akira Takarada) and
     Dr. Serizawa (Akihiko Hirata) try to score a hole-
     in-one with an atomic golf ball.

5   Fishing for compliments: Dr. Serizawa's secret
     weapon turns his aquarium into dust.

6   Oh, the grass is always greener on Godzilla's
     lawn. Paleontologist (Takashi Shimura) is sick of
     models and longs for a close-up view of a real-life
     dinosaur.

7   Today Tokyo, tomorrow the world!

8   War on terror: Professor Yamane puts together
     a slideshow presentation on the anti-democratic
     menace that is out to destroy their way of life.

"This is a bad movie, but it has earned its place in history, and the enduring popularity of Godzilla and other monsters shows that it struck a chord." *Chicago Sun-Times*

had all been testing newly developed atomic weapons in the Pacific. One such American test exposed the entire crew of a Japanese fishing vessel to nuclear radiation. It is therefore no surprise that Godzilla does not stem from mythological tradition as such, but is to be seen as the embodiment of a ubiquitous, post-war atomic threat. Initially, the catastrophe is treated as environmentally related; something faceless that wreaks havoc on marine life and the water supply. Soon, however, the crisis is pegged to something more immediate; for *Godzilla* is actually a Japanese reflection on the outcome of the Second World War, and the cataclysmic violence experienced on the home front. We are shown images reminiscent of the nightly bomb raids, the flight for shelter, and the storms of poisonous black rain and nuclear fallout. A state of panic floods the streets. Crying children are stranded, forlorn fam-

ilies search frantically for missing loved ones. The battle against the unthinkable not only requires the most advanced technology and the solidarity of the Japanese people, but also a full demonstration of the nation's military muscle as tanks, aircraft, bombs and even documentary footage of Japanese soldiers practicing maneuvers. Only when Serizawa hears a song that reminds him of the victims at Hiroshima and Nagasaki does he feel compelled to build the bomb that will end the suffering. Yet the picture clearly states that only humanity is to blame for Godzilla's visit and his devastating rampage. We are left with the echo of Professor Yamane's chilling reminder that while Godzilla may be gone for now, the atomic forces that awakened him are far from being in check.

LA STRADA
La strada

1954 - ITALY - 104 MIN. - B & W - DRAMA

DIRECTOR FEDERICO FELLINI (1920–1993)
SCREENPLAY TULLIO PINELLI, FEDERICO FELLINI, ENNIO FLAIANO DIRECTOR OF PHOTOGRAPHY OTELLO MARTELLI
EDITING LEO CATOZZO MUSIC NINO ROTA PRODUCTION DINO DE LAURENTIIS, CARLO PONTI for
PONTI-DE LAURENTIIS CINEMATOGRAFICA.

STARRING GIULIETTA MASINA (Gelsomina), ANTHONY QUINN (Zampanò), RICHARD BASEHART (Matto),
MARCELLA ROVERE (Widow), LIVIA VENTURINI (Nun), ALDO SILVANI (Colombiani).

ACADEMY AWARDS 1956 OSCAR for BEST FOREIGN FILM.

FF VENICE 1954 SILVER LION (Federico Fellini).

"Zampano is here!"

When the decision was announced, the audience went crazy. One set of fans booed the other lot, and the whole thing culminated in a punch-up. Luchino Visconti's *Senso* (1954) had come away empty-handed, and Federico Fellini's *La strada* had won the Silver Lion. In the mid-50s, Italian cinema was divided into two camps: on the Left, the neorealists, whose star was gradually waning; on the Right, the conservatives, who wanted a cinema that propagated the values of Catholicism. The neorealists around Visconti saw *La strada* as an act of betrayal by their former ally Fellini; they found it abstract, individualistic, and even tainted with religiosity. As these critics saw it, *La strada* did nothing to further the cause of educating and informing cinema audiences, or did it accurately represent the real problems facing society.

It's true that *La strada* says nothing about the class struggle, and the film can indeed be interpreted religiously, as a parable about salvation. But Fellini rejected the accusation that his movie had nothing to do with reality. *La strada*, he said, most certainly did have a point to make about society, for it examined the shared experience of two individuals, and this was the very basis of any human community. Maybe it wasn't literally "a true story," said Fellini, but it was a product of his own personal reality, of his memories and feelings, which had conjured up this vision of two creatures bound together for life without ever knowing why.

"Gelsomina! Gelsomiiina! You've got to come home now!" Two girls on the beach are calling their blonde sister (Giulietta Masina), who's busy

> ## "Signor Fellini has used his small cast, and, equally important, his camera, with the unmistakable touch of an artist. His vignettes fill the movie with beauty, sadness, humor and understanding."
> *The New York Times*

1 Screen-smart sweetheart: Giulietta Masina gained international acclaim as Gelsomina. But the greatest praise came from film legend Charles Chaplin.

2 Can I tickle your pickle? Utterly naive Gelsomina is intrigued by the crude Zampanò (Anthony Quinn). All he's interested in, however, are cheap women and fast wine.

3 Creatures of the night: She's a bat, he's a beast. But by the time Zampanò realizes just how attached he is to this fragile, kooky soul he will have missed his chance with her.

4   54' Dodge Caravan: Poverty hits the open road in post-war Italy.

5   Brute force: In his autobiography, Anthony Quinn wrote that no character he ever played came closer to the real him than Zampanò.

collecting driftwood in the dunes: Zampanò (Anthony Quinn) has come to take her away. He's bought her, for 10,000 lira, and his converted motorcycle sidecar will be her future home. Zampanò is a showman, a muscleman, a one-man circus who performs his shabby show in the market squares of godforsaken villages. Gelsomina is to be his assistant, as a drummer, clown and money-collector. So she leaves her impoverished seaside home, forever.

They're an odd couple, this small, childish, naive, fun-loving young woman, who's looking forward to her life as a traveling artiste, and the crude, bear-like man who becomes her master, hardened by the streets and blind to the world around him. Years of grinding routine have made Zampanò's performances lifeless and mechanical; every time he bursts the chains on his massive, hairy chest, he utters the same tired patter for the crowd.

Gelsomina, by contrast, can't help clowning as soon she dons her hat at the correct jaunty angle, and the mere sight of a trumpet enchants her. When first presented with a drum, she immediately starts pounding away freestyle,

until she feels the sting of a blow to her bare legs – Zampanò won't tolerate indiscipline. He drills Gelsomina until she can introduce his act just the way he wants.

Zampanò is a laborer who sees his body art as nothing more than a means of earning a crust and a bottle of wine. His attitude contrasts sharply with that of Matto (Richard Basehart), whom Gelsomina and Zampanò encounter repeatedly in the course of their travels. For Matto, his high-wire act is a carefree game, and his art is indistinguishable from his life. There's something unearthly about his witty, gravity-defying performances; indeed, on one occasion, we see him in the circus ring with a pair of angel's wings on his back. So it's no wonder that he and Zampanò are sworn enemies – a rivalry that the weaker of the two will not survive.

Matto's death finally breaks Gelsomina. She could have gone with him, but she chose to stay with Zampanò, who never saw her as a wife or a woman, and who always brusquely rejected her shy attempts to support and understand him. In the dead of night, on the beach, his loneliness finally over-

"I was enthralled by the film's resolution, where the power of the spirit overwhelms brute force." *Martin Scorsese*

"It's Gelsomina's sad clown face that remains the film's most haunting image, vividly photographed in black-and-white by Otello Martelli. As French critic André Bazin pointed out, 'The Fellini character does not evolve; he ripens.' And so do his movies." *The Washington Post*

6

GIULIETTA MASINA

When Giulietta Masina visited her husband in Cinecittà, the studio workers gave a thunderous round of applause. A bunch of flowers appeared from nowhere, and work only resumed after she had taken her seat beside Fellini to watch the great man direct. Federico Fellini and Giulietta Masina were one of the most legendary couples in movie history. Under his direction, she became one of the greatest stars of the Italian cinema. Her best-known roles included the naive Gelsomina in *La strada* (1954) and the plucky prostitute in *Nights of Cabiria* (*Le notti di Cabiria / Les Nuits de Cabiria*, 1957), for which she won the Best Actress award at the Cannes festival. The critic François Truffaut was not pleased by the decision, but he was forced to agree that Giulietta Masina had marked a moment in cinema history, in a manner comparable to James Dean.

Giulia Anna Masina was born in 1920 in the province of Bologna and grew up mainly with her worldly, sophisticated aunt in Rome. She performed with theater groups and worked in radio. In 1942, she met Fellini there, and performed in a radio play he had written. She first attracted movie-goers' attention in a supporting role as a prostitute in Alberto Lattuada's *Without Pity* (*Senza pietà*, 1948); Fellini had co-written the script and also worked on the movie as an assistant. From then on, Masina worked mainly in her husband's films, from *Variety Lights / Lights of Variety* (*Luci del varietà*, 1950) to *Juliet of the Spirits* (*Giulietta degli spiriti / Juliette des esprits*, 1965). Then she retired from the movies, although she did continue to appear sporadically on TV. She later made a successful comeback in *Frau Holle* (*Perinbaba*, 1985) by Juraj Jakubisko, Fellini's *Ginger and Fred* (*Ginger e Fred / Ginger et Fred*, 1985) and *Aujourd'hui peut-être* (1991) by Jean-Louis Bertuccelli.

Giulietta Masina will go down in cinema history for her role as the puckish Gelsomina, a girl with a deep faith in the essential goodness of mankind. She died in 1994, only a few months after her husband had passed away.

6   The main attraction: Gelsomina meets the 'angelic'
     Matto (Richard Basehart) in the circus ring. But
     rather than running off with him, she runs herself
     into the ground.

7   Wrestle with the devil: Matto is Italian for loon, and
     this man's nature costs him his life.

comes him; he feels that he can feel something, and that he has lost some-thing priceless. Zampanò weeps, perhaps for the very first time in his life.

La strada is not merely a poetic social parable, not just a fairy tale in the form of a road movie. More than anything, it's a sad love story. Film critics the world over, and especially in France, celebrated this movie as "a lighthouse for the cinema" (Jacques Doniol-Valcroze), "a milestone in film history" (Georges Sadoul), "an encounter with an unknown world" (André Bazin). A world rejected by the Italian Marxists, because magic was not part of their

The surface of things is there to be penetrated, and he's determined to find the meaning that makes life worth living, however burdensome it may some-times be.

"Everything in the world is good for something," says Matto to Gelsom-ina, when the humiliations heaped on her by Zampanò almost destroy her will to live. Even stones have their part to play in the grander scheme of things. Matto picks up a stone from the ground, and says: "If this is mean-ingless, then everything else is, too – even the stars." He gives it to Gel-somina, who nods, understands, and smiles.

ON THE WATERFRONT

⛓⛓⛓⛓⛓⛓⛓⛓⛓

1954 - USA - 108 MIN. - B & W - DRAMA

DIRECTOR ELIA KAZAN (1909–2003)
SCREENPLAY BUDD SCHULBERG, based on a series of articles by MALCOLM JOHNSON
DIRECTOR OF PHOTOGRAPHY BORIS KAUFMAN EDITING GENE MILFORD MUSIC LEONARD BERNSTEIN PRODUCTION SAM SPIEGEL for
COLUMBIA PICTURES CORPORATION, HORIZON PICTURES.

STARRING MARLON BRANDO (Terry Malloy), KARL MALDEN (Pater Barry), EVA MARIE SAINT (Edie Doyle),
LEE J. COBB (Johnny Friendly), ROD STEIGER (Charley Malloy), PAT HENNING (Timothy J. Dugan),
LEIF ERICKSON (Glover), JAMES WESTERFIELD (Big Mac), TONY GALENTO (Truck), TAMI MAURIELLO (Tullio).

ACADEMY AWARDS 1954 OSCARS for BEST FILM (Sam Spiegel), BEST DIRECTOR (Elia Kazan), BEST ACTOR
(Marlon Brando), BEST SUPPORTING ACTRESS (Eva Marie Saint), BEST SCREENPLAY (Budd Schulberg),
BEST CINEMATOGRAPHY (Boris Kaufman), BEST EDITING (Gene Milford),
BEST ART DIRECTION (Richard Day).

IFF VENICE 1954 SILVER LION (Elia Kazan).

"I coulda had class. I coulda been a contender. I coulda been somebody, instead of a bum, which is what I am, let's face it. It was you, Charley."

In the New York port of Hoboken, a corrupt, racketeering union enjoys un-limited power. Day in, day out, would-be workers gather on the dockside in the early morning, hoping to acquire a day pass to earn a few dollars. The union bosses rule the roost; their word is law, and anyone foolish enough to challenge them is risking his neck. That includes the young longshoreman Joey Doyle, who's preparing to testify before the Waterfront Crime Commis-sion: the union men use Terry Malloy (Marlon Brando) to lure Doyle into a trap that costs him his life. Terry, a former boxer who runs errands for the union

boss Johnny Friendly (Lee J. Cobb), had no idea it would come to this: "I thought they was gonna talk to him", he protests. Terry Malloy is not a bad guy, but he's certainly none too bright.

He's going to have to learn to think, though. Gradually, his guilt will grow on him, and in the end, he'll even have the guts to betray his false friends to the Commission: not just Friendly himself, who has made Terry into a willing slave, but Terry's own brother Charley (Rod Steiger). But it takes two other people to persuade Terry that he owes nothing to his brother: Father Barry

"In those early films, Brando cut through decades of screen mannerisms and provided a fresh, alert, quirky acting style that was not realism so much as a kind of heightened riff on reality."

Chicago Sun-Times

1 When doves cry: Terry Malloy (Marlon Brando) doesn't get what the world's about anymore. In *On the Waterfront*, the magic of Method acting and meticulous make-up elevate Brando to new heights. Hard to believe that the role was written with Frank Sinatra in mind.

2 Harboring resentments: Corrupt waterfront boss, Johnny Friendly (Lee J. Cobb), has a cutthroat reputation.

2

3   Love birds and chicken wire: Edie Doyle (Eva Marie Saint) only sees Terry's sensitive side.

4   Stool pigeon: Johnny tries to keep Terry from squealing, but peer pressure has little immediate impact on him these days. It won't be long before he'll suffer the consequences of his actions.

5   Fishermen's grotto: Terry seems to have left his membership card at home.

(Karl Malden), a tough priest who's long wanted to see Terry wake up and cast off his servile and apathetic attitude, and Edie (Eva Marie Saint), the angelic blonde sister of the murdered man. It's Edie who awakens in Terry the conscience he never knew he had.

For both moviegoers and critics, *On the Waterfront* was a bombshell. With its razor-sharp dialog and its somber black-and-white photography, the movie radiated an unprecedented, raw authenticity. Budd Schulberg's script was no mere work of the imagination. He based it on a series of articles by the journalist Malcolm Johnson on the intolerable conditions at the New York

docks. At that time, America's unions were at the height of their power. Having once formed the vanguard in the legitimate fight for workers' interests, they had long since grown hopelessly corrupt.

But the real sensation was Marlon Brando. He had already made a huge impression in Elia Kazan's Tennessee Williams adaptation, *A Streetcar Named Desire* (1951). Now, as Terry Malloy, he showed the underlying complexity of a simple man, torn apart by conflicting feelings and powerful external forces. It was a performance that notably enhanced the good-versus-evil straightforwardness of the plot. Two scenes in particular have entered into movie

> ## "Journalism may have made these ingredients familiar and certainly more inclusive and multi-dimensional, but Mr. Kazan's direction, Mr. Schulberg's pithy and punchy dialogue give them distinction and terrific impact."
>
> *The New York Times*

6   Catch of the day: After another murder takes place, Father Barry (Karl Malden) holds an impassioned, underground sermon.

7   Left in the lurch: The staunch man of the cloth is dismayed by Terry's indecisiveness. The fact that Terry recently converted to church-going isn't about to redeem him either.

8   To the lighthouse: Harsh reality is softened by a silver lining as Edie helps Terry reach a decision.

KARL MALDEN (b. 1914)

His nose became his trademark; as a schoolkid, he had broken it playing basketball. Mladen Sekulovich, the son of Serbian immigrants in the steel town of Gary, Indiana, only began learning English at kindergarten. Though it could hardly be said that a Hollywood career was pre-ordained, Karl Malden made his way with the same iron stubbornness that characterized his roles. He had a passion for the stage, and soon joined the legendary Group Theater on Broadway, where Elia Kazan discovered him and gave him his first important film role; and for his performance as Mitch in *A Streetcar Named Desire* (1951), Karl Malden received an Oscar. After *On the Waterfront* (1954), his friend Marlon Brando cast him as the sadistic sheriff in the first film he directed: *One-Eyed Jacks* (1961). Malden was soon established as the supporting actor *par excellence*, appearing in such outstanding films as *Birdman of Alcatraz* (1962), *The Cincinnati Kid* (1965) and *Wild Rovers* (1971). But he enjoyed his greatest popularity as Detective Lieutenant Mike Stone in the TV series *The Streets of San Francisco* (1972–1977). In February 2004, this fine character actor was given a Life Achievement Award by the Screen Actors Guild.

mythology. When Eva Marie Saint inadvertently drops a glove, Brando picks it up and pulls it onto his own hand. It's a perfect example of his gift for improvisation, and it lends a whole new dimension to Terry's relationship with Edie.

The second scene, on the back seat of a taxi, includes the most famous line ever spoken by Brando: "I coulda been a contender. I coulda been somebody." Terry feels his brother has sabotaged his chances of a boxing career. Both men are now beginning to realize something important; and when Charley pulls out a gun to persuade him to keep his mouth shut before the Commission, it's an act of pure desperation. Almost tenderly, Terry brushes the gun aside, and Charley's fate is sealed. It's a scene that shows the painful loss of brotherly love and the breadth and depth of Brando's acting.

Though *On the Waterfront* is a powerful and disturbing work of art, it has also aroused controversy as an alleged attempt by the director to justify his own actions. In 1952, Elia Kazan had betrayed a large number of his communist friends to the House un-American Activities Commission. It earned him the contempt of many of his colleagues. In *On the Waterfront*, Kazan's action undergoes a radical moral revaluation. At the end of the film, the bloody and beaten Terry Malloy leads the liberated workers into the stockrooms; like a boxing trainer, Father Barry offers him passionate encouragement from the sidelines. Terry Malloy is like Christ on his way to Calvary and Elia Kazan has never denied that this tale of guilt and salvation was intended as a reflection of his own fate.

PB

THE SEVEN YEAR ITCH

1955 - USA - 105 MIN. - COLOR - COMEDY

DIRECTOR BILLY WILDER (1906–2002)
SCREENPLAY BILLY WILDER, GEORGE AXELROD, based on his play of the same name
DIRECTOR OF PHOTOGRAPHY MILTON KRASNER EDITING HUGH S. FOWLER MUSIC ALFRED NEWMAN, SERGEJ RACHMANINOV Piano concerto no. 2) PRODUCTION BILLY WILDER, CHARLES K. FELDMAN for 20TH CENTURY FOX.

STARRING MARILYN MONROE (the Girl), TOM EWELL (Richard Sherman), EVELYN KEYES (Helen Sherman), SONNY TUFTS (Tom MacKenzie), ROBERT STRAUSS (Mr. Kruhulik), OSKAR HOMOLKA (Doctor Brubaker), MARGUERITE CHAPMAN (Miss Morris), VICTOR MOORE (Plumber), DONALD MACBRIDE (Mr. Brady), CAROLYN JONES (Miss Finch), ROXANNE (Elaine), DORO MERANDE (Waitress), BUTCH BERNARD (Ricky), DOROTHY FORD (Native American), MARY YOUNG (Woman at the train station), RALPH SANFORD (Ticket checker).

"You certainly don't have to worry about me. I'm a married man. Oh, am I ever a married man! I'm probably the most married man you'll ever know."

Devil, thy name is woman. Marilyn, to be precise …

Billy Wilder pops the cork on bottled desire in *The Seven Year Itch*, a frivolous comedy about imagined adultery. New York paperback book editor Richard Sherman (Tom Ewell) has sent his wife Helen (Evelyn Keyes) and kids off to the countryside for their summer break so that he can finally relax in the comfort of his own home. But it's hot in the city, and the dog days begin to eat at Sherman even before he makes the acquaintance of his extraordinary upstairs neighbor (Marilyn Monroe). Once bitten by the lust bug, Sherman quickly feels its sting, and a nasty infection threatens his fidelity. He actively pursues the object of his affection, albeit with somewhat rusty tactics, inviting her to an evening of wine and Rachmaninov or a night out at the movies. But the sweet young thing finds the guy from downstairs far goofier than sexy – at first …

Producing a "subversive" comedy like this in morally upstanding 1950s America was nearly unthinkable. And indeed, the Hays Office, in charge of upholding the stringent Hollywood Production Code, watched *The Seven Year Itch's* shoot like a hawk. Originally, Wilder had intended to show a hairpin in the bed sheets to insinuate the protagonists' extramarital act, but the censors

"*Itch* is beautifully mounted in DeLuxe-color CinemaScope, and Marilyn Monroe's eye-catching gait is more tortile and wambling than ever." *Time Magazine*

"The Seven Year Itch is a film about adultery, but the narrow-minded morals of the 50s made sure the climax could only take place in the dreams of the audience."

...ly Wilder

...n't having any of that. A scene with Monroe in the bathtub also had to be ...And so, unlike in the stage original, the Shermans' marriage vows are ...erved. Yet these same restrictions ended up feeding Wilder's creativity ...consequentially endowing *The Seven Year Itch* with a timeless comic ...istication built on erotic innuendo and ambiguity.

The picture gained a reputation for being the crowning achievement in ...istory of the UFF a.k.a. unfinished fornication. As Mr. Sherman is robbed ...s jollies, the viewer likewise effectively endures sex with no climax; but ...ite the agony, the audience exits the movie as satisfied and blissful as ...ale protagonist.

Based on George Axelrod's play of the same name, there's no mistaking ...*Seven Year Itch's* theatrical roots; in addition to a limited number of

locations and characters, Sherman has a stagy tendency to verbalize ever... thing that's on his mind whenever he's left alone in front of the camer... Wilder tries to compensate for the lengthy monologs and occasionally st... scene-work with pointedly cinematic sequences. Such is the case at the t... of the film when we see the behavior of contemporary New Yorkers mirrore... in that of Manhattan's original Native American inhabitants; and at a lat... point in the story, Wilder exploits Sherman's daydreams as a means of pa... odying *From Here to Eternity*'s (1953) famous kiss scene. But rather tha... emerging as an autonomous adaptation, *The Seven Year Itch* reads like th... filmed version of a play, made memorable by the "situational chemistry" ... Ewell's bland, if not forgettable characterization and Monroe's unleashed se... appeal.

1. Cat's cradle: She's ready to live life, with or without her husband. Helen Sherman (Evelyn Keyes) leaves a tangled web in her wake when she and her children go off for some fun in the sun.

2. A breath of fresh air: Even if his neighbor gives him the shaft, Richard Sherman (Tom Ewell) has been awarded quite the consolation prize. Marilyn Monroe lights up every star in Hollywood in *The Seven Year Itch*.

3. Tearing at the fabric of reality: Richard starts to see every woman he meets in terms of sexual conquest.

4. Freudian slips: Among his editorial responsibilities, Richard Sherman is in charge of marketing literary classics... and it's no secret that se... ...

SECOND CHOICES Filling the lead role in *The Seven Year Itch* (1955) led to complications among screenwriter-director Billy Wilder, producer Charles Feldman and studio executive Darryl Zanuck. After Marilyn Monroe signed onto the project, the search began for her male co-star. Gary Cooper, Jack Lemmon, William Holden and James Stewart were all in talks with the studio, but Wilder had his heart set on casting the then unknown Walter Matthau in the role of Richard Sherman. Feldman and Zanuck, however, favored Tom Ewell, who had created the role on Broadway. In Cameron Crowe's book *Conversations with Wilder*, the filmmaker recalls their saying "we want to go with someone we can rely on, so we're using the man who acted in the play, Tom Ewell … The man I used in screentests was Walter Matthau. He would've been brilliant. He was a fresh face, and had never made a film before."

Billy Wilder was forced to concede to Feldman and Zanuck's better-known actor, but was still grumbling about the studio exec and producer's decision years after the project. Nonetheless, he did eventually get to shoot pictures with Matthau, including *The Front Page* (1974), *The Fortune Cookie* (1966) and *Buddy Buddy* (1981). The DVD version of *The Seven Year Itch* features bonus material with Walter Matthau's original screentests.

"Monroe plays the usual male fantasy, but you have to admit that her radiance redeems the eternal stupidity of her characters."

Brian Koller, Epinions.com

Monroe had claimed her title as *the* Hollywood sex symbol long before shooting commenced. Wilder immortalized this status with a shot that remains the one most associated with the actress, filming her above a subway grate while a car races by beneath and sends a rush of air up her dress. The scene, filmed in Manhattan at the corner of Lexington and 52nd St., not only created an uproar among the moviegoing masses, but also flushed Monroe's marriage to baseball legend Joe DiMaggio down the tubes. With his star's private life in shambles, Wilder suddenly found that Monroe had become an unreliable leading lady, relapsing into depression and substance addiction when they shot *Some Like It Hot*, 1959) together four years later, her insta-

bility sealed the fate of their professional relationship once and for all). was not altogether uncommon on the set of *The Seven Year Itch* for Wilder to go through 40 takes before getting a decent performance out of a distracted or forgetful Monroe. In fact, Wilder was so dissatisfied with the original filming of the airshaft scene that he ultimately shot it again at the studio. Not everybody was upset by this. In Cameron Crowe's book *Conversations with Wilder* the director revealed that "the technicians fought amongst themselves for the privilege of operating the ventilator from beneath the grate."

E

Love sick: It's hard to tell just which part of Richard's body is aching.

6 Hot flashes: Given the summer heat, his hot-to-trot neighbor, and the hot seat at work, it's wonder Richard needs a therapist.

6

REBEL WITHOUT A CAUSE

1955 - USA - 111 MIN. - COLOR - DRAMA

DIRECTOR NICHOLAS RAY (1911–1979)
SCREENPLAY STEWART STERN, IRVING SHULMAN, NICHOLAS RAY DIRECTOR OF PHOTOGRAPHY ERNEST HALLER
EDITING WILLIAM H. ZIEGLER MUSIC LEONARD ROSENMAN PRODUCTION DAVID WEISBART for WARNER BROS.

STARRING JAMES DEAN (Jim Stark), NATALIE WOOD (Judy), SAL MINEO (John 'Plato' Crawford),
JIM BACKUS (Frank Stark), ANN DORAN (Mrs. Stark), COREY ALLEN (Buzz Gunderson), DENNIS HOPPER (Goon),
EDWARD PLATT (Ray Fremick), FRANK MAZZOLA (Crunch), ROBERT FOULK (Gene).

"Want my jacket?"

It was a film that made history even before it hit the screens. On September 30th, 1955, just four weeks prior to its premiere, its leading actor rammed into a limousine in his silver Porsche 550 Spyder and died on impact. It was as if 24-year-old James "Jimmy" Byron Dean intended to live out the role he played in *Rebel Without a Cause*, which along with *East of Eden* (1955) and *Giant* (1956) is one of the only three films he made. *Rebel*, however, was the one that shaped Dean's image, making film and star into an inseparable whole.

The fused Dean-rebel unit is the product of Nicholas Ray's deft and compassionate directing. Ray allowed Dean and the other young actors plenty of room for improvisation. Dean's Method acting imbued the Jim Stark character with attributes above and beyond those inherent in the script, and the film became a cult classic overnight. Actor and role were one and the same, and the rebel smoker in a red windbreaker and blue jeans became synonymous with the iconography of the off-camera Dean.

Even before the opening credits, the film presents us with one of Hollywood's all-time most touching moments. On an ordinary night in small-town America, a man in a drunken stupor loses his balance and lands flat on the asphalt. That man is Jim Stark, and beside him is a wind-up monkey, whose mechanical dance is coming to a halt. Smiling gently, he tends to the toy as if it were something more. He lovingly wraps it in a crumpled sheet of newspaper, lays it down on the street as if putting it to bed, and then curls up next to it. A triumph in improvisation, the scene is indicative of the tragic plight the film's teen characters are about to endure. And, oddly enough, it was an entirely unscripted sequence.

The story centers around a day in the life of three troubled adolescents living in the suburbs of Los Angeles. A Romeo and Juliet tale in a compact time frame, the characters meet, forge ties, fall in love and are separated by death before dawn. New to town, outsider Jim Stark lays eyes on gorgeous

1   Rebel, rebel: An actor with a lifestyle as fast and furious as the Jim Stark character he played. James Dean improvises his way into the hearts of world audiences in *Rebel Without a Cause*.

2   Forever in blue jeans: plus white t-shirt and red windbreaker gives you Jim Stark traipsing through the night in patriotic colors. By contrast, Stark's rival Buzz Gunderson (Corey Allen) only lets symbol-free leather caress his loins.

3   Drunk as a skunk: A night of binge drinking lands Jim Stark in the slammer

4   The in-crowd: Buzz's gang gives Jim directions to school – via Albuquerque.

"*Rebel Without a Cause* is a reasonably serious attempt to show that juvenile delinquency is not just a local outbreak of tenement terror but a general infection of modern U. S. society." *Time Magazine*

NICHOLAS RAY (1911–1979)

He was immortalized as the man with free-flowing, cotton-white hair, clad in a fur-lined leather coat and a cowboy kerchief tied round his neck. With a patch over his right eye and a cigarillo dangling from his lips, Nicholas Ray stood before the Manhattan skyline like a supernatural spirit returned from beyond as Derwatt the painter in Wim Wenders' *The American Friend* (*L'Ami américain*, 1977), a screen adaptation of Patricia Highsmith's thriller *Ripley's Game*. It was a role that also caught Ray in the final stages of cancer, just before he lost his life to the disease in the summer of 1979. His role in this film was an allegory of his own lifework, which encompassed some thirty filmmaking projects: Derwatt, a painter publicly declared dead, sees his artwork go up in value as a result of this media-propagated hoax. At the time, Ray's best directing years were more than a decade behind him, for he virtually withdrew from the movie industry at the beginning of the 1960s.

The man born Raymond Nicholas Kienzle was Hollywood's filmmaking rebel during the 1940s and 50s, emerging as a force that refused to be tamed by the studio system. He fought vigorously against the sensibilities of big-budget Hollywood, preferring to pursue his strongly narrative and visually overwhelming obsessions that resulted in such unmistakable films as: *Knock on Any Door* (1949), a non-linear social study about a young man whose life goes off track, and *In a Lonely Place* (1950), Ray's scathing critique of Hollywood. His diversity is also exhibited in works like the polarizing city-country drama *On Dangerous Ground* (1952/53) and the sumptuously colorful Western ballad *Johnny Guitar* (1954).

Ray's pictures are distinguished by their excellent sense of color, composition and supreme mastery of the CinemaScope format. Their power had its greatest impact on voices that would rise to fame in the decade to come: the auteurs of the Nouvelle Vague, New British Cinema and New German Cinema. They took Ray's individualistic, alienated heroes as a model for personal expression in cinema itself. As Jean-Luc Godard said of him, "If cinema hadn't existed, Nicholas Ray could have invented it himself."

Judy (Natalie Wood) during his first day at school. Ignored by an uncaring father, Judy is a member of a gang of rebels led by Buzz (Corey Allen), who does his best to make Jim feel entirely unwelcome. Tagging along for the ride is the runty Plato (Sal Mineo), a child from a broken home as extraneous to his family as he is to the other kids at school, until the unbiased Jim takes him under his wing. Feeling Jim moving in on his turf, Buzz challenges him to a game of chicken that ends in the accidental death of the leader of the pack. When Jimmy turns himself in to the authorities, despite his parents' advice, his guilty conscience falls upon deaf ears.

Gang members Goon (Dennis Hopper) and Crunch (Frank Mazzola) decide to avenge Buzz's untimely demise. Things come to a head on an abandoned Hollywood estate, where Jim, Judy and Plato live out the family

"But it takes only a blink to visualize *Rebel Without a Cause* as a movie so audacious it can only be poetry, a kind of cinematic free verse whose tone saves it from caricature and the now disregarded sociological assertion that parents are entirely to blame for the alienation of kids." *San Francisco Chronicle*

5   Reckless abandon: The call of the wild ends in disaster when Buzz races over the edge of a cliff and loses his life. The incident incites a witch hunt and forever alters the course of Judy (Natalie Wood), Jim and Goon's (Dennis Hopper) lives.

"Ray's films refuse to become the stuff of cozy retrospectives, for they embody the great motive force of the era in which they were made. Only someone who lived through that period could do justice to it. This is all the more true because these films are content to be films,

6 Balancing act: Plato (Sal Mineo) performs a stunt above an empty swimming pool that reflects his precarious emotional state. He'd better watch his step, for he has neither friends nor family to break his fall.

and the truths they express are only expressible in this form. It's the images themselves that move, and move us; palpable, visible, audible traumata. Ray's restlessness created films of feverish beauty, and they still have the power to disturb." *Süddeutsche Zeitung*

life they lack at home. As the other gang members storm the premises, Plato shoots at them and flees the scene. Wanted by the police and utterly disoriented, he runs for cover at the local planetarium. Jim intends on smoothing things over for Plato, but catches up with him just as a cop shoots him down. In a gesture that recalls the movie's introduction, Jim lays Plato to rest, covering his friend's body in the red windbreaker he lent him to protect him from the cold. "He's always cold," Jim says to a stunned crowd of bystanders.

"It's the story of a generation that grew up overnight," dialog writer Stewart Stern once said of the film. *Rebel Without a Cause* is among Nicholas Ray's most outstanding pieces. Here, he addresses his audience with a blind confidence that makes for an arrestingly direct storytelling style, whose plot

"James Dean was so cool in the film that guys ached to be him and spent hours training their hair into messy pompadours. He's like a lost puppy being hunted by trouble. But he's also a cat stalking elusive prey, and he even seems at times a sinewy cool serpent ready to strike. But he's always lonely."

San Francisco Chronicle

7 Chin up: Judy's father (William Hopper) tries to act impartially towards the womanly daughter who has replaced daddy's little girl.

8 Damned if you do, and damned if you don't: Jim contemplates whether he should take on Buzz at the drag race or stay at home like a sissy.

9 That's the concussion talking: Mrs. Stark (Ann Doran) just doesn't get her son these days. Why would Jim insist on turning himself in to the authorities when he hasn't technically committed a crime?

revolves around the character of his protagonists. Ray's heroes are grating individualists, and his films spotlight an indifferent, uncompromising reality. His is a ruggedly individual style of filmmaking, which was admired and emulated by French Nouvelle Vague greats Godard, Rivette and Truffaut, as well as the German Wim Wenders.

Part of an attempt to win a new contingent of moviegoers, *Rebel Without a Cause* was one in a series of pictures that responded to the spirit of rebellion that characterised America's youth in a decade dictated by complacency. It is only fitting that movies like *Rebel Without a Cause*, Laszlo Benedek's *The Wild One* (1953) starring Marlon Brando, and Richard Brooks' *Blackboard Jungle* (1955) with Glenn Ford and Sidney Poitier captured the hearts and minds of audiences at the very moment that rock 'n' roll took the airwaves by storm.

SR

THE MAN WITH THE GOLDEN ARM

1955 - USA - 119 MIN. - B & W - DRAMA

DIRECTOR OTTO PREMINGER (1905–1986)
SCREENPLAY WALTER NEWMAN, LEWIS MELTZER, based on the novel of same name by NELSON ALGREN
DIRECTOR OF PHOTOGRAPHY SAM LEAVITT EDITING LOUIS R. LOEFFLER MUSIC ELMER BERNSTEIN PRODUCTION OTTO PREMINGER
for CARLYLE PRODUCTIONS.

STARRING FRANK SINATRA (Frankie Machine), ELEANOR PARKER (Sophie / Zosh Machine),
KIM NOVAK (Molly), ARNOLD STANG (Sparrow), DARREN MCGAVIN (Louie), ROBERT STRAUSS (Schwiefka),
GEORGE MATHEWS (Williams), JOHN CONTE (Drunky), DORO MERANDE (Vi), LEONID KINSKEY (Dominiwski),
EMILE MEYER (Detective Bednar).

"Here we go – down and dirty."

Frankie's back. One sunny morning, the bus drops him off at his familiar surroundings on a lively Chicago street. Wearing a fresh set of clothes and a smile on his face, he looks like a new man. The two suitcases at his side contain his hope for a better future, a new set of drums. Today, Frankie Machine (Frank Sinatra), the city's most able cardsharp, will renounce a life as a gambler and start anew as a jazz musician. It's a decision that has taken him six long months for to make. Months he's spent at a detox clinic, where he's learned to roll out rhythms and kicked a heroin habit. The former drug addict has shed his skin and been reborn as an optimistic young man, full of vigor; even the weight of the drums can't drain the spring in his step as he saunters down the street, the camera following behind.

"Girls, Girls, Girls," and other promises in neon greet Frankie as he walks by a nightclub, where a lady welcomes him by name. Continuing along his stroll, he makes his way past a few shabbily clad guys, a pool hall, and a policeman, who's just made an arrest and has his eye out for potential hooligans. Then, after paying the hock shop little mind, he stops abruptly in front of a bar storefront. At the counter, he spots his former drug dealer Louie (Darren McGavin) beleaguered by a swarm of lost souls: unkempt figures in tattered suits, perspiring faces, mouths missing teeth, blind eyes, and suffering alcoholics. These people are the collective behind the haphazard assortment of businesses in what is clearly a run-down part of town, an amalgamation of human misery, crime and a sinister lady luck.

Director Otto Preminger doesn't waste any time in confronting Frankie with the world he so desperately wants to escape. As we can already see, changing for the better will be no short order. As unfaltering as Frankie appeared at the bus stop just moments ago, within days he feels the burn of the old neighborhood and his iron will starts to bend. For his old buddies are adamant about making sure he remains the man he has always been: soon Schwiefka (Robert Strauss), his former boss, makes Frankie take up card playing again by means of extortion. Similarly, Frankie's wife Zosh (Eleanor

1   Marching to different drums: Zosh (Eleanor Parker) doesn't want to hear another word from Frankie (Frank Sinatra) about his musical ambitions, and he feels the same about her moaning and groaning.

2   Dealer's call: As the hottest cardsharp in town, Frankie uses his hands for more than just waving batons.

"Sensational on its first release with its cold turkey scenes."

Halliwell's Film and Video Guide

Parker) ridicules his new musical ambitions rather than offering support. Before he knows it, Frankie, overcome by deep-seated insecurities and poor moral fiber, is up to his old tricks. All his attempts at making a fresh start blow up in his face and life becomes a perpetual balancing act between bright prospects and burdensome addictions.

Preminger holds Frankie's living environment and social stratum accountable for his woes. Still, the Austrian-born director doesn't just address yet another socially critical issue in *The Man with the Golden Arm*; he challenges Hollywood taboos. Before this film, the industry's censoring mechanism, the so-called Production Code, had prohibited any direct depiction of drug abuse on screen.

Having set up a legitimate artistic debate, Preminger had hoped to circumvent the Production Code and receive a seal from the Motion Picture Association of America. Instead, his film was tabled for a year. When it finally was released as unrated, many film critics played down the controversy.

Bosley Crowther of *The New York Times* described it as, "nothing very surprising or exciting," neglecting to mention that heroin withdrawal was being presented for the first time on the American screen. Apparently, Crowther didn't listen closely to the film's soundtrack either. For despite voicing sustainable criticisms about the picture's rusty look and conventional narrative, he completely ignored Elmer Bernstein's riveting score.

While it certainly wasn't the first film to integrate jazz elements into its fabric, *The Man with the Golden Arm* redefined its role in cinema. Meticulously fused with the screen images, Bernstein's music steered the entire picture. It set the tone and tempo of the action: moving Frankie's story vigorously forward with pulsating beats, drawing it out with melodic pianos, or warning of a potential relapse with blaring trumpets.

Enhanced by Saul Bass' career-making opening credits sequence, the music creates an atmosphere of slow-building suspense and latent instability. Bass' almost minimalist design is dominated by slanted white streaks

3   When it comes to enemies, Frankie's got 'em in
    spades.

4   Not in the cards: Even Frankie gets stuck with a
    bum hand every once in a while.

5   He's up, he's down: Fingers shake as the pressure
    sets in, and beads of sweat fall from his brow. At
    this rate, Frankie need not show up to his audition
    in the morning.

against a black surface. It's zigzag logic, and much like the jazz composition, the streaks seem free-floating. This, in turn, relates back to both the protagonist's shaky existence, brought on by drug dependency, and the constant motion and intensity of a poker game. The sequence's lines are like intersecting lanes of a highway, which, when the camera pulls back, reveal a greater visual pattern – a hand dangling from the end of a broken arm.

Given the one-dimensionality of all the other characters, Sinatra's absorbing portrayal of Frankie is an outstanding performance, and certainly one of the best of his career. Sinatra totally surrenders himself to the character in

the climactic withdrawal scene. Sweating, shivering, quivering – he curls up into a ball, collapses on the floor, and then drags himself across the side of the wall in utter despair. It is a gripping illustration of a battle with drugs, accompanied by a compassionate camera that abstains from trite tricks of the trade and trusts the actor to take the reigns. From today's perspective, where drugs have become the commonplace fare of after-school specials, the film's reserve in showing life on drugs runs the risk of appearing dated. Upon closer inspection, we see it for what it is – a groundbreaking moment in cinematic history.   OK

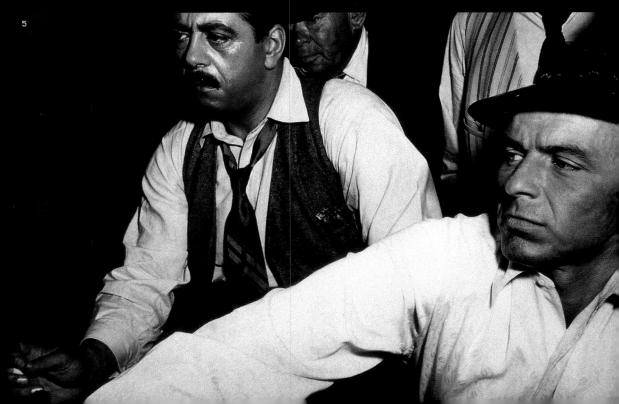

6 Pillar of strength or pillar of salt? Molly (Kim Novak) is there for Frankie when the chips are down; but he can't distinguish between friend and foe.

7 Who's got the upper hand? Zosh and Louie (Darren McGavin) compare notes on their favorite golden boy.

"The monkey never dies. When you kick him off he just hides in the corner, waiting his turn."

Film quote: Louie (Darren McGavin)

DRUGS IN FILM

Enjoying success at the box office, *The Man with the Golden Arm* (1955) was the first picture to thrust a heroin addict's life into the cinematic foreground for mainstream audiences. Prior to this picture, the movie industry had only addressed serious drug use either within the framework of mysteries as a symbol for moral decrepitude or as a plague affecting invisible minorities. Thus Hollywood often took the opportunity to show Chinese running wayward opium dens. Although such stereotypes were prevalent long after *The Man with the Golden Arm* had come and gone, the picture still raised awareness for a more unbiased depiction of drug consumption. Traditionally, most of the pictures dealing with drug abuse had focused on alcoholism, as was the case with Billy Wilder's *The Lost Weekend* (1945). This film sought to identify society as at least partially responsible for habitual drug abuse while relying on voyeuristic camera techniques to shadow the life of an addict. Two questions frequently come to the fore: who is to blame for the addict's drug dependency, and will the addict be able to free him or herself from a life of drugs?

Society re-defines the meaning of the word drug with each coming generation. Thus the hippie movement allowed marijuana to become accepted as the rugged type or free spirit's drug in films like *Easy Rider* (1969). Shortly thereafter, marijuana reached its cinematic climax in 1970s lampoon comedies à la *Cheech and Chong* (1978, 1980, 1981, 1982, 1983). The other, crasser end of the spectrum can be seen in pictures like Uli Edel's *Christiane F. – Wir Kinder vom Bahnhof Zoo* (*We Children from Bahnhof Zoo,* 1981). Mainstream movies in particular to take cheap shots at drug use or veer toward cliché in their depiction. Familiar, psychedelic color filters meant to indicate LSD use is among the most salient examples of this.

In the early 1990s, a new approach was taken toward the subject matter. Films like *Trainspotting* (1996) pair comic elements of drug culture with uncompromising realism. In *Traffic* (2000), Steven Soderbergh examines drug trafficking as a component of mainstream society, and Sam Mendes' *American Beauty* (1999) elevates the cannabis dealer to a teen status symbol, who uses drug money to escape his familiar trappings. Still darker effects have not entirely disappeared from the scene, as evidenced in Mike Figgis' *Leaving Las Vegas* (1995). Here, alcohol is at the heart of a planned suicide that even true love cannot prevent.

7

LOLA MONTES

Lola Montès

955 – FRANCE / WEST GERMANY - 110 MIN. - COLOR - DRAMA

DIRECTOR MAX OPHÜLS (1902–1957)
SCREENPLAY MAX OPHÜLS, ANNETTE WADEMANT, JACQUES NATANSON, FRANZ GEIGER, based on the novel _A VIE EXTRAORDINAIRE DE LOLA MONTÈS_ by CÉCIL SAINT-LAURENT **DIRECTOR OF PHOTOGRAPHY** CHRISTIAN MATRAS
MUSIC GEORGES AURIC **EDITING** MADELEINE GUG, ADOLPH SCHLYSSLEDER **PRODUCTION** ANDRÉ HAGUET, ALFRED ZAPPELLI, ANTON SCHELKOPF, EMIL E. REINEGGER for GAMMA FILM, FLORIDA FILMS, OSKA-FILM GMBH, UNION FILM GMBH.

STARRING MARTINE CAROL (Lola Montes), PETER USTINOV (Ringmaster), ADOLF WOHLBRÜCK, a.k.a. ANTON WALBROOK (King Ludwig I), HENRI GUISOL (Maurice), LISE DELAMARE (Mrs. Craigie), PAULETTE DUBOST (Josefine), OSKAR WERNER (Student), JEAN GALLAND (Secretary), WILL QUADFLIEG (Franz Liszt), WILLY EICHBERGER (Doctor), IVAN DESNY (Lieutenant James), FRIEDRICH DOMIN (Circus director).

"La vie pour moi, c'est mouvement."

When _Lola Montes_ was released in 1955, it caused a scandal. Many movie-goers were not amused by Max Ophüls' film biography of the notorious Scot-ish-Irish courtesan and dancer, whose most famous conquest was King Ludwig I of Bavaria. Yet the production company had originally been sure they had a huge hit on their hands, for the historical material was decidedly spicy. Moreover, they had allowed Ophüls to make the film in color and Cinemascope, and they had cast the French sex symbol Martine Carol in the leading role. Carol was already a well-known actress, thanks mainly to a series of costume dramas in which her splendid _décolleté_ was a sight to behold.

And then this: Martine Carol as Lola, clad mainly in high-necked dress-es, and exhibited in a circus like a waxwork dummy; a narrative structure with several non-chronological plot-levels, each commenting on the others; experiments with the widescreen format; and finally – at least in the so-called "international version" – an "impressionist" soundscape, with dialog in French, German, English and Italian, much of it almost drowned out by vari-ous other noises.

To add insult to injury, it seemed as though Ophüls was also mocking the audience's expectations. On one occasion, Lola rips open her bodice to show King Ludwig (Adolf Wohlbrück) how admirably well-built she is – and the director cuts away without letting us get an eyeful. All we see – and it _is_ a funny scene – is the King calling for a needle and thread and pestering a horde of lackeys till they've mended the gaping hole in Lola's dress.

When the film was first shown in Paris, there were actually minor riots. Disappointed moviegoers demanded their money back and warned others

not to waste their time with such "_merde_." As reactions in Germany were no much more positive, _Lola Montes_ was a flop. It had cost around three-and-a-half million dollars to make, and it recovered only a tenth of that sum at the box office.

But that wasn't all. Disregarding the director's wishes, the production company then insisted that Ophüls make a dubbed version for the German market, in which all the characters spoke clear, understandable German. The English version was partly re-dubbed, this time in the absence of the director. The clash between Ophüls and the producers hit its absolute low point with a version in which the circus story – the "frame" of the film – was removed, except for the final episode. What remained of the movie was rearranged to create a chronological narrative. None of this helped in the slightest. The production company went bust, and Ophüls was made the scapegoat.

Originally, the director had been far from enthusiastic about the project. Ophüls stated that he had little interest in such an action-packed biography as _Lola Montes_, and that he preferred making films in which nothing much happened. In addition, he found the widescreen format hard to deal with, and he had never yet made a movie in color. But then Ophüls did manage to find a way into the material: he discovered that Lola had once appeared in an Amer-ican circus, and this gave him the idea for the story that forms the framework of the film. Peter Ustinov gives one of his finest performances as the loqua-cious ringmaster who presents Lola in a New Orleans circus and "stages" var ious scenes from her turbulent and allegedly glorious life. But Lola's memorie of her unhappy love affairs, shown in flashback, tell a very different story.

According to Ophüls, the screenplay was partly inspired by the Hollywood scandals of the time, from Zsa Zsa Gabor's affairs to Judy Garland's depression. While writing the script, Ophüls had followed the newspaper reports and noted the reactions of a public hungry for the latest sensation. *Lola Montes* holds a mirror up to moviegoers, which presumably goes some way towards explaining why they hated the film so much.

The circus scenes have a decidedly unreal atmosphere: Lola is the rigid star of the show, an object passed around from hand to hand, from man to man. A horse rider gallops past and throws her to another, two trapeze artists repeat the same trick, and Lola ascends ever higher into the circus dome until she reaches the top of the tent, which symbolizes her affair with King Ludwig; then she leaps off into thin air. All around her, people and objects are

"On its debut, in 1955, an unfortunate scandal ensured that a near-masterpiece would not receive its due. This important film was undoubtedly damaged less by Lola's 'immorality' than by the exceptionally elaborate sets and the positively baroque quality of the intrigues it dealt with." *Le Nouvel Observateur*

4

1 Rich with experience: Lola Montes (Martine Carol) is coming to the close of a deliciously scandalous life, but has little left to show for it.

2 Old-school Rockettes: With a knockout figure like this, whether or not Lola can dance is clearly immaterial. Light up the stage she will.

3 From 'big top' to flop: Circus owner and star clown (Friedrich Domin) discusses Lola's predicament with doctor (Willy Eichberger).

in motion: the artistes – who also serve as a choir, echoing the words of the ringmaster – whirl around madly, lights and set elements rise and fall and rise again, the camera circles deliriously. At the still center of it all is Lola: alone, stock-still and expressionless, her face as impassive as a mask. It's a powerful contrast to the Lola we see in the flashbacks, who is constantly traveling, always on the move. Now she is a sick woman grown old before her time, and she will end as an object of idle curiosity, caged like a circus lion.

Ophüls tames the widescreen format by dividing the space with poles, curtains and other set elements, thus creating one or more frames within the picture to focus the audience's attention. He had also had a technical device constructed and placed before the camera: a kind of theater curtain which could cover parts of the picture whenever necessary. Where other directors might have switched to close-up, Ophüls simply draws the curtain.

The various stages in Lola's life are clearly distinguished by a careful use of color. In the circus, everything is gaudy and garish against a dark

4   One for the money, two for the show: Lola warms up her past and serves it to the public as a circus act.

5   Whatever Lola wants …: Lola's love affair with Bavarian King Ludwig I (Adolf Wohlbrück) ushers in the climax of her sideshow career.

6   Selective hearing: The king cultivates a disability and plays it for all it's worth.

7   Helen of Troy: War catapults Lola out of one man's arms and into those of another when a student (Oskar Werner) rescues her from the madness of revolution and proposes marriage.

8   One last romp in the hay before being sent off to pasture: The sinister ringmaster (Peter Ustinov) milks the aging Lola for all she's worth – alone in the bedroom and in front of a packed house.

"The nature and characteristics of the film medium, its ability to free itself from time and space, the cinematographic challenge of creating a dreamlike whole out of parts that won't fit together, the subtly dialectical interplay between picture and sound … director Max Ophuls handles all this with remarkable brilliance. He shows the audience the stuff that cinematic myths are made of."

Frankfurter Rundschau

background (we never see the audience); when Lola says farewell to Franz Liszt (Will Quadflieg), the scene is shot in autumnal tones; sad grays, blues and browns dominate Lola's unhappy youth and her first marriage to the drunken brute Lieutenant James (Ivan Desny), whereas the scenes at the Bavarian court are radiant in white and gold. Lola is a driven woman, and only in her love of King Ludwig does she achieve a brief period of comparative tranquility. Some of these scenes display an almost lighthearted humor. Adolf Wohlbrück plays the King with typical irony and elegance, as a nearsighted, somewhat deaf old gentleman who deliberately ignores anything he'd rather not have heard. While his ministers are just dying to get rid of Lola, he tries to make her stay, insisting she must have her portrait painted. He chooses a painter who's known to take ages to complete his work; and because the artist is well aware of what motivates the King, he keeps scrapping the

picture and starting over again. Lola begins by sitting for her portrait in a winter coat, but the finished painting depicts her as a naked Venus. The problem now is where to hang it, for neither the university nor the art gallery wants anything to do with it. By now, Lola has become the Countess of Landsfeld and has a castle of her own; but she too has no desire to have the portrait on her wall; for as she says, it would look a little too much like advertising. Even this amusing episode ends in tragedy, though: almost in passing, we hear that the portrait affair has moved Ludwig to fire some of his ministers and shut down the university. But the King's autocratic style is no longer in fashion. A revolution drives Lola out of Bavaria and into the arms of her very last lover – the ringmaster, who had already made his cynical intentions clear: "Come with me. I'll sell you for a very good price."

LP

**ADOLF WOHLBRÜCK
(ANTON WALBROOK)**

Adolf Wohlbrück, the son of a clown, was born in Vienna in 1896. He was undoubtedly one of the most elegant men ever to grace a cinema screen. His audience knew and loved him as the gent in the tailcoat with a flower in his lapel and one hand placed nonchalantly in his trouser pocket. Wohlbrück studied acting at the Max Reinhardt Seminar in Vienna, and his first successes were in the theater. But it was the cultivated comedy talkies of Reinhold Schünzel and Willi Forst that really made his name in the 30s. In 1936, he moved to England and changed his name to Anton Walbrook. Now the British had a chance to experience his wonderful acting. He became popular in two films as Queen Victoria's German husband, Prince Albert. During the war, he was cast as the "good German" in two Powell & Pressburger productions: *The 49th Parallel / The Invaders* (1941) and *The Life and Death of Colonel Blimp* (1943). Besides his elegance, it was Wohlbrück's cool, ironic and distanced acting style that defined his screen persona. Yet his finest moments include those in which this façade could be seen to crumble: in Willi Forst's *Maskerade* (1934), for example, his sheer bashfulness eventually leads him to yell a declaration of love in Paula Wessely's face; and as the ballet impresario Lermontov in Powell and Pressburger's *The Red Shoes* (1948), he announces the death of the ballerina in a voice almost crazed with grief. In Max Ophüls' *La Ronde* (1950), adapted from the stage play by Arthur Schnitzler, he gave another memorable performance as the raconteur, a figure specially invented for him by Ophüls. In the 60s, Wohlbrück spent more time in Germany, working in TV and at the theater. In 1967, he died of heart failure.

THE NIGHT OF THE HUNTER

1955 - USA - 93 MIN. - B & W - FILM NOIR, PSYCHO THRILLER

DIRECTOR CHARLES LAUGHTON (1899–1962)
SCREENPLAY JAMES AGEE, based on the novel of the same name by DAVIS GRUBB
DIRECTOR OF PHOTOGRAPHY STANLEY CORTEZ **EDITING** ROBERT GOLDEN **MUSIC** WALTER SCHUMANN
PRODUCTION PAUL GREGORY for PAUL GREGORY PRODUCTIONS, UNITED ARTISTS.

STARRING ROBERT MITCHUM (Harry Powell), SHELLEY WINTERS (Willa Harper),
LILLIAN GISH (Rachel Cooper), EVELYN VARDEN (Icey Spoon), PETER GRAVES (Ben Harper),
BILLY CHAPIN (John Harper), SALLY JANE BRUCE (Pearl Harper), JAMES GLEASON (Birdie),
DON BEDDOE (Walt Spoon), GLORIA CASTILLO (Ruby).

"I'll be back, when it's dark."

The actor Charles Laughton directed only one film, and there is nothing else like it. Darkly poetic and deeply moving, *The Night of the Hunter* is a work of horror and enchantment, a hypnotic fairy tale for grown-ups. Laughton's cinematic tableau distils the worst terrors of childhood into a beautiful fable about a brother and sister on the run from a demonic preacher. It's the very stuff of nightmare: two defenseless children pursued relentlessly by an unpredictable and pathologically violent adult.

America is in the grips of the Depression, demoralized and prey to hysterical religiosity. Two rural children, John (Billy Chapin) and his younger sister Pearl (Sally Jane Bruce) watch helplessly as their father is arrested. He had murdered two people for the money to ensure his family's survival. But seconds before the cops catch up with him, he succeeds in handing over the booty to his son John. He makes the boy swear to protect his sister with his own life – and never to talk about the money. It's an almost monstrous burden to place on a child's soul, and it's also the beginning of a nightmarish odyssey for John and Pearl. The father is executed for murder; and a short time later, a sinister wandering preacher appears on the scene. Not content to woo the widow, he appears to know something about the kids and the carefully hidden loot …

Hollywood's most charismatic bad guy, Robert Mitchum, gives another brilliant performance as the mysterious Harry Powell, serial murderer and itinerant "man of God." With the words LOVE and HATE tattooed on his knuckles, Powell stages bizarre fights between his left and right hands, symbolizing the eternal struggle between Good and Evil. From the very start, he dominates every room he enters, every space he inhabits – an impression reinforced by some powerful and unorthodox framings and camera angles. Harry Powell is practically ubiquitous and seemingly inescapable. *Something wicked this way comes* – on a train, in a car, or on a horse. And to John and Pearl's dismay, it seems Harry Powell is even capable of entering locked rooms. In short, he is a figure of almost mythical power, a manifestation of evil in human form.

And he's irresistible: Harry Powell marries the widowed mother (Shelley Winters) and crushes her spirit with talk of sin and salvation, before murdering her in cold blood to clear his way to her children. To make it look like an accident, he places her body in the driver's seat and rolls her car into the river. The underwater sequence that follows has since acquired an almost legendary status. We see the dead woman in the submerged automobile, her loose hair swaying softly above her like seaweed. Poetry and horror, beauty

1   Toying with her affections: Reverend Harry Powell (Robert Mitchum) takes advantage of little Pearl Harper's (Sally Jane Bruce) good nature without a morsel of shame.

2   As I lay dying: Harry Powell pulls an inconceivable con with fatal consequences for the children's mother (Shelley Winters).

3   Cheers and sneers: A diabolical mind lies behind this man's bright smile.

"I can hear you whisperin' children, so I know you're down there. I can feel myself gettin' awful mad. I'm out of patience children. I'm coming to find you now."

Film quote: Harry Powell (Robert Mitchum)

4   The little man takes a stand: Young John (Billy Chapin) launches a surprise attack on Harry Powell.

5   Bustin' out: The children orchestrate a plan for survival from the confines of their basement.

and terror, grace and decay: a fabulously melancholic sequence quite without parallel in the cinema.

Indeed, the whole film is unique in the way it combines an almost mannered expressionist style with motifs from the realms of dream and nightmare. The result is a well-nigh surrealist masterpiece, profoundly strange and subtly frightening.

The Night of the Hunter gives us a child's-eye-view of the world, in which nocturnal terrors become manifest in the person of a monstrous man. At the moment of greatest threat, on the banks of the river, John and Pearl just manage to escape into a tiny boat; their pursuer, Harry Powell, scrambles after them in the shallows, howling like a beast as the boat drifts away from his grasping hands. The children's ordeal finally ends when they find refuge with Mrs. Cooper, a steadfast and warm-hearted woman who takes in and cares for the waifs and strays that come her way. As Rachel Cooper, the former silent-movie star Lillian Gish is another glory of this film. She is the antithesis of Harry Powell, the light that banishes his darkness, a kind of ideal mother, in fact. And it's Rachel Cooper who finally defeats the evil preacher and hands him over to the police. The circle closes when John, finally freed from his unbearable burden, reveals where the money had been hidden all along: in Pearl's rag doll. By the end of this film, the little girl's doll has come to symbolize far more than a stolen childhood.

BR

LILLIAN GISH   Born in 1893, she is still regarded as "The First Lady of the Silent Screen." Lillian Gish came to fame through the good offices of Mary Pickford, another star of the day, who introduced her to the pioneering director David W. Griffith; and it was in Griffith's thriller *An Unseen Enemy* (1912) that Lillian Gish made her debut. She was an ideal protagonist for the sentimental Victorian world of Griffith's films, often playing deceptively fragile figures with a strong spiritual core. Under Griffith's aegis, she became perhaps the best actress of her day, appearing in movies such as *The Birth of a Nation* (1915), *Intolerance* (1916) and *Broken Blossoms* (1919). In the early 20s, after she and Griffith went their separate ways, Lillian Gish's career went into a slow decline. Nonetheless, she still enjoyed star status for some time to come. Thus the production company MGM allowed her to have a say in the making of *The Scarlet Letter* and *La Boheme* (both 1926).

In 1928, having been supplanted at MGM by Greta Garbo, Lillian Gish turned her back on Hollywood, returned to the theater and worked for radio and TV. Later, she received many awards for her life's work, including an Oscar in 1971 and an award from the American Film Institute in 1984. Lillian Gish died of heart failure on February 27, 1993.

KISS ME DEADLY

1955 - USA - 104 MIN. - B & W - CRIME FILM, FILM NOIR

DIRECTOR ROBERT ALDRICH (1918–1983)
SCREENPLAY A. I. BEZZERIDES, based on the novel of the same name by MICKEY SPILLANE
DIRECTOR OF PHOTOGRAPHY ERNEST LASZLO EDITING MICHAEL LUCIANO MUSIC FRANK DE VOL
PRODUCTION ROBERT ALDRICH for PARKLANE PICTURES INC.

STARRING RALPH MEEKER (Mike Hammer), CLORIS LEACHMAN (Christina), MAXINE COOPER (Velda),
GABY RODGERS (Lily Carver, Gabrielle), ALBERT DEKKER (Doctor Soberin), PAUL STEWART (Carl Evello),
JUANO HERNANDEZ (Eddie), WESLEY ADDY (Pat), MARIAN CARR (Friday), JACK ELAM (Charlie Max).

"Don't open the box!"

Why are all the boys hot on the heels of the woman in the light-colored trench coat? Barefoot, she roams the streets at all hours of the night and the police feel compelled to shut off the streets to arrest her. Does she really present a danger to society? There is something is strikingly wrong with this set-up, a feeling that sticks with the viewer right up until *Kiss Me Deadly*'s fast and furious finale.

At first glance, the film's premise seems cut and dry. Private investigator Mike Hammer (Ralph Meeker), a gang of thugs and the police are all trying to locate a missing suitcase with radioactive contents. But nothing is as it appears. The superficially smooth detective turns out to be a big dolt who gets swept up in the events of the case rather than utilizing his powers of de-

duction; in fact, his machismo altogether prevents him from grasping what's going on. An inordinately large number of women surround Mike and lure the shortsighted crime fighter from locale to locale. First there's the woman from the street, Christina (Cloris Leachman), who catches his curiosity; then there's Velda (Maxine Cooper), his smart and attractive secretary who'd jump through hoops of fire to be near him, but only ends up getting burned; and finally there's the impenetrable Lily (Gaby Rodgers), a game-playing dame ready to turn the tables on Hammer and seize the stuff that dreams are made of. That would be "the great whatzit," Velda's term for the radioactive material supposedly sniped from the Manhattan Project, the secret atom bomb research project conducted by the U.S. government in the 1940s ...

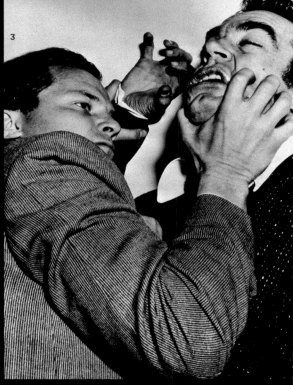

2   3

Kiss Me Deadly succeeds in disorienting its audience by means of its topsy-turvy story and expressive visual style. It is as if we are trapped in the eye of the hurricane and unable to ever see the bigger picture. True, the movie always has us on a par with its protagonist Mike Hammer; trouble is that Mike is always one step behind everybody else. And thus at no time does either he or the viewer know where they stand. Only this much is clear. The mysterious Christina quite literally holds the key to the puzzle, as we realize once it is extracted from her stomach during a medical autopsy. The key leads Hammer to a locker at a posh Hollywood sports club and a suitcase-shaped container housing a mind-boggling mystery. Opening the strange box but a crack, Hammer's eyes are flooded by a blinding light and a piercing screech grabs hold of the soundtrack: the film's underlying eeriness has finally taken form. Not that it takes a genius to know that this would happen sooner or later. For after all, the way towards this Pandora's box was paved with horrors: fear-

struck people, the victims of an abstruse brainchild of modern science that leaves indelible brands on their skin; inexplicable, deadly accidents as unscrupulous killers and an inept police force try to locate the spooky substance with about as much of a game plan as the homme fatale Hammer.

All roads lead to doom as the story's third female character enters the picture. Lily, in truth the wicked Dr. Soberin's (Albert Dekker) assistant Gabrielle, aids the mastermind by supplying him with the dimwitted detective's hard-won clues whilst she tries to snatch the goods out from under Hammer's nose. Needless to say, the P. I. is hung out to dry and the radioactive loot lands in the hands of the bad guys. But Gabrielle proves no better than Mike, when at the film's conclusion she too can't help but peek inside the box, letting loose an atomic fireball. In the midst of the resulting apocalyptic tumult Mike Hammer and Velda stagger towards the sea, and therefore back to the origin of all life.

UNITED ARTISTS   By the 1920s, Hollywood stars had realized just how much influence they had on audiences and correspondingly began to demand greater independence. Actors Mary Pickford, Douglas Fairbanks, Charles Chaplin and director David W. Griffith therefore decided to found the independent production company United Artists in 1919. Their goal was to release star-produced movies whose earnings would flow back directly into their own pockets. Pictures like *The Mark of Zorro* (1920), *Little Lord Fauntleroy* (1921) and *The Gold Rush* (1925) gave clout to the burgeoning studio. While United Artists' limited production capacity proved a great disadvantage in the face of ever-increasing demand from movie house owners, the company still managed to turn a respectable profit in a depression economy. Pictures like Charlie Chaplin's *City Lights* (1931), *Modern Times* (1936) and *The Great Dictator* (1940) were immensely popular with audiences as were stars like Gloria Swanson, Buster Keaton and Rudolph Valentino. Producers like Samuel Goldwyn and Howard Hughes cranked out one winning film after another. Financial complications in the 1950s led to the company's sale and U. A. shifted its focus to the financial backing and distribution of pictures. Productions like *Some Like It Hot* (1959) and *West Side Story* (1961) got the company back on its feet and box-offices smashes like the James Bond flicks and *Rocky* (1976) helped keep it there. Today, United Artists is owned and operated by Metro-Goldwyn-Mayer (MGM).

This surreal jigsaw puzzle in the guise of a detective caper ultimately emerges as a 50s farce. Many subjects are touched on and flippantly analyzed, from architecture via common-law marriage to the finer points of music. Underscoring this is the perpetual threat of human annihilation by the wonders of modern science, with unsubtle discussions about the general abuse of technology for purposes like splitting atoms, as well as humanity's inability to responsibly manage the vast technology it has created. But despite the mix of genres, *Kiss Me Deadly* has a striking clarity, and the complex theme of the responsibilities that accompany technological developments and the very real possibility of mankind's end in a nuclear Armageddon are illustrated in gripping cinematic form.

BR

"This pressing need to talk in order to avoid disaster, even death, is a recurrent noir motif, and one that finds its most dramatic statement in *Kiss Me Deadly*."

Journal of Popular Film & Television

1 Hard-pressed: In his quest for the truth, detective Mike Hammer (Ralph Meeker) falls willingly into the clutches of one conniving woman after another.

2 Disposing of the evidence: The low-key style, shadows and angular shots suggest that those gloves have been party to something sinister.

3 Now talk! Mike Hammer puts his powers of persuasion to good use.

4 Mood lighting: Tuxedos, cocktail dresses and a secluded booth for two evoke an air of stifling claustrophobia and mystery in this late noir classic.

5 When the thugs come knocking, Mike Hammer makes a run for the covers.

ALL THAT HEAVEN ALLOWS

1955 - USA - 89 MIN. - COLOR - MELODRAMA

DIRECTOR DOUGLAS SIRK (1897–1987)
SCREENPLAY PEG FENWICK, EDNA L. LEE, HARRY LEE DIRECTOR OF PHOTOGRAPHY RUSSELL METTY EDITING FRANK GROSS
MUSIC FRANK SKINNER PRODUCTION ROSS HUNTER for UNIVERSAL INTERNATIONAL PICTURES.

STARRING JANE WYMAN (Cary Scott), ROCK HUDSON (Ron Kirby), GLORIA TALBOTT (Kay Scott),
WILLIAM REYNOLDS (Ned Scott), AGNES MOOREHEAD (Sara Warren), CONRAD NAGEL (Harvey),
VIRGINIA GREY (Alida Anderson), CHARLES DRAKE (Mick Anderson), JACQUELINE DE WIT (Mona Plash),
HAYDEN RORKE (Doctor Hennessy).

"But that was different; you didn't really love him, did you?"

"Watching Douglas Sirk leads me down the path of human despair," Rainer Werner Fassbinder wrote more than thirty years ago. *Fear Eats the Soul* (*Angst essen Seele auf*, 1974) is the result of Fassbinder's own filmmaking journey along this way, following in the footsteps of Douglas Sirk's 1955 picture *All That Heaven Allows*. A melodrama of the highest order, the Sirk piece investigates the plight of an affluent widow in the 1950s, who falls in love with a considerably younger and socially unacceptable man. Forced to face a world ruled by intolerance, small-mindedness and double standards, she quickly discovers that the road to love can be paved with life-shattering despair. In 2002, Todd Haynes breathed new life into Douglas Sirk's legacy with the film *Far from Heaven*, which critically investigated issues still taboo in the 1950s such as racial discrimination and homosexuality. It is thus not

surprising that Douglas Sirk is highly regarded by both filmmakers and cineasts alike, and that, as one film critic put it, "his movies age beautifully." *All That Heaven Allows* is one of the most visually striking pictures Sirk ever made and a fine example of his so-called "weepies" – gut-wrenching cinematic soap operas with great symbolic depth. In the 1980s, critical views of this sort of melodrama were radically revised when feminist film theory re-appropriated the genre as a specifically female cinematic form. In fact, *All That Heaven Allows* was one of the first films to express the basic themes of melodrama, i. e. love, agony, and the power of social conventions in a visual and symbolical language, and was a watershed in defining the genre.

Like so many melodramas, *All That Heaven Allows* takes place in a nondescript corner of rural America. The film opens with the camera slowly

descending upon the hamlet of Stoningham. It's fall, and we enter a picture-book world of pristine homes and manicured lawns soaked in golden-brown sunlight. On one of these plots resides Mrs. Cary Scott (Jane Wyman), a middle-aged widow, who, though well provided for, has lived a secluded life since her husband's death. She receives no company other than the occasional visit from her two grown children, Ned (William Reynolds) and Kay (Gloria Talbott), or her friend Sara (Agnes Moorehead). Hers is what one might call a less than satisfying life with few prospects: Cary is too old to be publicly regarded as a woman with sexual desires and too young not to be free of them. Oblivious to Cary's state, her wisecracking daughter tells her of macabre practices in Ancient Egypt, where widows were locked in their husband's tombs along with the rest of his possessions. It's a quip that gives the

"In Hollywood's estimation, the middle-class American woman would sooner give up her honor than her social standing." *Time Magazine*

1   The young and the restless: Cary (Jane Wyman) and Ron (Rock Hudson) couldn't be happier, but nobody else approves of their unorthodox affair.

2   Kids is kids: Cary's children don't take kindly to the prospects of having a young gardener for a stepfather.

3 Keeping up appearances: Despite her love for him, Cary has reservations about introducing her new beau to the nosy neighbors.

4 Everything you always wanted to know about sex, but were afraid to ask: Cary tries to figure out what makes her nature boy tick by catching up on her Henry David Thoreau.

film one of its central metaphors; for Cary, too, feels as if she'd been buried alive in her beautifully furnished albeit sterile home, depicted by Sirk as the ultimate 1950s 'Home & Garden' magazine monstrosity. Considering her predicament, it's only logical that Cary would be attracted to a man in his prime, and the guy she sets her sights on fits the bill. He's young, virile, attractive – and he's her gardener. Although a personal relationship with Ron Kirby (Rock Hudson) would be – socially speaking – out of the question, she is too drawn to him to resist falling in love. Like Cary, the introverted Kirby, who seems as rooted to the earth as the trees he tends, also resides in a

private world. His love for Cary is deep and genuine, and he is unhampered by the shackles of social convention. His lives by his own golden rule, which is never to blow insignificant matters out of proportion. It's a credo that opens a debate on what really counts in life, contrasting two great schools of thought. One of these is the Freudian viewpoint purported by Cary's daughter; time and again, she superciliously cites the psychoanalyst's theories, but beats the sense out of them whenever she attempts to put them into practice. On the other side is the Henry David Thoreau (1817–1862) school of thought, summed up in his book "Walden" (1854), which is at once a factual

account of the author's personal withdrawal from small-town American life and a theoretical discourse on the virtues of a simple, self-directed life in harmony with nature. The embodiment of this ideal, Ron lives in a mill outside of town. And Cary, swept up by the world he introduces her to, is ready to marry him at once and start up a new life. But the snide comments of her community, emotional ties to her house and social conventions, and finally her children's damning view of their mother marrying beneath her class slowly erode her confidence. Both Ned and Kay have a bigoted approach to life that values keeping up appearances over personal happiness, and egotistically pressure Cary to act in their interests rather than her own. It is their potential rejection that seals her decision to call off her engagement with Ron. Ned and Kay thus emerge triumphant in locking Cary inside the cage society has con-

structed for her. As a token of consolation, they give her a television set, hoping to compensate for the real life they have robbed her of with a virtual surrogate. But at first all the screen shows is Cary's shadowy reflection – as if she'd been buried alive once and for all like an Egyptian widow. Had Sirk ended on the film on this note, *All That Heaven Allows* would have been chilling indeed. What he does, however, is grant his audience the happy ending they so desire, climbing a Kilimanjaro of melodrama to do so. A wreck after the separation from Cary, Ron has an accident that leaves him severely injured. At long last, Cary realizes where she belongs, and decides to take up with Ron in the old mill after all. We leave her, viewing the end of the movie through her eyes, as she peers out the window onto the woods lying beyond – a vision of utopia as only Thoreau could have painted it.   KK

6

5   Bambi meets Tinkerbell.

6   Snow white: Rock Hudson would prefer Prince Charming to wake him from frozen slumber, but he'll settle for Jane Wyman if need be.

7   Why be satisfied with silver when you can go for gold? Cary isn't about to live out the rest of her years with an old geezer. Conrad Nagel as Harvey.

"Having seen this film, I know that the last place on earth I'd want to go is a small town in America." *Positif*

DOUGLAS SIRK (1897–1987)

He is the unequivocal master of melodrama, and shot "women's pictures," that were revered for the same reasons they were despised. Douglas Sirk faded into a decade of oblivion, and it was only with the 1971 publication of Jon Halliday's interview with the filmmaker entitled "Sirk on Sirk" that audiences began to rediscover him. Pictures like *Magnificent Obsession* (1954), *All That Heaven Allows* (1955) and *Written on the Wind* (1956) were held in high esteem by renegade German director Rainer Werner Fassbinder. Sirk's "weepies" captured the day-to-day malaise and social conflicts of 1950s America's like no other filmmaker in parables of passion, disaster and redemption – the more melodramatic, the better. In his final and arguably best picture, *Imitation of Life* (1959), a white man beats his girlfriend after discovering that she has Negro blood in her – it is a scene that compellingly shows how closely related racial abuse is to the abuse of women.

Before Douglas Sirk started shooting American melodramas in the 1950s, he directed Zarah Leander to stardom in Nazi Germany with pictures like *La Habanera* (1937) and *Life Begins Anew* (*Zu neuen Ufern*, 1937). Born Hans Detlef Sierck 1897 in Hamburg, Sirk studied philosophy and art history before launching a directing career in theater and then eventually shifting to film. Nonetheless, Sirk was by no means a puppet of the Nazis. In 1938, he stopped working in Germany and emigrated to the United States. Once in Hollywood, he went on to direct *Hitler's Madman* (1943), which along with Frank Borzage's *The Mortal Storm* (1940) and Edward Dmytryk's *Hitler's Children* (1942), is considered one of the best films on fascism the American cinema produced at the time. Sirk left America and big-time filmmaking for good in 1959, living out the rest of his days in Switzerland until his death in 1987. Douglas Sirk was an intellectual who was always a league apart. He loved grand, sweeping emotion and expressed it in his own cinematic language, inspiring a long line of directors, right down to the present day.

RIFIFI
Du rififi chez les hommes

1955 - FRANCE - 120 MIN. - B & W - THRILLER, CRIME FILM

DIRECTOR JULES DASSIN (b. 1911)
SCREENPLAY JULES DASSIN, RENÉ WHEELER, AUGUSTE LE BRETON DIRECTOR OF PHOTOGRAPHY PHILIPPE AGOSTINI
EDITING ROGER DWYRE MUSIC GEORGES AURIC, M. PHILIPPE-GÉRARD & JACQUES LARUE (Song: "Rififi")
PRODUCTION RENÉ GASTON VUATTOUX for INDUSFILMS, PRIMA FILM, SOCIÉTÉ NOUVELLE PATHÉ CINÉMA.

STARRING JEAN SERVAIS (Tony le Stéphanois), CARL MÖHNER (Jo le Suedois), ROBERT MANUEL (Mario Farrati),
JANINE DARCEY (Louise), PIERRE GRASSET (Louis Grutter), JULES DASSIN (as PERLO VITA) (César le Milanais),
MARIE SABOURET (Mado), ROBERT HOSSEIN (Rémi Grutter), CLAUDE SYLVAIN (Ida Farrati),
MARCEL LUPOVICI (Pierre Grutter).

IFF CANNES 1955 BEST DIRECTOR (Jules Dassin).

"Wake up dog, I want you to be afraid – how does it feel?"

A huge, crudely decorated dummy guitar dominates the room, so that the man standing beside it is almost reduced to an afterthought. He's standing upright, tied to a joist, in the backstage area of a seedy subterranean nightclub. Behind him, the paw of a cardboard tiger; in the semi-darkness around him, papier-mâché cacti, palm leaves, a jungle of unidentifiable junk. Bars of light fall on the filthy cellar floor while the man stares calmly into the camera. A shot rings out; his body twitches briefly, and everything dissolves behind a cloud of black smoke. With no fuss and no nonsense, Jules Dassin has just directed his own execution. The scene was in fact never planned in this form; Dassin had only taken on the role of the Italian safecracker César after the original actor dropped out shortly before filming began.

The killer, Tony le Stéphanois (Jean Servais), is the real hero of the film. His sad eyes practically tell the whole story. After five years in jail, he's lost his girlfriend, he has pneumonia, and he no longer enjoys the respect of his

1   The whole world in his hands: But no amount of wealth can erase the disillusion from his face. Jean Servais as Tony le Stéphanois.

2   Thick as thieves: Relying on daredevil acrobatics, the gang pulls off the crime without a exchanging a single word.

3   Getting fired up! The gangsters arm themselves for the final showdown like true urban cowboys.

underworld buddies. His friendship with the young crook Jo (Carl Möhner) seems to be the only glimmer of hope in his life – until Tony gathers the strength for one final major coup. Together with Jo, César and Mario (Robert Manuel), he starts preparing a break-in at the exclusive jewelers Mappin & Webb. Once they have worked out how to disable the alarm system, the heist can begin. It's a gripping sequence: without a word, the four men make their way to the scene of the crime, accompanied by the edgy music of Georges Auric. But when they get to the hallway of the building, the music stops. The men pull on ballet shoes to muffle their footsteps, and they begin to pry open

the parquet flooring. The slightest tremor could set off the alarm. For almost a full half-hour, Dassin relies entirely on the strength of the images: there's no music and no dialog whatsoever. It's a stroke of genius, for in this austere silence, the suspense gradually becomes almost unbearable.

At first, Georges Auric refused to believe the scene could work this way, so he composed a suitable musical soundtrack for the break-in; but when he saw the result, he was happy to dispense with his composition. And so, while Jo removes the flooring in the midst of a terrible silence, the tension rises steadily. Layer by layer, the floor is removed; and as the men tap away softly,

4 Underworld highlife: Tony's archenemy owns a nightclub where thugs hide out behind bizarre backdrops, and buxom beauties sway to the sounds of Georges Auric chansons. What more could a gangster movie ask for?

5 Child's play: However, Tony and Jo have no enthusiasm for the caper, only the prize.

"It makes the hair on the back of your neck stand on end." *The New York Times*

JULES DASSIN In *Rififi* (*Du rififi chez les hommes*, 1955), director Jules Dassin also played the role of a traitor. In real life, it was Dassin himself who was betrayed. Born in 1911, Dassin was the son of a Jewish hairdresser. At the age of 20, he took a trip around Europe, acting, painting stage sets and studying dramaturgy for a while. After returning to the States, he visited and soon joined the Jewish Theater. Meanwhile he took part in various small experimental theater productions and wrote plays for the radio. Soon, he was attracting Hollywood's attention. He worked as an assistant to Alfred Hitchcock before he began making B-movies for MGM in the 40s.

He enjoyed a quick commercial success with *The Canterville Ghost* (1944), but his big breakthrough came in the late 40s, with movies such as *The Naked City* (1948) and *Night and the City* (1950). He was now regarded as an American neorealist with a lot of talent, and a successful career was at his fingertips. Then the anti-communist witch-hunters destroyed his future within weeks. Dassin had been a member of the Party for a short time in the 30s, and Edward Dmytryk denounced him as a communist. He was placed on Hollywood's blacklist. From then on, any actor, producer or director who worked with him would have been risking his own career. Dassin hoped to find work abroad, but the long arm of Hollywood reached across the seas, and frightened colleagues often backed out of planned projects at the last minute. Only after three years was he able to make another film – and *Rififi* was a splendiferous success. Dassin's situation remained unaltered, though; again and again, he had to change countries in order to find work. Such conditions made it difficult for him to develop a definite style of his own; his oeuvre is bitty, and it contains numerous mediocre films. In 1964, he made one more American film: the comedy thriller *Topkapi*, a parody of heist films like *Rififi*. Once again, he had landed a big box-office hit. Since the end of the 80s, he has chosen to work only in the theater, emerging into the media limelight only to receive prizes for his life's work.

6

6 All in a day's work: César (Jules Dassin) and Mario (Robert Manuel) finetune their safecracking skills and prove that success depends on the pride one takes in the job – no matter how unethical.

7 I got rhythm: Whether on the dance floor or in the midst of a heist, no-one is suaver than César.

8 Having his way with her: Tony forces ex-girlfriend Mado (Marie Sabouret) to strip, only to beat her to a bloody pulp.

"*Rififi* contains a 30-minute sequence of wordless moviemaking that is one of the most engrossing sequences since the invention of the motion picture."

Time Magazine

the viewers' nerves are stripped bare. These guys are so careful, and so inventive: it's a joy to see how they prevent the dust from landing on the room below, or how they open the massive safe like a tin can.

When the job's been done, all's right with the world, or so it would seem; but the title song sums up the plot – there's always some kind of trouble in the end. César makes a stupid mistake and betrays the gang's secret. The code of the Mafia demands that Tony kill him. "You know the rules?" he asks. César nods.

The film's presentation of violence was a sensation at the time. Tony forces his ex-lover Mado (Marie Sabouret) to strip off, so that he can beat her with a belt for being unfaithful; meanwhile, Tony's enemy Louis Grutter (Pierre Grasset) treats his junkie brother (Robert Hossein) like a mangy dog. Yet,

188

tough as it is, the film has the balance and integrity of a work of art. This is due in no small part to the fantastic camerawork of Philippe Agostini. The interiors are skillfully lit, so that the hard world of the criminals is filled with niches of soft darkness. The exteriors have a raw documentary beauty that points towards movies like *The French Connection* (1971), partly because Dassin would only shoot when the sky was overcast. All the while, he makes almost playful use of standard film noir elements, and the obligatory nightclub sequence that accompanies the title song is an unashamed parody, with a mime artist in shadow play, lighting his cigarette from the barrel of a smoking gun.

Rififi's frank treatment of sex and violence didn't stop the Cannes jury from presenting Dassin with the prize for Best Director. In other countries, the film was banned immediately, and was therefore known only to a few until fairly recently. Only at the turn of the century was it released in U. S. cinemas, and the DVD version is now increasingly popular, for *Rififi* is rightly seen as a prototype of the ice-cold thriller. The film is a real shocker. It uses the means of the European cinema to drive the American film noir to its stylistic limits, before the pessimism of the post-war years gives way to the escapist tendencies of the 60s. In particular, it leaves the two-dimensional quality of earlier noir films far behind it. Movie maestros such as Kubrick and Tarantino were inspired by the sheer technical perfection of *Rififi*, but its particular blend of hardness and grace still remains unmatched.

OK

EAST OF EDEN

1955 - USA - 115 MIN. - COLOR - DRAMA, LITERARY ADAPTATION

DIRECTOR ELIA KAZAN (1909–2003)
SCREENPLAY PAUL OSBORN, based on the novel of the same name by JOHN STEINBECK
DIRECTOR OF PHOTOGRAPHY TED MCCORD **EDITING** OWEN MARKS **MUSIC** LEONARD ROSENMAN
PRODUCTION ELIA KAZAN for WARNER BROS.

STARRING JAMES DEAN (Cal Trask), RICHARD DAVALOS (Aron Trask), RAYMOND MASSEY (Adam Trask),
JULIE HARRIS (Abra), JO VAN FLEET (Kate), BURL IVES (Sam), ALBERT DEKKER (Will Hamilton),
LOIS SMITH (Anne), HAROLD GORDON (Gustav Albrecht), NICK DENNIS (Rantani).

ACADEMY AWARDS 1955 OSCAR for BEST SUPPORTING ACTRESS (Jo Van Fleet).

IFF CANNES 1955 BEST FILM (Elia Kazan).

"It's awful not to be loved.
It's the worst thing in the world."

Restless impatience is a privilege of the young, who have to find their way in a world ruled by their fathers. Along with Marlon Brando, James Dean was *the* rebellious adolescent of 1950s cinema, and *East of Eden*, directed by Elia Kazan, is a powerful Cinemascope epic that lends a positively Biblical dimension to the sons' rebellion against their fathers. From the title to the characters' names to the various motifs – ranging from the Prodigal Son to Cain and Abel – this is a work that's awash with Christian mythology. There's a certain grandeur about the whole enterprise: scenes are composed and framed like works of art, while the general sense of restlessness and unease is made palpable in the film's use of light and shade, in the dynamic interplay of vertical, horizontal and diagonal lines, and in the use of skewed camera-angles. The characters are precisely drawn and convincingly developed, never clichéd or one-dimensional and always psychologically plausible. Most memorable, of course, is the rebellious, introverted, doubt-ridden, edgy, manic-depressive Cal (James Dean), son of the self-righteous farmer Adam Trask (Raymond Massey) and twin brother of the conformist Aron (Richard Davalos). Faced with an overbearing pious father and a guileless, straitlaced brother, Cal struggles to come to terms with his past and find his own iden-

1 More than just a movie star: James Dean became synonymous with the rebellious desperadoes he portrayed. He left Eden the icon of a generation.

2 Chip off the old block: Even Cal's brother Aron (Richard Davalos) can't escape the familial legacy unscathed.

3 Tell it like it is: A son discovers that sometimes the only way to get answers out of your father is to back him into a corner.

"Paul Osborn has written a splendidly warm and living screenplay, vibrant with Steinbeck's classic theme, and telling it in motion picture terms which are always clear, always pictorially legible and always effective." *Motion Picture Herald*

tity. Eventually, his struggle takes on the dimensions of an existential battle against the hypocrisy and tyranny of a moribund patriarchal order. It's no accident that the film is set in the first quarter of the 20th century, with America making the difficult transition from an agrarian to an industrial society. As the U.S. prepared to enter the First World War, traditional values were cast into doubt, while new ways of life had yet to develop and take their place.

The film begins, with unusual directness, where other movies might end: with Cal's discovery that his mother (Jo Van Fleet) is running a whorehouse. Her life story is a tragic refutation of the family legend so carefully tended by Cal's father. Not only had she had dared to rebel against her own husband; she had shot him and left her children in order to build up a life of

4 The land of Nod: Thankfully, Abra (Julie Harris) isn't the only one who's been expelled from the garden.

5 Running red lights: Young Cal (James Dean) insists on seeing his mother outside of visiting hours.

JAMES DEAN James Byron Dean was born in 1931, and his career was short but brilliant. He made three films in very quick succession – *East of Eden* (1955), *Rebel Without a Cause* (1955) and *Giant* (1956) – and was immediately hailed as Hollywood's brightest hope. Dean's acting training included spells at the Actors' Studio in New York, where he studied under Lee Strasberg and Elia Kazan. He worked in the theater, made ads, appeared on TV and had small roles in various movies before the breakthrough came in 1954: while performing on Broadway in a play called "The Immoralist," he came to the attention of Warner Brothers.

As the embodiment of youthful rebellion against family, tradition and social constraints, Jimmy Dean became the role model for an entire generation of young moviegoers. He soon acquired cult status, and he is still an icon of American youth culture. Sadly, *East of Eden* was the only one of his films that he ever saw. On September 30, 1955, James Dean died in a car crash.

her own. The boys have been brought up believing a lie, knowing nothing of their mother's fate, for their father had always told them she was dead. Only when Cal forces his father to speak does the older man finally admit the truth: she's still alive – but where she is, he cannot say.

With a past like this, Cal's future seems sealed. Again and again, his father rejects him and favors his brother Aron. Cal does his best to adapt and adjust to the way things are, but nothing he does has any effect. Then Adam Trask's frozen-fruit business hits the rocks, and he starts to founder financially. Cal tries to help him out by paying off his debts with the profits from his own bean farm, but Trask rebuffs his son's offer with unexpected harshness. The cracks in this family are now clearly irreparable. In utter dejection, the outcast son realizes he has nothing more to lose, and he leads

film is wise enough not to exploit this situation for the sake of a cheap effect, using it rather to demonstrate once again an astonishing ability to find powerful images for a situation that cannot be expressed in words. After meeting the mother he had long thought dead, Aron is so shattered that he joins the army and goes to war. A disturbing scene on the station platform encapsulates the spiritual anguish of a betrayed generation: as Aron's father calls his name in despair, the boy – half-drunk, half-crazy, and laughing like a wild man – smashes his head through the window of the train. For the Hollywood studio bosses, this was an intolerably pessimistic ending, so they had the destruction of the family followed by signs of imminent renewal, as Cal and his father are reconciled at the old man's sickbed.

INVASION OF THE BODY SNATCHERS

1956 - USA - 80 MIN. - B & W - SCIENCE FICTION, HORROR FILM

DIRECTOR DON SIEGEL (1912–1991)
SCREENPLAY DANIEL MAINWARING, based on the novel *THE BODY SNATCHERS* by JACK FINNEY
DIRECTOR OF PHOTOGRAPHY ELLSWORTH FREDERICKS EDITING ROBERT S. EISEN MUSIC CARMEN DRAGON
PRODUCTION WALTER WANGER for ALLIED ARTISTS PICTURES CORPORATION, WALTER WANGER
PRODUCTIONS INC.

STARRING KEVIN MCCARTHY (Doctor Miles Bennell), DANA WYNTER (Becky Driscoll), LARRY GATES (Doctor
Dan Kauffman), KING DONOVAN (Jack), CAROLYN JONES (Theodora), JEAN WILLES (Nurse Sally Withers),
RALPH DUMKE (Chief of Police, Nick Grivett), VIRGINIA CHRISTINE (Wilma), TOM FADDEN (Uncle Ira),
KENNETH PATTERSON (Stanley Driscoll).

"Tomorrow you'll be one of us!"

After a two-week absence, Dr. Miles Bennell (Kevin McCarthy) returns home to sleepy Santa Mira, his piece of Californian utopia to find the community stricken by a bizarre outbreak of mass hysteria. A young boy insists that his mother just isn't his mother anymore. An agitated woman doesn't recognize her uncle. And during a visit to the home of his horror novelist friend, Bennell spots a gigantic embryo the size of a full-grown man.

The next morning, both the grotesque fetus and the psychological afflictions of his patients have vanished. Still, Dr. Bennell can't shake the feeling that an unseen force is closing in on his world, and his worst fears are confirmed when he stumbles upon enormous peapods containing spitting-image replicas of Santa Mira inhabitants. An alien life form, growing in his own backyard, is conspiring to take over the town. Soon Miles is the last human being alive, and must run for his life in a desperate attempt to escape the mind-controlled masses better known as "pod people."

Now one of the great classics of sci-fi cinema, Don Siegel's *Invasion of the Body Snatchers* took years to catch on with audiences and critics.

Compared to the standards of the time, it was a study in understatement (look closely and you'll even get a glimpse of uncredited co-writer Sam Peckinpah as a gas station attendant). Special effects were kept to a minimum, and horror was evoked without a monstrous face. Here, paranoia is not a symptom of xenophobia, but rather the fear of a sinister force at the heart of normality. The pod people are humanoid doppelgangers, incapable of emotion or individuality. In a chilling scene, Miles observes how nondescript passers-by respond to orders from an unseen commander and cluster together into a workers battalion to receive a new shipment of pods from a delivery truck. But only much later, after kissing his beloved Becky (Dana Wynter), does he feel the full horror of the mindlessness and blind obedience that has the town in its grip; for Becky's cold lips reveal that she too has become one of them, having surrendered her humanity in exchange for sleep.

As with so many science fiction films of the decade that depicted an invasion from outer space, the mind-stealing element of the Body Snatchers

1 Split pea soup: What Miles (Kevin McCarthy) and Becky (Dana Wynter) will become, if they don't find another hiding place pronto.

2 Taking a stab at genetic engineering: Cold War hysteria lets off steam in horror novelist Jack's (King Donovan) hot house.

"In a California town not too far away practically the entire population turned into a vegetable salad of sorts and the results — well, see this picture, *Invasion of the Body Snatchers*, this almost terrifying science-fiction yarn."

Los Angeles Examiner

3 Utopian lynch mob or weeding out individuality:
Miles and Becky decide it's time to check out of
suburbia.

4 Obedient, organized and orderly: Pod people or
neo-conservatives? You decide.

5 Home grown: By equating Americans with veget-
ables, Don Siegel puts film noir and horror in one
neat husk.

facilitated an anti-communist reading of the picture. Other interpretations
saw it as a reflection on the wave of fascism inspired by McCarthyism or on
Middle America's consumer conformity. Don Siegel's ingeniously subversive
tactic was, of course, to question the state of so-called normality rather than
any particular political ideologies. As the director said in an interview: "People are pods. Many of my associates are certainly pods. They have no feelings. They exist, breathe, sleep. To be a pod means that you have no passion,
no anger; the spark has left you." And a population of drones is naturally the
ideal basis for all forms of state control.

Sadly, Siegel himself also conceded to conformist pressures within the
industry. The studio forced him and producer Walter Wanger to embed the
main plot within a framing story that showed Miles raving about his run-ins
with the pod people to a psychologist. Finally, they buy his story and the FBI
intervenes. Don Siegel took pride in the fact that for years many underground
movie houses would stop the film prematurely at its originally foreseen end
point: the viewer is left with an extreme close-up of Miles, almost out of his
mind, as he fervently preaches his warning into the camera, "They're here
already! You're next, You're next . . ."

5

6   Cool as a cucumber: Jack doesn't seem the least bit disturbed to see his spitting image gestating in his living room – a reaction that's almost inhuman.

7   Car hop: In an effort to alert the authorities about the space invaders, Miles tries to keep his wits about him while grabbing a lift.

8   Break it up, you guys: Miles kills alien impostors before they kill his neighbors.

> ## "Well, I think there's a strong case for being a pod. These pods, who get rid of pain, ill health, and mental disturbance are, in a sense, doing good. It happens to leave you with a very dull world. But that, my dear friend, is the world that most of us live in." *Don Siegel*

7

Because of its short length and spartan budget of 417,000 dollars, *Body Snatchers* is categorized as a B-movie. But what really makes the film stand head and shoulders above the crowd of cheaper flicks is its clever integration of elements from other genres. The stark black-and-white contrasts, the motifs of sleep and underlying social instability are straight out of film noir; the same applies to Siegel's original title "Sleep no more," which was most likely rejected by the studio because of its cross-genre implications. Two successful remakes attest to the universal appeal of the story: Philip Kaufman's *Invasion of the Body Snatchers* (1978)) reworks the piece as a look at modern urban isolation, and Abel Ferrara's *Body Snatchers* (1993) relocated the action to an army base.

PB

Although by no means a household name, Walter Wanger had a career that spanned almost 50 years and is among Hollywood's most intriguing personalities. In 1919, he signed with the legendary Paramount Pictures forerunner Famous Players-Lasky Corporation. Later on, he became a free-lance producer working with almost all the major studios. As one of the few intellectuals holding such a position, he spoke out for the cinema's social responsibilities, a stance which was, however, only reflected in a handful of his 65 projects. His best-known work includes *Queen Christina* (1933) with Greta Garbo, *Stagecoach* (1939) and the Hitchcock thriller *Foreign Correspondent* (1940). At one point, he came close to a professional crash, although not as a result of his box-office flop *Joan of Arc* (1948), but because of a personal tragedy in 1951. Having discovered that his wife, actress Joan Bennett, was two-timing him with her agent, Wanger shot him in the groin, and spent four months behind bars as a result. Wanger rebuilt his reputation with the independent films *Riot in Cell Block 11* (1953/54) and *Invasion of the Body Snatchers* (1956). In 1958, he produced *I Want to Live!*, directed by Robert Wise, for which Susan Hayward won an Oscar as death row's Barbara Graham. In the early 60s, 20th Century Fox got him to climb aboard *Cleopatra* (1963), the 44-million-dollar bomb that nearly bankrupted the studio. This was to be his last picture. In 1968, Walter Wanger died in New York.

8

MOBY DICK

1956 - GREAT BRITAIN - 116 MIN. - COLOR - LITERARY ADAPTATION, DRAMA
DIRECTOR JOHN HUSTON (1906–1987)
SCREENPLAY RAY BRADBURY, JOHN HUSTON, based on the novel *MOBY DICK, OR, THE WHALE* by
HERMAN MELVILLE DIRECTOR OF PHOTOGRAPHY OSWALD MORRIS EDITING RUSSELL LLOYD MUSIC PHILIP SAINTON
PRODUCTION JOHN HUSTON, VAUGHAN N. DEAN for MOULIN.

STARRING GREGORY PECK (Captain Ahab), RICHARD BASEHART (Ishmael), LEO GENN (Starbuck),
JAMES ROBERTSON JUSTICE (Captain Boomer), FREDERICK LEDEBUR (Queequeg), HARRY ANDREWS (Stubb),
ORSON WELLES (Father Mapple), ROYAL DANO (Elijah), JOSEPH TOMELTY (The innkeeper),
TAMBA ALLENBY (Pip, the cabin boy).

"I'll follow him around the Horn, and around the Norway maelstrom, and around perdition's flames before I give him up."

Christmas 1848, New Bedford, New England. With swelling sails, the Pequod departs to hunt sperm whales in the Atlantic. The entire crew is hoping for a good catch, for a hold full of whale meat and whale oil. But the one-legged, sombre-visaged Captain Ahab (Gregory Peck) has something else in mind. He cares nothing for wealth or morality, as long as he can find and kill Moby Dick: the white whale, the king of the ocean, the sea-monster that robbed him of his left leg and made him a cripple in body and in mind.

Obsessed with thoughts of his private revenge, Ahab knows he needs to get the crew on his side, so he promises a gold doubloon to the man who first spots Moby Dick. He nails the coin to the main mast, where all can see it glittering in the sun. But Ahab is challenging not only the crew, but Nature – and therefore God himself. The ominous voyage proceeds, through storm and calm, until Moby Dick finally surfaces ahead of the prow. Only one member of the crew will survive the showdown: Ishmael (Richard Basehart), a simple sailor and the narrator of the story. Moby Dick sinks the ship, and Ishmael saves his own life by clinging to a watertight coffin that's floating amongst the flotsam until another whaler picks him up.

Director John Huston had wanted to film Herman Melville's great novel for more than a decade. At the start of the 50s, he met Ray Bradbury, author of the science fiction novel *Fahrenheit 451*, and asked him to condense Melville's sprawling epic to the length of a film script. Bradbury's screenplay is indeed a radically slimmed-down version of a bizarrely erudite literary masterpiece that covers everything from whaling to sailing to meteorology. One incidental curiosity: the process of making the film was actually more time-consuming than Ahab's insane hunt for the whale (as described by Melville).

For over three years, the film crew labored under considerable difficulties off the coast of Ireland and Madeira, and later in the studio too. It was

"Scene after scene is imprinted on the mind's eye: the smoky, weathered interior of Spouter Inn; a blazing sun distending against a lemony sky; the tall ship becalmed and quivering in the heat of an oily ocean; the encarnadined seas thrashed to a froth by harpooned whales; the dizzying leap of whale boats coursing in a 'Nantucket sleigh ride;' the green St. Elmo's fire dancing from the ship's spars."

Time Magazine

3

important to Huston to film outdoors, for he wanted the movie to look as real and vivid as possible. But *Moby Dick* also required a little help from the Dream Factory's box of tricks. For the titanic chase scenes on the open sea, three dummy white whales were constructed, each of them over 30 yards long, steel-framed monstrosities, covered with pale plastic. Two of them were lost in the Irish Sea; the first sank, and the second broke free of its moorings. For a long time, the newspapers delightedly reported that these "ghost whales" were still at liberty, drifting happily around somewhere in the Atlantic.

Huston and his cameraman Oswald Morris wanted a particular color-scheme for the film, comparable to the sepia tones of 19th-century whale-ship engravings. Together, they worked out a special process that gave the

film a grainy appearance and made the light appear strangely raw and "dirty." Somehow, it evoked or expressed Ahab's character perfectly. Huston had originally wanted to cast his own father in the leading role, but the Hollywood moguls would have none of it: Gregory Peck got the role, for the studio needed to attract a large audience in order to recoup the five million dollars the film had cost.

Though many people felt that Peck was miscast, he did lend thorough-ly convincingly expression to Ahab's manic, tormented soul, with his dark eyes grimly scouring the sky and the sea. The make-up department lent him a facial scar, some white streaks in his hair, and a false leg made of whale-bone. The only slight problem was Peck's soft, sensual mouth; framed by an Abe Lincoln beard, it radiated gentleness rather than iron resolution.

1 Honest Ahab: Despite Gregory Peck's impeccable performance as the ruthless Captain Ahab, critics just weren't convinced. Could it have had something to do with his presidential demeanor?

2 What a dick: Ahab becomes a hazard to the Pequod when he Moby gets the better of him. Note the whale bone peg-leg.

3 Overboard: First mate (Leo Genn as Starbuck) and captain get into each another's hair and rock the boat in already murky waters.

4 Daydream believers: The pagan Ishmael (Richard Basehart) has to save his own hide and that of islander Queequeg (Frederick Ledebur) from the wrathful hands of a superstitious crew.

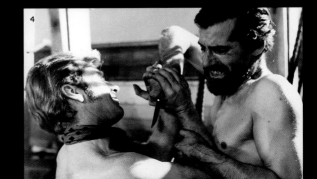

5

5   Die for your art: Moby Dick pulls Ahab down for the third time and Gregory Peck nearly lost his life while filming the sequence. Indeed, two whale set pieces, made of a steel skeleton with rubber exterior, ended up at the bottom of the sea.

6   Hooked: One of Ahab's men plans to audition for a part in *Peter Pan* when his stint on the Pequod is over.

7   Travel the world and the seven seas: Ahab throws caution to the wind and follows the whale to the tip of Cape Horn. It is here that the ship is seduced by the demonic green light of Antarctica, which he takes for the Aurora Mobialus.

8   A whale of a tale: Only Ishmael survives the horrors of Moby Dick. Using Queequeg's coffin as a raft, he goes off in search of help in the maritime wasteland.

"Like the book, the film is liquid – the rhythmic, tidal pulse of the ocean shades imperceptibly into the throb of blood in human arteries." *Time Magazine*

Frederick Ledebur, an aristocratic Austrian from Galicia, gave a memorable performance as Queequeg, the heavily tattooed Micronesian harpooner. In another supporting role, Orson Welles, as Father Mapple, stands in his prow-shaped pulpit in the seamen's chapel and tells the Biblical story of Jonah and the Whale. Even during the test takes, he performed with such passion and precision that everyone on the set was overwhelmed – and the rehearsal take became part of the finished film.

It was an intriguing adaptation of the book, the action scenes on the high seas were exhilarating, and the film's coloring is in itself a work of art; yet *Moby Dick* failed to attract the moviegoers *en masse*. Today, however, it has acquired the undisputed status of a classic.

SR

"Screenwriter Ray Bradbury masterfully captures the allegorical elements in the Herman Melville original without sacrificing any of the film's entertainment value ... Cinematographer Oswald Morris' washed-out color scheme brilliantly underlines the foredoomed bleakness of the story. *Moby Dick*'s one major shortcoming is its obviously artificial whale – but try telling a real whale to stay within camera range and hit its marks." *The New York Times*

OSWALD MORRIS AND THE NEW TECHNICOLOR DESATURATION PROCESS

As early as *Moulin Rouge* (1952), director John Huston and cameraman Oswald Morris (b. 1915) had experimented successfully with a controlled deployment of color. In order to achieve a color-scheme based on Toulouse-Lautrec's palette, they had entire sections of the film material colored. In *Moby Dick* (1956), it was the bleached-out sepia tones of 19th-century steel engravings that Huston and Morris wanted to emulate. Morris developed a process that enabled him to combine color and monochrome films. To do so, he used the old Technicolor processing technique, which allowed each of the three matrices to be worked on individually and complemented with a black-and-white image. When these were combined, the end result was the desired sepia tone. After the introduction of triple-layered Eastman Color film, Morris' ingenious method was no longer used. In order to achieve the same kind of bleached-out effect, Technicolor in Rome developed their New Technicolor Desaturation Process. This involved holding the film copies in a sepia bath during the developing process, with some sections of the picture colored reddish-purple. Once again, it was John Huston who initiated this technically complicated process, and a decade after *Moby Dick*, he perfected it further for the similarly desaturated *Reflections in a Golden Eye* (1967). Huston and Morris collaborated on other films, too: *Heaven Knows, Mr. Allison* (1957), *The Roots of Heaven* (1958), *The Mackintosh Man* (1973), and *The Man Who Would Be King* (1975). Morris' best-known work also includes Stanley Kubrick's *Lolita* (1962), Carol Reed's *Our Man in Havana* (1959), Martin Ritt's *The Spy Who Came In from the Cold* (1965), and a James Bond film, *The Man with the Golden Gun* (1974).

GIANT

1956 - USA - 201 MIN. - COLOR - DRAMA

DIRECTOR GEORGE STEVENS (1904–1975)
SCREENPLAY FRED GUIOL, IVAN MOFFAT, based on the novel of the same name by EDNA FERBER
DIRECTOR OF PHOTOGRAPHY WILLIAM C. MELLOR EDITING WILLIAM HORNBECK MUSIC DIMITRI TIOMKIN
PRODUCTION GEORGE STEVENS, HENRY GINSBERG for GIANT PRODUCTIONS, WARNER BROS.

STARRING ELIZABETH TAYLOR (Leslie Lynnton Benedict), ROCK HUDSON (Jordan "Bick" Benedict),
JAMES DEAN (Jett Rink), CARROLL BAKER (Luz Benedict II.), JANE WITHERS (Vashti Snythe),
CHILL WILLS (Uncle Bawley Benedict), MERCEDES MCCAMBRIDGE (Luz Benedict), DENNIS HOPPER (Jordan Benedict III),
SAL MINEO (Angel Obregon II), ROD TAYLOR (Sir David Karfrey), JUDITH EVELYN (Mrs. Nancy Lynnton),
EARL HOLLIMAN (Bob Dace), ROBERT NICHOLS (Pinky Snythe), PAUL FIX (Doctor Horace Lynnton).

ACADEMY AWARDS 1956 OSCAR for BEST DIRECTOR (George Stevens).

"Bick, you should have shot this fellow long time ago. Now he's too rich to kill."

Stripped of its stars, this picture would still be a cinematic giant. It is a tale of family lineage and legacy with epic magnitude, and the proud recipient of ten Oscar nominations, hailed by critics and audiences alike. But George Stevens' land baron saga became an instant classic for another reason altogether: it was James Dean's final movie. The 1950s Hollywood icon, whose fast and furious film career consisted of just two other features, *Rebel Without a Cause* (1955) and *East of Eden* (1955), died unexpectedly in a car crash on September 30th 1955 – a year before *Giant*'s official world premiere.

Dean plays cowboy Jett Rink, the third of his three big-screen rebels, and a man with an iron will tormented by eternal jealousy and unrequited love. Rink is what you might call *Giant*'s third wheel; for the two main characters are wedded couple Leslie and Jordan "Bick" Benedict (Elizabeth Taylor and Rock Hudson). Their story begins in Maryland during the early 1920s. Bick, a rich Texas rancher, falls for sassy East Coast beauty Leslie while trying to acquire a horse from her father. It's love at first sight, so the two quickly tie the knot and Leslie follows her beau to Texas to live on his

Reata ranch. But acclimating to her new environs proves a trial for the fragile flower of the East as Bick's sister Luz (Mercedes McCambridge) is harsher than the Texas sun. And being progressively minded, Leslie finds it hard to look the other way when her husband demeans Mexican immigrants or ruthlessly exploits his staff. This pressure cooker comes to a head when she befriends the introverted farmhand Jett Rink, and Bick gets a bad case of sour grapes. A full-blown marital crisis ensues when Leslie, continuing to press her luck, fights for the welfare of the Mexicans living in the neighboring town. Just as the couple seem to be patching things up, Luz dies in a riding accident and leaves a dark legacy that will forever bear upon the Benedicts: she bequeaths the hard-working Jett a small piece of homestead, and it soon transpires that he's sitting on a fortune in black gold. Overnight, the young man becomes one of Texas' most powerful oil barons and Bick's most ruthless competitor.

Giant spans twenty-five years at Reata. The film chronicles Leslie and Bick's lives both as a married couple and parents, documenting their per-

"The performances by Dean, Taylor, Hudson, et al, remind us of the days when 'movie star' wasn't a dirty phrase."

E! Online

1 A giant among men: He only made three films, but he left Hollywood a legend. James Dean as talk of the town, Jett Rink.

2 Cream of the crop: Leslie (Elizabeth Taylor) has a soft spot for pretty boy Jett Rink, but her heart belongs to handsome husband and cattle baron Bick.

3 Relationship derailed: Jordan "Bick" Benedict (Rock Hudson) can only sit and watch as his wife packs up with the children. He'll have to lay plenty of new track if he intends on winning her back.

3

sonal crises on the ranch alongside those of the other members of the Benedict family and the farmhands. The story's second tier follows Jett's metamorphosis from dirt-poor laborer to super-rich tycoon, who will not rest until he either wins Leslie's hand or drives Bick into the ground, going so far as to seduce their daughter (Carroll Baker) to achieve his ends. As the title suggests, *Giant* is a grand, sweeping film: well over three hours in length, and saturated with breathtaking shots of Texas landscapes as fertile as they are unforgiving. It is a film that delves into the complexities of racism, emancipation, and family; and its exceptional cast bring the minutiae of their world to life with razor-sharp accuracy and conviction. A generous amount of screen time is devoted to Bick's lifelong struggle with his own fatherly ambitions, for even at a young age the Benedict children defy the values of their father.

A four-year old Jordan breaks into tears when mounted on a pony. Disgusted at the sight before him, Bick snorts, "I could ride before I could walk," never suspecting that this event is a premonition of the trajectory their relationship will take. As an adolescent, Jordan (Dennis Hopper) has already voiced his lack of interest in ranching, wishing instead to pursue a career in medicine. Adding insult to injury, he later weds a Mexican. But this act of defiance also becomes a turning point in Bick's life, as he finally overcomes his deep-seated racism: when his daughter-in-law is refused service at a hotel beauty parlor during a reception honoring Jett Rink, Bick gives Jett a piece of his mind. However, this new mindset soon has negative repercussions in a separate incident at an eatery, when he tries to share his enlightened ways with a waiter unwilling to serve a Mexican family, and is beaten to a pulp.

"*Giant* is as intimate as a letter from home. A masterpiece."

·The Chicago Daily News

4

4 Breakfast of champions: Bick's eldest son Jordan Benedict III (Dennis Hopper) breaks with tradition as he pours himself a bowl of wild oats and heads off to medical school to sow them.

5 With the wind in their mares: Bick and Leslie
Benedict take a morning ride across Reata and
enjoy the advantages of private property.

6 South Fork meets Manderley: It's a good thing
these walls can't talk, because we'd never hear
the end of it.

7 Family foibles: After 25 years of hard work, Leslie
manages to work some of the kinks out of her
grassroots husband. Only now the hotheaded Bick
picks fights with strangers rather than his loved
ones.

Reforming his social views proves a long and arduous task, and time and again Bick falls victim to his own machismo and prejudice. Like a living cog in a cycle of hate, he blindly sings the praises of the Lone Star State – just one example of how the Texan mentality emerges as an invisible supporting player within the drama – and internalizes its implicit mantras as he dismisses Mexicans as lesser mortals, or silences his spouse when she dares to contribute to an exclusively male discussion about politics. Leslie, meanwhile, is the personification of moral goodness. As *Giant*'s sole Texas outsider and narrative counterpoint, actress Elizabeth Taylor subtly layers her character by displaying the undying devotion and patience of a loving wife, while astutely ridiculing the powers that be. While the Benedicts' repeated tiffs and lovers' quarrels never threaten to destroy their marriage, the brawl at the diner inadvertently renews their vows and reaffirms their relationship. By putting both his social status and his life on the line, Bick at long last wins his wife's respect.

ES

**GEORGE STEVENS
(1904–1975)**

Although George Stevens was responsible for classics like the comedy *Woman of the Year* (1941), the Western *Shane* (1953) and the Biblical epic *The Greatest Story Ever Told* (1964), Hollywood's upper echelons were forever to evade him. The son of actors Landers Stevens and Georgie Cooper, he was born in Oakland, California and started off as a cameraman in what would amount to an extremely diverse career. In the 1920s, he served as cinematographer to Hal Roach on Laurel & Hardy comedies like *Big Business* (1929) and *Men O'War* (1929). It was Roach who gave the ambitious young cameraman a chance to shoot his own short films. Stevens then began to gain further experience at Universal and RKO, eventually shooting his first feature-length film, *The Cohens and Kellys in Trouble* (1933).
An important development in Stevens' life and artistic work came during the Second World War as cameraman for a U.S. army outfit, with whom he would film the Allied invasion of Normandy. His camera crew also documented the Dachau concentration camp, resulting in the film *Nazi Concentration Camps* (1945), which was first shown at the Nuremburg Trials.
Over the course of his career, perfectionist George Stevens went from being a director of light comedies to a masterful genre chameleon, gradually gaining total control as producer on many of his filmmaking endeavors. He received his first Oscar nomination in directing for *The More the Merrier* (1943). His work as producer was recognized the previous year when *Talk of the Town* (1942) was nominated for Best Picture. *A Place in the Sun* (1951) marked his final departure from comedy – but earned Stevens his first Oscar in directing. His second came for his adaptation of Edna Ferber's *Giant* (1956). George Stevens died of a heart attack in March 1975.

THE SEVENTH SEAL

Det sjunde inseglet

956 - SWEDEN - 96 MIN. - B & W - DRAMA

DIRECTOR INGMAR BERGMAN (b. 1918)
SCREENPLAY INGMAR BERGMAN, based on his play *TRÄMÅLNING* **DIRECTOR OF PHOTOGRAPHY** GUNNAR FISCHER
EDITING LENNART WALLÉN **MUSIC** ERIK NORDGREN **PRODUCTION** ALLAN EKELUND for SVENSK FILMINDUSTRI.

STARRING GUNNAR BJÖRNSTRAND (Jöns), BENGT EKEROT (Death), NILS POPPE (Jof), MAX VON SYDOW (Antonius Block),
BIBI ANDERSSON (Mia), INGA GILL (Lisa), MAUD HANSSON (Witch), INGA LANDGRÉ (Karin),
GUNNEL LINDBLOM (Dumb Woman), BERTIL ANDERBERG (Raval).

"How can we believe in anything when we're no longer capable of trusting life?"

On a craggy Nordic coastline in the hours before dawn, a black eagle circles under mountainous clouds. Close to the surf, two men lie sleeping beside their horses: Antonius Block (Max von Sydow), a knight, and his squire Jöns (Gunnar Björnstrand). As the sun comes up, the knight rises with it – and a pale apparition in a monk's habit emerges from the shadows: Death (Bengt Ekerot). Block has been expecting him, yet he's unwilling to give up his life without a struggle, so he challenges the uncanny figure to a game of chess.

The dramatic light and shade of the opening is already enough to make it clear that this film has an allegorical dimension. *The Seventh Seal* tells the story of a crusader who returns to his Scandinavian homeland and finds it ravaged by the plague. There's misery everywhere, and the people are in a

state of moral degeneracy. While the squire Jöns confronts this situation with a mixture of cynicism and pragmatism, Block is thrown even further into his crisis of faith, restlessly questioning the existence of God. And only in the presence of the juggler Jof (Nils Poppe), his wife Mia (Bibi Andersson) and their small son can he find moments of inner peace.

Even today, the name Ingmar Bergman seems practically synonymous with an intellectually demanding and ethically relevant European cinema. In its existential pessimism and formal stringency, *The Seventh Seal* is widely regarded as the quintessence of the Swedish director's work. Based on a play written by Bergman himself, entitled "Trämålning" ("Woodcut"), the film version contains numerous motifs borrowed from early medieval Swedish

"The directness of *The Seventh Seal* is its strength. This is an uncompromising film, regarding good and evil with the same simplicity and faith as its hero."

Chicago Sun-Times

1   It won't be trumpets: Bard Jof (Nils Poppe) and his wife Mia are the last bastion of hope in a world dominated by pestilence and warfare.

2   Dance with death: Ingmar Bergman's spectacular mise-en-scene was inspired by medieval paintings and ornamental woodcarvings.

3   Curtain call: A gruesome promise is fulfilled with the breaking of the seventh seal. Bengt Ekerot as Death.

2

church paintings as well as from the woodcuts of Albrecht Dürer. These include Death personified, typically seen playing chess or sawing down the tree of life. The various characters encountered by the knight are also powerfully drawn; in their archetypal presence, they constitute a kind of typology of the human race. No doubt the preacher's son Ingmar Bergman felt closest to Antonius Block, the ascetic seeker after life's essential truth and meaning. It's easy to see Block as the director's alter ego, for Bergman has openly stated that the film's apocalyptic plague scenarios were an expression of his own terror in the face of the nuclear threat.

Gunnar Fischer's masterly black-and-white cinematography also has the clarity of a medieval print. Block's homecoming, his desperate search for

God, is shown in rigorously composed monochrome images that are laden with symbolism. The almost archaic power of these images is often reminiscent of the Scandinavian and German Expressionist films of the silent era. The close-ups, above all, make it clear how much Bergman admired the films of Carl Theodor Dreyer. And like Dreyer's two masterpieces, *The Passion of Joan of Arc* (*La Passion de Jeanne d'Arc*, 1928) and *Day of Anger* (*Vredens dag*, 1943), *The Seventh Seal* climaxes with the burning of a witch.

On one dark night in the course of their journey, Block and his companion emerge from a forest to find a place of execution: a girl is to be burnt at the stake. Before the executioners light the pyre, Block approaches the alleged witch, but she too has no answer to his questions. In the young

3

GUNNAR BJÖRNSTRAND No other actor worked with Ingmar Bergman as often as Gunnar Björnstrand. The son of a famous theater actor, he was born in Stockholm in 1909. After trying out various other occupations in his youth, he eventually took private acting lessons: he then went on to the Royal Drama School in Stockholm, where Ingrid Bergman was a student in the same year. After completing his studies, Björnstrand worked in the theater, before his film career began in the early 1930s. He was soon appearing alongside rising stars such as Zarah Leander and his former classmate Ingrid Bergman. Though Björnstrand would later work with many other well-known film, TV and theater directors, it was the movies of Ingmar Bergman that made him internationally famous in the 50s. In his early comedies, Bergman made ideal use of Björnstrand's impish talents. *Smiles of a Summer Night* (*Sommarnattens leende*, 1955), for example, featured a wonderful performance by Björnstrand. In one superb scene, he is discovered, clad only in his nightshirt, in the company of a former mistress, with the episode culminating in a brilliantly witty verbal exchange. His best-known perform-ance, however, was as the squire Jöns in *The Seventh Seal* (*Det sjunde inseglet*, 1956). Sardonic and disillusioned, Jöns represents a kind of coun-terweight to Antonius Block, his spiritually tormented master. Gunnar Björnstrand gave memorable performances in several other Bergman films, including *Through a Glass Darkly* (*Såsom i en spegel*, 1961) and *Winter Light* (*Nattvardsgästerna*, 1962). In his old age, he also took on a minor role in *Fanny and Alexander* (*Fanny och Alexander*, 1982). He died four years later in Stockholm.

4

4 Keeping Death in check: 29 years prior to taking on Satan, Max von Sydow (right) fought valiantly in a battle of life and death that made him a household name overnight.

5 Masked avengers: The church spooks the locals into behaving piously.

6 Apocalypse now: With the end in sight, mortals begin to castigate themselves for their ungodly ways …

7 … or opt to get bombed at the local watering hole. Whatever the poison, temporary numbness is their only escape from eternal damnation.

woman's face we see no profound insight, only fear. Uncomforted, she suffers a senseless, barbaric death.

Yet Bergman declines to let his film end in unmitigated gloom. During the travelers' next pause for rest, they begin the final round in their game of chess. Block knows he has lost, but he does manage one final "good deed:" in order to distract Death, he knocks over some of the figures, seemingly inadvertently – and Mia and Jof are able to flee. But it's checkmate for the crusader, and the cowled victor demands the tribute Block had been anticipating: all those still with him must now accompany him all the way … As the sun rises, the film ends with a Dance of Death. The juggler and his wife and child are the only ones to escape, and they remind us of the Holy Family. It's an ending that at least leaves us with some hope of a better future.

UB

5

"The power of these images is stronger than the intellect. Bergman makes our hearts pound, as and when he will." *Die Welt*

THE SEARCHERS

1956 - USA - 119 MIN. - COLOR - WESTERN

DIRECTOR JOHN FORD (1894–1973)
SCREENPLAY FRANK S. NUGENT, based on the novel of the same name by ALAN LE MAY
DIRECTOR OF PHOTOGRAPHY WINTON C. HOCH EDITING JACK MURRAY MUSIC MAX STEINER, STAN JONES (Song: "The Searchers")
PRODUCTION C. V. WHITNEY for C. V. WHITNEY PICTURES, WARNER BROS.

STARRING JOHN WAYNE (Ethan Edwards), JEFFREY HUNTER (Martin Pawley), VERA MILES (Laurie Jorgensen),
WARD BOND (Reverend Captain Samuel Clayton), NATALIE WOOD (Debbie Edwards),
JOHN QUALEN (Lars Jorgensen), OLIVE CAREY (Mrs. Jorgensen), HENRY BRANDON (Chief Scar),
WALTER COY (Aaron Edwards), DOROTHY JORDAN (Martha Edwards).

"We'll find them in the end.
We'll find them. I promise you."

The Searchers is a classic Western, but by no means a classical one. Good fails to defeat evil, and civilization certainly doesn't triumph over nature. Contradictions and mysteries remain, and most of them have to do with a man it's hard to call a hero.

Three years after the end of the Civil War, Ethan Edwards (John Wayne) visits the farm owned by his brother Aaron (Walter Coy) in Texas. It's a brief reunion. Ethan returns from an unsuccessful search for poachers to a scene of pure horror: Aaron and his wife Martha (Dorothy Jordan) have been murdered by Comanches, and their daughters Lucy and Debbie have been abducted. Ethan immediately organizes a search party and sets off in pursuit of the culprits. With them is young Martin Pawley (Jeffrey Hunter), the adopted son of the family, whom Ethan himself had once found wandering in the desert. Soon, they stumble upon Lucy's corpse. The rest of the search party

give up. Ethan and Martin continue on their quest, alone. In the course of the following five years, a terrible suspicion will form in Martin's mind: Ethan is less interested in finding his niece than in killing her, for her long captivity has now made Debbie a Comanche.

Without robbing the Western of its mythic power, John Ford shows that he is capable of keeping a distance from the genre with which he is identified. Ethan is a puzzling figure, a man surrounded by unasked and unanswered questions. What has he been doing since the Civil War ended? Was he a hero? A bandit? Is his deeply racist attitude really based only on a desire to avenge his brother's family? He hates the Indians, especially the Comanche tribe; yet it becomes increasingly clear that he has a profound knowledge of their customs and way of life. When the search party passes an Indian grave, Ethan shoots out the eyes of the corpse, so the deceased will

1

2

A bitter racist, quick to anger and take offense, the implacable foe of all tribes but especially the Comanche, Edwards is one of the most astonishing portraits of unapologetic, unmotivated fury ever put on screen, an unvarnished, frightening glimpse of the darkest side of the men who subdued the plains." *Los Angeles Times*

have to "wander amongst the winds for all eternity." And when Ethan meets his deadly enemy Scar (Henry Brandon) – the demonic Comanche chief – it's as if he were looking into a mirror.

Everything Ethan does makes one thing clear: this is a man without a tribe. In white society, he remains an outsider. The most famous shots are at the beginning and end of the film: they show him alone at the door of the farmhouse. This door marks the boundary between civilization and wilderness, and Ethan never goes through it. Nor did he even do so in the days

when he and Martha were a couple, as we see from the few scenes in the family home. Ford closes the door with a wipe to the next scene: Ethan alone in the depths of Monument Valley. Like the dead Indian, Ethan will find no peace, for he is haunted and pursued by the demons of his own past.

Many years passed before Ford's film was accused of being racist; and it took even longer until people were ready to do justice to its unusually modern episodic structure. Ford's attitude is as hard to pin down as that of his protagonist, and can perhaps only be construed by viewing the entire film.

1 The search is over: Searchers Martin (Jeffrey Hunter), Ethan (John Wayne) and the Reverend (Ward Bond) find themselves at a dead end when internal squabbles come to a head.

2 Monument Valley: The Grand Canyon excluded, John Ford and John Wayne are the cornerstones of the American West.

3 Little Debbie: Despite Ethan's assumptions, Debbie's (Natalie Wood) destiny looks even sweeter than ice cream.

4   Up to his eyeballs in it, chief: The rangers are aghast as they trample over sacred Indian burial ground while conducting their search.

5   Some things never change: Ethan and Martin lose their posse and get stuck alone with one another yet again. Their quest to retrieve Debbie lasts five long, arduous, painful, and backbreaking years. How's that for a mouthful?

6   Elbow room: John Wayne strips himself of his Hollywood veneer to deliver a performance as awe-inspiring as it is repugnant.

We are never shown an Indian committing a murder; yet Ethan kills Indians as they flee – a senseless deed, which shocks even his thick-skinned companions. The U. S. Cavalry, the pride of many earlier Ford films, is also guilty of terrible crimes. Ethan is a stark contrast to the peaceable Martin, who is one-eighth Cherokee, and whom Ethan clearly rejects from their first meeting onwards. That he finally does accept this man effects a change within Ethan: when the searchers finally find Debbie (Natalie Wood), he is capable of embracing her. Not without scalping her husband, though, for she has indeed become Scar's squaw.

The Searchers is John Ford's darkest and most complex Western, its tragic weight barely lightened by a minor sub-plot concerning the Edwards' Swedish neighbors. The leading actor also described the movie as Ford's best, and it certainly features one of John Wayne's most impressive performances. His irrepressible strength and individuality lends this movie even more power. The Searchers became a milestone of American cinema, and motifs from the movie can be found in countless later films, including Martin Scorsese's Taxi Driver (1975) and George Lucas' Star Wars (1977).

PB

JOHN WAYNE (1907–1979)

America's most popular actor was born in Iowa as Marion Michael Morrison. At the University of Southern California, "the Duke" was mostly known as a football player. From 1928 onwards, he played minor roles in films directed by his friend John Ford, until he finally made his breakthrough in Ford's classic Western, Stagecoach (1939). The two of them would go on to make around 20 films together, including She Wore a Yellow Ribbon (1949), Rio Grande (1950) and The Man Who Shot Liberty Valance (1962). These were films that stamped his image as a Western roughneck: craggy, tenacious, tightlipped and unwavering – the quintessential American hero, often in uniform. Wayne was thoroughly unfazed by the accusation that he only ever played himself. Ford's nostalgic Irish comedy The Quiet Man (1952), in which he partnered Maureen O'Hara, featured Wayne in one of his few comic roles. Even in other genres, such as the safari adventure Hatari! (1962) or the war film The Green Berets (1968), Wayne remained true to himself and his image.

A Hollywood strongman who never tried to conceal his reactionary views, John Wayne was nevertheless capable of treating his own myth with considerable irony. El Dorado (1967) and Rio Lobo (1970), two of Howard Hawks' famous late Westerns, featured the elderly Wayne as a washed-out gunslinger. For his performance as the drunken Marshal in Henry Hathaway's True Grit (1969), he received his only Oscar. His last role was as a cancer-ridden gunslinger in Don Siegel's The Shootist (1976). John Wayne died of lung cancer in 1979. It's said that he wasn't averse to a little punch-up right up until the very end.

THE TEN COMMANDMENTS

1956 - USA - 220 MIN. - COLOR - HISTORICAL EPIC, BIBLICAL EPIC

DIRECTOR CECIL B. DEMILLE (1881–1959)

SCREENPLAY ÆNEAS MACKENZIE, JESSE LASKY JR., JACK GARISS, FREDRIC M. FRANK
DIRECTOR OF PHOTOGRAPHY LOYAL GRIGGS EDITING ANNE BAUCHENS MUSIC ELMER BERNSTEIN
PRODUCTION CECIL B. DEMILLE for MOTION PICTURE ASSOCIATES, PARAMOUNT PICTURES.

STARRING CHARLTON HESTON (Moses), YUL BRYNNER (Rameses II), ANNE BAXTER (Nefretiri),
EDWARD G. ROBINSON (Dathan), YVONNE DE CARLO (Sephora), DEBRA PAGET (Lilia), JOHN DEREK (Joshua),
CEDRIC HARDWICKE (Sethi), NINA FOCH (Bithiah), MARTHA SCOTT (Yochabel),
JUDITH ANDERSON (Memnet), VINCENT PRICE (Baka), JOHN CARRADINE (Aaron).

ACADEMY AWARDS 1956 OSCAR for BEST SPECIAL EFFECTS (John P. Fulton).

"God made men.
Men made slaves."

God made heaven and earth, but Cecil B. DeMille gave us *The Ten Com-mandments* – the greatest Biblical epic ever made. It tells the story of Moses, his abandonment as a baby, his dealings as a prince at the court of the Pharaoh, the discovery of his Hebrew origins, the Israelites' Exodus from Egypt, and the delivery of the tablets bearing the Ten Commandments on Mount Sinai. DeMille, "The High Priest of Hollywood," knew how to lure the public from their TVs to the movie theaters: with dozens of star actors, bombastic sets, astounding special effects, and an army of extras as numerous as the slaves of Pharaonic Egypt. What impresses most? The sheer number of people involved in the Exodus scenes? The trick by which Moses turns the water of the Nile into blood? The parting of the Red Sea? Or is it in fact the holy man and liberator of his people, Moses himself?

Generations are still of the opinion that Moses looked like Charlton Heston. Or vice versa. DeMille, for his part, had chosen his leading actor after seeing Michelangelo's famous statue of Moses in the Roman church of San Pietro in Vincoli. In the Hollywood of the 50s, Heston was in any case the heroic actor *par excellence*. Like *Ben-Hur* (1959) three years later, *The Ten Commandments* gave him the chance to put his athletic body to work in the service of a good cause. We're shown the prince in all his youthful splendor, his fall into backbreaking slavery, and his rebirth as a prophet, filled with

divine fury and blessed with a resplendent head of hair. His adversary is Yul Brynner as Rameses II, a stubborn and vengeful tyrant. As the Bible was a little thin on supporting figures, DeMille provided a few amusing ones of his own, including the lecherous Queen Nefretiri (Anne Baxter) and the villainous overseer Dathan (Edward G. Robinson).

Before the story even begins, DeMille makes a dramatic personal appearance, gently breaking the news that the film that follows will be nearly four hours long. He goes on to emphasize the extensive amount of "historical" research that went into the project, before revealing the point of the whole monstrous endeavor: Moses' struggle against Rameses, DeMille tells us, is a struggle for freedom. Skillfully, he links the terms "freedom" and "liberty" with the message of the Ten Commandments. The Pharaoh's rule allows plenty of opportunities for speaking ill, worshipping false gods, and not loving your neighbor but hurting him. Revealingly, the obsessive moralist DeMille is much more interested in sin on the Nile than in any kind of spiritual message. We're shown the intrigues that go on at court, Nefretiri's constant wooing of her former lover ("Oh Moses, Moses, you stubborn, splendid, adorable fool!"), the eroticism of half-naked bodies, the sadistic maltreatment of the sweaty slaves. DeMille and his Hollywood heroes clearly know what they're up to. The director's first attempt at this story (made in 1923) had in fact been even more risqué, with bare-bosomed women dancing around the Golden Calf; by the 50s, however, such barefaced titillation had become taboo.

DeMille's love of inflated kitsch explains the unbroken popularity of this movie, whether one experiences it as a religious revelation or simply laughs at the unintentional comedy of it all. Most of the actors settle in with Heston's

1 Wielding weapons: Before the advent of firearms, men made themselves heard with staffs. Charlton Heston as Moses, the great prophet of the 1950s.

2 Set me free, why don't you babe: Moses implores Pharaoh Rameses (Yul Brynner) to let his people go.

3 Speak softly and carry a big stick: For his next trick, Moses will use his magic wand to turn the Nile River into blood. Hollywood senses Oscars all around.

4 A new reading of the Bible: Adhering to the commandment, "Thou shalt not steal" Cecil B. DeMille based his movie neither on historical nor Biblical fact. Cedric Hardwicke as Sethi and Anne Baxter as Princess Nefretiri – the minions of a dogmatic dictator.

"The 70th motion picture produced by 75-year-old Cecil B. DeMille is the biggest, most expensive, and in some respects perhaps the most vulgar movie ever made." Time Magazine

CECIL B. DEMILLE (1881–1959)

Alongside D. W. Griffith, Cecil B. DeMille is regarded as inventor of the still-popular Hollywood narrative style. He was also the prototype of the powerful Hollywood director-producer. In 1913, he teamed up with Jesse L. Lasky and Samuel Goldwyn to form the Jesse L. Lasky Feature Play Company, which later became Paramount Pictures. He set his first milestone as a director with *The Squaw Man* (1914), a Western that was so successful that he made two separate remakes, in 1918 and 1931, with ever-bigger budgets. Innumerable comedies with titles like *Don't Change Your Husband* (1918/19) and *Why Change Your Wife?* (1920) consolidated his reputation as a brilliant storyteller, and as an unrestrained moralist on very slippery terrain. *The Ten Commandments* (1923) depicted the Exodus from Egypt and the delivery of the tablets on Mount Sinai; a leap forward in time to modern San Francisco served to demonstrate the Commandments' timeless validity. For all his pioneering qualities, DeMille never enjoyed the approval of the critics. None of them saw him as the equal of D. W. Griffith, which may have had something to do with DeMille's weakness for bombastic Biblical and sword-&-sandal epics. *The King of Kings* (1927), *The Sign of the Cross* (1932), *Cleopatra* (1934) and *Samson and Delilah* (1949) were all big-budget productions. By the 50s, this often-imitated concept was past its sell-by date. DeMille's far-right political views cost him further sympathy, for the dictatorial man with the megaphone was a supporter of McCarthy's anti-communist witch hunt. Nonetheless, he did win a single Oscar, for the charming circus story *The Greatest Show on Earth* (1951). *The Ten Commandments* (1956) was the last film made by "Mr. Movies."

5   Jews to the Promised Land: Moses recruits slaves to join his mass exodus and the crowd goes wild first, godless second.

6   Flashy pharaohs: Nefretiri loves little orphan Moses, but she's not about to protest a future as Rameses' pampered queen.

7   Holy cow! Moses returns from Mt. Sinai and presents the Jews with the Ten Commandments.

> "With all due regard for the technical difficulties besetting Mr. DeMille, we must say his special effects department was not up to sets or costumes. The parting of the Red Sea is an obvious piece of camera trickery in which two churning walls of water frame a course as smooth and dry as a race track." *The New York Times*

melodramatic acting style; indeed, the static directing style hardly allows them to avoid it. But would any other form have been adequate for this "greatest show on earth"? With a budget of 13 million dollars, this was, at the time, the most expensive film ever made, though it did take in several times that amount at the box office. In the Exodus scenes alone, 2000 extras were deployed, twice the number of people estimated to have taken part in the actual historical event. The city of the Pharaoh was built near Cairo, and it was the biggest Egyptian construction project since the Suez Canal. Cecil B. DeMille didn't just contribute substantially to the creation of the Hollywood style; with his last movie, he also founded the modern genre of the blockbuster. It's been said that the voice of God in this film belonged to him or to Charlton Heston. But that's just a rumor.

12 ANGRY MEN

957 - USA - 96 MIN. - B & W - COURTROOM DRAMA

DIRECTOR SIDNEY LUMET (b. 1924)

SCREENPLAY REGINALD ROSE DIRECTOR OF PHOTOGRAPHY BORIS KAUFMAN EDITING CARL LERNER MUSIC KENYON HOPKINS PRODUCTION HENRY FONDA, REGINALD ROSE for ORION-NOVA PRODUCTIONS.

STARRING HENRY FONDA (Juror #8), LEE J. COBB (Juror #3), ED BEGLEY (Juror #10), E. G. MARSHALL (Juror #4), JACK WARDEN (Juror #7), MARTIN BALSAM (Juror #1), JOHN FIEDLER (Juror #2), JACK KLUGMAN (Juror #5), ED BINNS (Juror #6), JOSEPH SWEENEY (Juror #9), GEORGE VOSKOVEC (Juror #11), ROBERT WEBBER (Juror #12), John Savoca (The Accused), RUDY BOND (Judge).

IFF BERLIN 1957 GOLDEN BEAR (Sidney Lumet).

"I don't have no personal feelings about that, I just want to talk about facts."

Hustle bustle fills the streets; the sounds of horns, motors and urban buzz immerse us in the cacophony of city life. But suddenly the waves of sound hit a rock of noble columns, and fade away as our eyes are guided upwards to the inscription above the proud Corinthian capitals. "The True Administration of Justice is the Firmest Pillar of Good Government," we read; a phrase, as every American will tell you, that comes from a letter George Washington wrote to the U.S. Attorney General Edmund Randolph in 1789. Emphasizing the central role of justice in a young democracy, the words adorn the entrance of the New York Supreme Court, the very symbol of American values.

Inside the courthouse, the sounds of the city die away in the imposing corridor of the marble entrance hall with all its human dramas: on one side, we see a weary man in his mid-fifties with beads of perspiration dripping from his brow; not far away, some people are jumping for joy over an acquittal. Meanwhile, in courtroom 228, a judge presides indifferently if not disinterestedly over a murder trial. After the cases have been heard, he leaves the jury to their grave task of deciding whether there is reasonable doubt with regard to the defendant's guilt. The door to the jury's bare deliberation room shuts, thus ending the prolog to one of the cinema's most extraordinary courtroom dramas.

On this, the hottest day of the year, Sidney Lumet locks us in a room with 12 angry men who must determine whether or not a young man stabbed his father to death. A guilty verdict is almost unanimous: only juror number eight (Henry Fonda) remains unconvinced, and with sound arguments he begins to cast doubt on the alleged means and motive of the crime, and the credibility of the eyewitnesses. As condemning as the evidence initially appears to be, before long the audience is certain that the jury will turn in a verdict of "not guilty." The truth proves to be relative, and the suspense created by the doubt that is brewing among the jury soon overshadows the question of the defendant's guilt, with the audience guessing who will be the next to change his verdict. Arguments escalate, and soon polarized jurors are at each other's throats.

ONE-ROOM DRAMAS "It never occurred to me that shooting an entire movie within a single room could be problematic. In fact, I thought of it as something I could use to my advantage." Such are the sentiments Sidney Lumet voices about *12 Angry Men* (1957) in his book *Making Movies*. Indeed, extreme spatial constraints give films a unique psychological edge; they focus the viewer's attentions on the characters to such an extent that, beyond the walls of the setting, there is nowhere else to look but deep into their flawed souls. In *Der Totmacher* (*The Deathmaker*, 1995), Romuald Karmakar traps the audience in an interrogation room with serial killer Fritz Haarmann, where the psychopath relates his gruesome acts with horrifying ease. Based on original police records from the 1920s, the film presents a shocking psychological portrait, made all the more compelling by Götz George's stunning performance. The genre itself, however, produces more than just this type of character-driven suspense as Carl Schenkel's situationally pressurized film *Abwärts (Out of Order*, 1984*)* makes clear. Here, four people fight for survival in a stuck elevator, the plot's action triggering the characters to bare all psychologically. In the one-room drama, the space itself is the unifying constant: the condensed sense of reality makes the venue the locus of the final revelation. In his film adaptation of the play *Who's Afraid of Virginia Woolf?* (1966), Mike Nichols showed the gruesome depths such dialog-based quests for truth can sink to when the most intimate secrets of a college professor and his wife are bared in an emotional bloodbath. Although well-drawn characters form the heart of any one-room drama, lighting and cinematography are also of fundamental importance. In *12 Angry Men*, perpetually changing perspectives and camera lenses create an almost unbearable sense of claustrophobia. In *Rope* (1948), Alfred Hitchcock ingeniously intensified the genre's spatial constraints by giving the film the illusion of playing out over a single continuous shot. Years later, in a widely-acclaimed interview with director and film critic François Truffaut, Hitchcock ridiculed the film's experimental, stylistic technique as "idiotic."

"Ever since you walked into this room you've been acting like a self-appointed public avenger. You want to see this boy die, because you personally want it, not because of the facts. You're a sadist."

Film quote: Juror #8 (Henry Fonda)

1   Exhibit A: Twelve angry men try to assess whether they've got their hands on an ordinary piece of cutlery or a red-hot murder weapon. What starts off as an open-and-shut case, soon fans out into reasonable doubt.

2   Blue in the face: Initially, all the talking in the world doesn't seem to get these guys any closer to a consensus. Until the jury's own skeletons start making their way out of the closet and into the courtroom, that is.

3   Of men and mice: Twelve commoners deliberate about another man's life, and have their morals put through the wringer. An omniscient camera communicates their respective mindsets by cornering them in the jury room.

4   Fight club: Juror number 5 (Jack Klugman) teaches the others the basics of ghetto warfare.

Sidney Lumet took Reginald Rose's television play and shot this outstanding courtroom drama, his debut feature, in just three weeks. As is often the case with Lumet's work, *12 Angry Men* delves to the depths of the human soul. Neither the psychological recreation of the crime nor the incessant battle of words among the jury are the film's true focus. Instead, Lumet uses the jury to look at the mechanisms of justice, usually depicted as a blind but impartial governing hand.

Lumet removes its godly aura, presenting us instead with a jury of thoroughly human components, full of prejudices and personal shortcomings. Bound by a vow of secrecy while the court is in session, the jury room discussions reveal many of the jurors' judgments to be of a personal nature, founded more on their social status than on facts. One of the men is more concerned about the evening baseball game than he is about the defendant's life; another sees the accused as nothing more than a foreigner and a scapegoat for his frustrations; and yet a third projects his deep-seated anger towards his own son onto the defendant.

In line with traditional techniques of courtroom drama, a beloved genre in American cinema whose emergence coincided with the advent of talkies, Lumet turns rich dialog into a catalyst for suspense. But rather than polished

rhetoric and clever pro-and-con debates, he presents base arguments that develop into far-reaching conflicts over the course of the story, provoking wild tirades and fits of rage. The camerawork reflects this progression, initially showing the characters in midrange shots filmed from slightly overhead. Over time, a noticeable shift in visual perspective gives rise to extreme close-ups or action filmed from an angle below; at once, the jury room ceiling pushes its way into the picture while lenses with longer focal lengths shrink the space, creating a powder keg atmosphere, defused only by the wide-angle shot that opens up the room at the film's conclusion.

Despite the jury's verdict, the innocence of the accused is far from certain. The court proceedings and handling of evidence are presented as superficial and faulty. We exit the movie believing that the eighth juror's stubborn defense of his own point of view is the sole undisputed virtue. The film must therefore be understood as a plea for democracy, a system that gives voice to the individual. Even so, the jury's rational methodology is depicted as the exception rather than the rule. The outcome makes us question the administration of justice and, given the jury's initial lethargy, the death penalty in particular. Perhaps this socially critical view was responsible for the film's flop at the box office; only later did it achieve its status as a classic.   OK

THE BRIDGE ON THE RIVER KWAI ♸♸♸♸♸♸♸

1957 - GREAT BRITAIN / USA - 161 MIN. - COLOR - WAR FILM

DIRECTOR DAVID LEAN (1908–1991)
SCREENPLAY PIERRE BOULLE, MICHAEL WILSON, CARL FOREMAN, based on the novel *LE PONT DE LA RIVIÈRE KWAI*
by PIERRE BOULLE DIRECTOR OF PHOTOGRAPHY JACK HILDYARD EDITING PETER TAYLOR MUSIC MALCOLM ARNOLD
PRODUCTION SAM SPIEGEL for HORIZON PICTURES, COLUMBIA PICTURES CORPORATION.

STARRING WILLIAM HOLDEN (Major Shears), JACK HAWKINS (Major Warden), ALEC GUINNESS (Colonel Nicholson),
SESSUE HAYAKAWA (Colonel Saito), JAMES DONALD (Major Clipton), GEOFFREY HORNE (Lieutenant Joyce),
ANDRÉ MORELL (Colonel Green), PETER WILLIAMS (Major Reeves), JOHN BOXER (Captain Hughes),
PERCY HERBERT (Grogan).

ACADEMY AWARDS 1957 OSCARS for BEST FILM (Sam Spiegel), BEST DIRECTOR (David Lean), BEST ACTOR (Alec Guinness),
BEST ADAPTED SCREENPLAY (Pierre Boulle, Michael Wilson and Carl Foreman [awarded posthumously in 1984]),
BEST CINEMATOGRAPHY (Jack Hildyard), BEST EDITING (Peter Taylor), BEST SCORE (Malcolm Arnold).

"Madness! ... Madness!"

Japanese-occupied Burma, 1943. War is madness; and it's madness to build a bridge that will give your enemies an advantage great enough to decide who wins the war. It's even crazier to devote enormous technical ingenuity to building a bridge capable of standing forever – only to destroy it shortly after completion. For Colonel Nicholson (Alec Guinness), however, it's a question of honor. He's the Commanding Officer of a British battalion in a Japanese POW camp deep in the Burmese jungle; and right at the start of the film, he shows us just how stubborn he can be. The camp commander Colonel Saito (Sessue Hayakawa) orders the British prisoners to construct a rail bridge over the River Kwai. Nicholson, who always carries a copy of the Geneva Convention, insists that he and his officers may not be compelled to perform manual labor. Saito reacts with fury, but even several days in "the oven," without food or light, fail to break Nicholson's will.

Not only does Nicholson get his way on this, he also has the incompetent Japanese constructors replaced, thus ensuring that his personal fate will depend on the bridge being built correctly. It's a bridge made of blood, sweat and tears, and in his vision, the entire British Empire rests on the pillars of this edifice. Meanwhile, a three-man team of explosives experts is on its way through the jungle, hoping to destroy his work. Among them is Shears (William Holden), an American who had previously managed to escape from the camp.

2

1   Blasting through Her Majesty's heart: The American Shears (William Holden) is commissioned by the British to blow the bridge into an empire known as Kingdom Come.

2   Never let them see you sweat: No amount of pressure can break the iron will of Colonel Nicholson (Alec Guinness).

3   Cut off: The men have to pull off the blast without a lifeline to the government that has employed them to do so.

4   Hara-kiri: Colonel Saito (Sessue Hayakawa) ignores modernity, preferring to defend his honor the old-fashioned way.

5   March of the green berets: And when the troops get tired of that tune, they'll switch over to the Colonel Bogey 'Shuffle.'

He's not the only one who thinks Nicholson is crazy, but it won't be Shields who ultimately presses the lever and blows the whole thing sky-high …

The film is based on a novel by Pierre Boulle, which didn't include the movie's thrilling finale. (In fact, the script was reworked incessantly until it reached its final form.) David Lean, however, felt the explosive ending was an absolute necessity, for *The Bridge on the River Kwai* was not just his first major epic, but his first film in widescreen format. And it was a huge popular success, largely because it's so incredibly spectacular – something that Lean's trailers and advertising campaign had taken great pains to emphasize.

Filming took place under difficult conditions in the jungles of Sri Lanka. The enormous wooden construction took eight months to build and cost a quarter of a million dollars. The train that crashes into the water had belonged to a maharajah 65 years previously. Indeed, the whole thing was

"Alec Guinness does a memorable — indeed, a classic — job in making the ramrod British colonel a profoundly ambiguous type. With a rigid, serene disposition, he displays the courage and tenacity of a lion, as well as the denseness and pomposity of a dangerously stupid, inbred snob. He shows, beneath the surface of a hero, the aspects of an inhuman fool. He gives one of the most devastating portraits of a militarist that we have ever seen." *The New York Times*

"Do not speak to me of rules. This is war! This is not a game of cricket!"

Film quote: Colonel Saito (Sessue Hayakawa)

...esigned to be a magnificent spectacle, and to that end, William Holden was ...are-chested for much of the movie's duration.

Many people regard *The Bridge on the River Kwai* as the last David Lean ...ilm that actually focuses on individual human beings. Nicholson and Saito ...re basically two sides of a single character. While one is driven to commit ...reason by his belief in British discipline and the superiority of his own cul-...ure, the other is prepared to commit hara-kiri after suffering a humiliation. ...hat eventually drives both of them mad is not the distant war, but the mili-...ary principle of unconditional duty. Alec Guinness later commented that he ...ad found Nicholson insufferable from the very beginning, yet the character's ...bsessive formality also reveals a deep human tragedy. Guinness' perform-...nce makes the tension between military selflessness and personal integrity

positively palpable, and it marked a significant step forward in the English man's career. By contrast, Sessue Hayakawa – the Japanese actor who played his adversary – had to be called out of retirement. In the early years of the Dream Factory, he had been a star of the silent movies, and that turned out to be pretty useful experience for his role in *Kwai*.

The Bridge on the River Kwai came to symbolize the senselessness of war, and everyone who saw it came out humming the Colonel Bogey March Nicholson's roll-call to his sweat-soaked workforce. The movie won sever Oscars and took in around 30 million dollars at the box office. Its success paved the way for further David Lean blockbusters with similarly extravagant and eccentric protagonists, including *Lawrence of Arabia* (1962) and *Docto Zhivago* (1965).

PE

6 Elevator shoes: Saito rises above the protocol of the Geneva Convention by getting up on an orange crate and redefining the parameters of martial law.

7 Twin towers: According to Colonel Nicholson, attacking this structure is like piercing the heart of the British Empire.

8 Keeping a stiff upper lip: Colonel Nicholson is the epitome of military virtue – far more than an ordinary officer and a gentleman.

DAVID LEAN (1908–1991)

David Lean, born in Surrey, England in 1908, started his film career as a clapper boy, went on to become a successful film editor, and eventually became the unrivalled master of the widescreen epic. On the first film he directed – *In Which We Serve* (1942) – he actually shared the directing honors with Noel Coward. The wartime tearjerker *Brief Encounter* (1945) brought him his first Oscar nomination, and he went straight on to direct two impressive Dickens adaptations: *Great Expectations* (1946) and *Oliver Twist* (1948), both of which featured Alec Guinness in major roles. This fruitful collaboration was continued in *The Bridge on the River Kwai* (1957), which marked the maturing of Lean's inimitable style, and in several later movies. Indeed, Lean had a habit of turning his leading actors into major movie stars, from Peter O'Toole in the desert epic *Lawrence of Arabia* (1962) to Omar Sharif and Julie Christie in the Russian Revolution romance *Doctor Zhivago* (1965). These three big-budget productions raked in 19 Oscars between them. Though Lean himself won the Best Director award twice, he could never quite shake off his reputation as a solid but uninspired Hollywood craftsman. It was allegedly Pauline Kael's ferocious review of *Ryan's Daughter* (1970) that crippled his career for the following 14 years. David Lean's last film was the E. M. Forster adaptation, *A Passage to India* (1984).

JAILHOUSE ROCK

1957 - USA - 96 MIN. - B & W - ROCK MUSICAL, PRISON FILM

DIRECTOR RICHARD THORPE (1896–1991)
SCREENPLAY GUY TROSPER, NEDRICK YOUNG DIRECTOR OF PHOTOGRAPHY ROBERT BRONNER EDITING RALPH E. WINTERS
MUSIC JEFF ALEXANDER SONGS JERRY LEIBER, MIKE STOLLER PRODUCTION PANDRO S. BERMAN for AVON
PRODUCTIONS, MGM.

STARRING ELVIS PRESLEY (Vince Everett), JUDY TYLER (Peggy Van Alden), MICKEY SHAUGHNESSY (Hunk Houghton),
VAUGHN AYLOR (Mr. Shores; The Narrator), DEAN JONES (Teddy Talbot), JENNIFER HOLDEN (Sherry Wilson),
ANNE NEYLAND (Laury Jackson), DON BURNETT (Mickey Alba), WILLIAM FORREST (Head of the Studio),
BILL HICKMAN (Guy who whips Vince).

"Let's rock, everybody, let's rock. Everybody in the whole cell block was dancin' to the Jailhouse Rock."

Arched on his toes and gyrating his stuff, Elvis sings of a time when "the war-den threw a party in the county jail..." So begins the show-stopping *Jailhouse Rock* number from which this picture takes its named. The climactic scene is staged as a televised rock concert, featuring Elvis, star composer-producer Mike Stoller at the piano, and the entire band all costumed in horizontal striped prison uniforms. The cell doors set off the scene with a vertically striped backdrop. It''s an eye-catcher in black and white that shows just what the extra-wide CinemaScope screen format is capable of. Elvis and his fellow inmates break out of their cells and dance along the corridor, swinging down the spiral staircase. In song, Elvis recalls how "number forty-seven said to number three, 'you're the cutest jailbird I ever did see.'" Then the tune comes to a halt as the cellblock return to its cages, doors slam shut behind them, and cut! The number lasts but two minutes: two minutes that shook up rock and roll, re-established its icons and prophesized the dawn of the music video.

Today, Elvis' self-choreographed, geometrically stylized dance number is as captivating and invigorating as ever. For a better sense of the movie's impact, just consider the polarized reactions of the time: the adoring screams of impressionable young women nationwide and the violent uproar from the upholders of propriety. *The New York Times* went so far as to describe the controversial movie as "a fully-clothed striptease."

Jailhouse Rock is the story of one musician's rise to fame. Elvis starts off as construction worker Vince Everett, riding onto the first scene in his utility vehicle with the intention of collecting his paycheck. And what an entrance! Defending an innocent woman's honor, Everett feels obliged to knock an uncouth ruffian to the ground. Not ten minutes have gone by and our hero has landed himself in the slammer, where he learns to play the guitar and keys into his musical potential. Behind bars he meets Hunk Houghton (Mickey Shaughnessy), an uptight country singer initially bent on taking Vince for a ride. Houghton quickly changes his tune, acting as both the young man's promoter and mentor. Shortly after being released from prison, the talented, pulsating singer shoots to the stars as a rock and movie sensa-tion. However, the singer's sense of moral integrity falls by the wayside. The

**ELVIS AARON PRESLEY
(1935–1977)** One might describe Elvis' story as a series of one impressive event after another. While alive, the sale of his LPs and singles was reported at more than 500 million. Likewise, the worldwide audience of his 1973 TV special *Elvis: Aloha from Hawaii* (1973) was estimated at more than one million. Twenty years after his death, a remixed version of his "A Little Less Conversation" went straight to number one on the hit parade, proving that the King was indeed still alive and well, if only in spirit. Elvis' life can also be seen in terms of its remarkable rises and falls. From the truck driver who wanted to make a record for his momma, via his reign as the world's best selling recording artist, to his eventual decay as a portly, pill-popping junkie, who was discovered dead in a bathroom on his Graceland estate at the age of forty-two. Still, any retrospective analysis of his life can only touch on the legend that was and remains Elvis. He was a rebel, a white guy who sounded black, and crossed cultural and demographic boundaries as a result. He was the first country and western, blues and rock-and-roller whose on-stage demeanor was as energetic and dynamic as it was sexually charged. He was also the first modern-day pop star in that his records, films and television appearances received worldwide attention. Nonetheless, the era of Elvis the movie star is a knife that cuts both ways. Deciding to focus more on his film career, Elvis took an almost ten-year hiatus from the stage after returning home from service in 1960. He made a rapid succession of films, playing various parts such as an heir to a banana plantation who'd rather play tour guide in *Blue Hawaii* (1961), a lifeguard in *Fun in Acapulco* (1963) or a racecar driver in *Speedway* (1968). These films showcased his singing and guitar-playing talents, with the plots often being a loosely strung excuse for a star vehicle. Elvis ended his absence from the stage with a concert film entitled *Elvis: That's the Way It Is* (1970); it was the first concert film to focus exclusively on one person. The picture is pure Elvis, doing what he does best – singing and strutting his stuff.

character who started off as a good-natured hothead, willing to stand up for what he believes in, transforms into an arrogant ladder climber. As he kicks his way to the top, Peggy Van Alden (Judy Tyler), the woman who adores him and helped him found his own record label, is left holding the short end of the stick. Only after Houghton beats some sense into him does Vince become an upstanding citizen. All in all, Elvis' character is painted in such an unflattering, borderline despicable light character that it's hard to imagine why the writers would make such an alarming choice for a picture intended to be nothing more than a star vehicle.

Jailhouse Rock is the third of more than thirty movies Elvis made. Yet no matter what the medium, singing was always his forte and screen renditions of songs like "Treat Me Nice," "Baby, I Don't Care" and "Young and Beautiful"

"Elvis gives some classic performances of classic songs, topped off by the tremendous title number; the design, choreography, and gorgeous black-and-white photography have had incalcuable impact on rock styles ever since."

Linda J. Sandahl, Rock Films

1 Bosom buddies: Elvis Presley alias Vince Everett longs for his bygone army days, when torpedoes were always at a range this close.

2 "For love, your honor:" Better change your tune, Elvis …

3 … or the judge will do it for you by locking you up and throwing away the key.

4 Going platinum: Peggy Van Alden (Judy Tyler) believes she can turn a jailbird into a nightingale and starts up a record label.

5   How 'bout a few of them golden bars? Country singer and con-artist Hunk Houghton (Mickey Shaughnessy) teaches Vince how to play guitar and then waits out the return on his investment.

6   Mixing business and pleasure: Peggy wants Vince to love her tender, but he ends up smacking her around a little instead.

7   Jailhouse gyrations: In an Ed Sullivan Show-style 'music video' Elvis sings a hit that flies clear off the charts. There's nothing left to say except, "let's rock!"

"*Jailhouse Rock* captures early Elvis in all his leg-quivering, nostril-flaring, lip-snarling teen idol glory."

Motion Picture Guide

re examples of his finest Hollywood work. And indeed, *Jailhouse Rock* is one of the best, if not *the* best of his pictures. Although it can be slow-moving at times by today's standards, it still gets a crowd going even after all these years. That success is not just due to the music, but also to the plot and the social stratum it depicts. For here, more than in any of his other pictures, the King's acting draws from his own experiences. As if watching a fictionalized biography, we witness the overnight success of an entirely new kind of musician, both in terms of sound and style. Even the film's less spectacular details seem to parallel the actor's life. After all, much like his construction worker counterpart, the real Elvis was a truck driver who wasn't so hot on the guitar and loved nothing more than a good hamburger.

HJK

"The title song sold two million records within two weeks, and the picture, in turn, grossed several million, with Presley receiving 50 percent of the profits."

Motion Picture Guide

THE INCREDIBLE SHRINKING MAN

1957 - USA - 81 MIN. - B & W - SCIENCE FICTION

DIRECTOR Jack Arnold (1916–1992)
SCREENPLAY RICHARD MATHESON, based on his novel *THE SHRINKING MAN*
DIRECTOR OF PHOTOGRAPHY ELLIS W. CARTER EDITING ALBRECHT JOSEPH MUSIC FOSTER CARLING, EARL E. LAWRENCE
PRODUCTION ALBERT ZUGSMITH for UNIVERSAL INTERNATIONAL PICTURES.

STARRING GRANT WILLIAMS (Scott Carey), RANDY STUART (Louise Carey),
RAYMOND BAILEY (Doctor Thomas Silver), PAUL LANGTON (Charlie Carey), APRIL KENT (Clarice),
WILLIAM SCHALLERT (Doctor Arthur Bramson), FRANK J. SCANNELL (Carnival Barker), HELENE MARSHALL (Nurse),
DIANA DARRIN (Nurse), BILLY CURTIS (Midget).

"To God there is no zero. I still exist."

Those of you who wish that the inches would just melt away, take heed. Imagine you woke up one morning to find that – joy of joys – your wardrobe fit is a bit looser. Five minutes later you discover that the arms and legs of all your clothes are noticeably longer than they should be. Has panic already wiped the smile off your face? Whatever for? It's not as if people can inexplicably start shrinking. At least that's what the physician attending Scott Carey (Grant Williams) says. But expert opinion can't deny what's plain as day: Scott is getting slightly smaller with each passing minute.

As nothing was beyond the comprehension of science in the rational 1950s, medical experts eventually pinpoint the cause of the bizarre phenomenon: an unfortunate combination of toxins, brought on by contact with an insecticide and a radioactive cloud, has activated a steady shrinking process within Scott's body. An antidote is found shortly after diagnosis, but it only temporarily curbs the effects. In the meantime, Scott has no choice but to adjust his lifestyle, first relocating to his children's playhouse and then to the dollhouse in the family room as he proceeds to "out-shrink" his residences.

One day, while wife Louise (Randy Stuart) is off running errands, an unexpected turn of events sends Scott's life completely out of orbit. Trying to escape the clutches of his cat, teeny tiny Scott just manages to squeeze

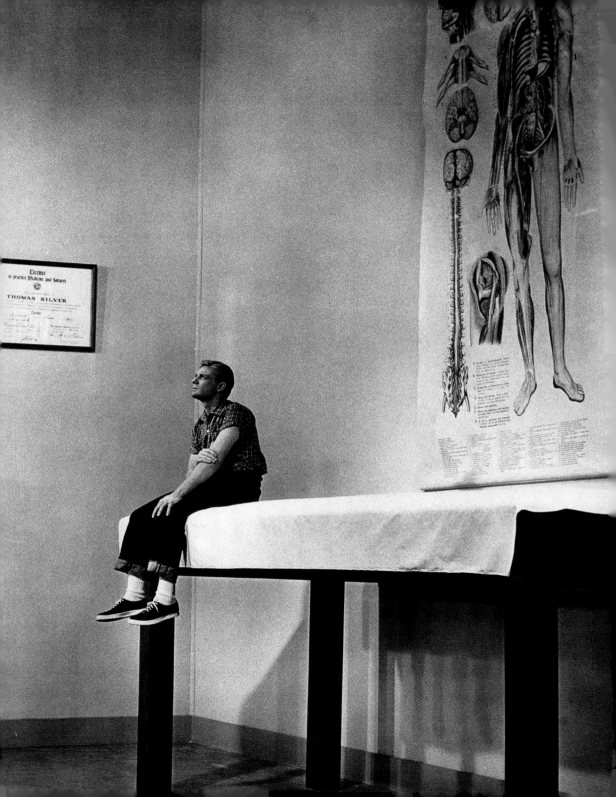

through a crack in the door, only to plummet into the basement. A tattered bit of bloodstained fabric convinces his loved ones that daddy's fallen victim to the family pet. Trapped in his new environs – which to him resemble an insurmountable, monster-laden war zone – Scott prepares to play the hand fate has dealt him …

While at first glance a sci-fi adventure, *The Incredible Shrinking Man* is actually an allegory about the alienation of modern man. Here, chance incidents effortlessly send ivory-tower concepts like private property and financial security tumbling down, leaving the cornerstones of society in ruins. Although he is otherwise physically and mentally healthy, Scott's diminishing stature is enough to ostracize him from his family, peers, and society at large. Regarded by the outside world as nothing more than a freak show curiosity,

"I am convinced that a film should also have a social meaning. And if it has a social meaning, then it also has a political meaning. These two things go hand in hand. But I think they both have to be approached with great care and sensitivity." *Jack Arnold*

4

1   Minor afflictions: After getting zapped by a mean dosage of radiation, Scott Carey (Grant Williams) is through complaining that nothing ever happens to little old him. And if his wife has anything to say about it, this will be Scott's last look at any sort of foreign anatomy.

2   The hypocrite's oath: When modern science provides no explanation, the doctors leave Scott to shrivel up and die.

.3   Moving house: After it becomes clear that her husband has lost all hope of the presidency, Mrs. Carey (Randy Stuart) enforces her prenuptial agreement and claims their stately residence for herself. She does, however, still treat hubby like a regular doll.

4   The cat's meow: When a feline from across the way makes a beeline toward Scott, he opts for self-imprisonment in the basement.

he quickly loses all footing in his trusted world. Estranged from his wife and emasculated, his dollhouse abode supplies him with a pathetic shell to crawl back into. His fall into the basement abyss, i. e. into oblivion, is the logical conclusion of his unfaltering degeneration.

Director Jack Arnold stages the film as a semi-documentary portrait of a middle-class married couple – a tactic that readily wins the audience's sympathies. The Careys live in a safe, pristine world. Even as Scott learns of his extraordinary affliction, we are reassured by a sober-minded, paternal doctor that science will succeed in remedying the matter. What makes *The Incredible Shrinking Man* so unnerving is that the trajectory of Scott's destiny cannot be averted, despite the supposedly ironclad safety of the world he lives in.

We watch as Arnold inconspicuously and masterfully introduces melodramatic elements into the plot: when Scott's wedding band, the symbol of

"I was continuing to shrink, to become … what? The infinitesimal? What was I? Still a human being? Or was I the man of the future?"

Film quote: Scott Carey (Grant Williams)

5 Sparks fly in the matchbox: Scott regrets not ever lugging that old TV down to the basement. Now that he's stuck there, he has a burning desire to live out his Shirley Temple and Snow White fantasies. How's that for trick photography?

6 The pencil is mightier than the sword: The question is whether it is weapon enough to help him avoid the veritable Charybdis that lies ahead – namely, the drain.

7 Lion tamer: Despite what this image suggests, no tarantula was hurt or injured during the shoot.

Much like the larger-than-life household objects – in truth gigantic set pieces – the entire shot is a brilliant trompe d'oeil.

8 Ain't nothing like a little ingenuity: Careful now, Scott. You don't want to cut the cheese.

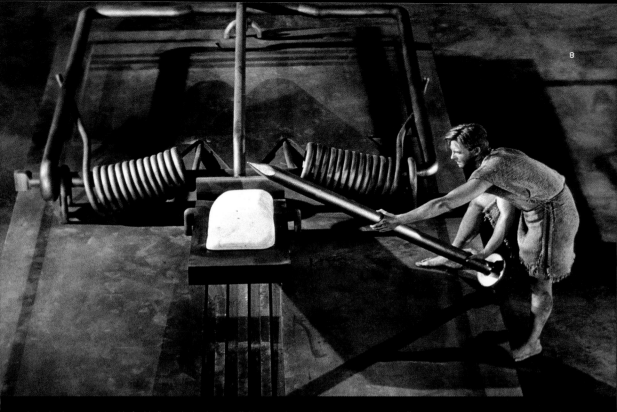

marital cohesion, proves too big for his finger, it simply slips off; it's no accident that this is also the first moment in which Scott is shown to be shorter than his wife, even if only by a drop. An eerier albeit subtler scene occurs immediately thereafter. A friend of the family is seen standing in front of an easy chair with its back to the camera. As the camera rotates 180° we lay eyes on Scott seated in the chair, now no bigger than a small child, and bear witness to what has become a shocking transformation.

Bit by bit, all the comforts of home start to present a serious threat. What was once a trusted living space mutates into an alien planet, on which a new power struggle between man and beast takes shape and life's essentials are redefined. This becomes especially clear when Scott uses a sewing needle as a lance to ward off a proportionately enormous garden spider, or nearly loses his life to a clogged drain.

It is thanks to a superior intellect that mankind manages to triumph even in such perilous realms. But this is cold comfort in a world where individuality has lost its intrinsic value, where your own cat thirsts for your life, and you've been abandoned by mankind to rot in the cellar. Jack Arnold's film accounts for the fragility and constant uncertainty of the human condition while managing to leave us with a grain of hope in the end, as if to say: as long as we continue to reflect upon ourselves and our actions, and refuse to blindly follow destiny, we can preserve our human integrity – no matter what the obstacle.   SH

JACK ARNOLD (1916–1992)

Born in New Haven, Connecticut, the so-called "neorealist of science fiction directors" got his start in the business as an actor. While in military service, Arnold tried his hand at documentary filmmaking and was promptly nominated for his first directing Oscar in 1950. Working for Universal Pictures from 1953-1959 he shot many an off-beat B-movie, whose fantastic subject matter was far removed from his former achievements. Nonetheless, Arnold films like *It Came from Outer Space* (1953), *Creature from the Black Lagoon* (1954), *Tarantula* (1955) and *The Incredible Shrinking Man* (1957) are today considered masterpieces in their respective genres. He made use of simple, yet highly effective trick photography in pictures that primarily dealt with external threats to well-ordered lives. These ominous clouds would often manifest themselves as a foreign power or – as was more frequently the case – a nasty side effect of human hubris and ignorance. Yet Arnold's work is not concerned with tackling issues like good and evil. His characters always act according to their nature, be it human, alien or that of an overgrown spider, making it almost impossible to apply a moral yardstick to their conduct.
In addition to the impressive range of technical innovations, Arnold's films stand out from countless others of the genre precisely because of their refusal to adhere to sci-fi and horror movie conventions. He is less known for his numerous Westerns, including *Man in the Shadow / Seeds of Wrath* (1957) with Orson Welles, and comedies. His over-the-top satire *The Mouse That Roared* (1959) starred legendary funnyman Peter Sellers as three characters at war with the United States. Throughout the 60s and 70s, Jack Arnold devoted his professional life to projects for television. He died of arteriosclerosis in Woodland Hills, California, in March 1992.

WILD STRAWBERRIES
Smultronstället

1957 - SWEDEN - 91 MIN. - B & W - DRAMA

DIRECTOR INGMAR BERGMAN (b. 1918)
SCREENPLAY INGMAR BERGMAN DIRECTOR OF PHOTOGRAPHY GUNNAR FISCHER EDITING OSCAR ROSANDER
MUSIC ERIK NORDGREN PRODUCTION ALLAN EKELUND for SVENSK FILMINDUSTRI.

STARRING VICTOR SJÖSTRÖM (Professor Isak Borg), BIBI ANDERSSON (Sara), INGRID THULIN (Marianne Borg), GUNNAR BJÖRNSTRAND (Evald Borg), FOLKE SUNDQUIST (Anders), BJÖRN BJELFVENSTAM (Viktor), NAIMA WIFSTRAND (Isak's Mother), JULLAN KINDAHL (Agda), GUNNAR SJÖBERG (Sten Ahlman), GUNNEL BROSTRÖM (Mrs. Ahlman), GERTRUD FRIDH (Karin, Isak's wife), ÅKE FRIDELL (Karin's lover), MAX VON SYDOW (Åkerman), SIF RUUD (Tante), YNGVE NORDWALL (Uncle Aron), PER SJÖSTRAND (Sigfrid Borg), GIO PETRÉ (Sigbritt), GUNNEL LINDBLOM (Charlotta), MAUD HANSSON (Angelica), LENA BERGMAN (Kristina), MONICA EHRLING (Birgitta).

IFF BERLIN 1958 GOLDEN BEAR (Ingmar Bergman).

"The question is no longer whether God is dead; the question is whether man is dead."

Dream, memory and the present: in *Wild Strawberries*, Ingmar Bergman combines several narrative levels with admirable dexterity. Here, there is no clear line between imagination and reflection, fantasy and contemplation of the thing fantasized. A dream sequence right at the beginning states the basic theme: fear of death. In the glow of dawn, an old man walks through an abandoned city. He sees clocks without hands, faces without eyes – surrealist images, born of a private nightmare. Ingmar Bergman himself has encouraged us to see it as an autobiographical film: "A hearse crashes into a pole, the coffin falls out and the corpse is flung to the ground: I had dreamt this myself, many times."

Wild Strawberries tells the story of a single day. Isak Borg, a 76-year-old professor of medicine, drives from Stockholm to Lund, an ancient Swedish university town, where he plans to join the celebrations for the anniversary of his doctorate. The journey takes him back through many episodes of his past life, both real and imaginary: he visits his mother (Naima Wifstrand), who produces a case full of toys, and he thinks back on his marriage, his first love and his parents. He gives a lift to a young hitchhiker, who strongly resembles Sara, the girl he loved in his youth (both roles are played by Bibi Andersson). At the summer house, memory takes possession of him. Wild strawberries still grow here, as they did in his childhood and youth. In

"Life as paradise lost." *Der Spiegel*

1 Dreams are my reality: Although Sara (Bibi Andersson, left) confides in her cousin Charlotta (Gunnel Lindblom) that she'd much rather have Sigfrid than her fiancé Isak, we'll never know whether it's true or just a figment of an old man's imagination.

2 Eternal youth: Isak Borg (Victor Sjöström) picks up three hitchhikers at the side of the road. The woman of the bunch, Sara, bears an uncanny resemblance to Isak's former fiancée of the same name. Bibi Andersson in a scintillatingly callous double-role.

3 Bearing fruit: Marianne (Ingrid Thulin) longs for a child, but her husband Evald (Gunnar Björnstrand) doesn't want to spoil yet another person's life.

4 Sweet dreams: By the end of his journey, Isak comes to amiable terms with the life he has led and the children who once shunned him.

5 Marianne Faithful: Though the others wrongly suspect her of infidelity, Marianne places honesty above all other human virtues. Why else would she be so rude to her father-in-law?

5

Swedish, "smultronstället" has two meanings: it denotes a place where wild strawberries grow, and it also signifies a *locus amoenus*, a secret garden, a place of magical serenity, outside of everyday existence. These wild strawberries appear in many of Bergman's films, and in *Fanny and Alexander* (*Fanny och Alexander*, 1982), for example, they symbolize paradise lost – youth, happiness and pure unadulterated love.

In a second dream sequence, the failures and character defects of the dreaming man are listed: he is selfish, cold and egotistical. As a basis for this character analysis, Isak Borg undergoes a kind of test: his teacher leads him through a dream landscape to a place where he's forced to watch his wife commit adultery. The old man awakens, tormented but reconciled to the truth. Far from allowing Borg to "reap the harvest" of his life and work, the film depicts a journey into the interior: self-knowledge is the ultimate goal, even if it means facing some very bitter facts. The moral is clear: a life story is only worth telling if it refuses to sentimentalize the past.

"I imagined this man to be a jaded egotist who has broken every link to the world around him – just as I had done." Bergman claimed that *Wild Strawberries* had been an unconscious attempt to depict his difficult relationship with his parents. The final scene, he said, had been a projection of his own deepest yearnings: Sara takes Borg by the hand and leads him to a glade, where he sees his mother and father waving to him from the other side of the water. It's a highly personal film, but thanks to Victor Sjöström, a great

Wild Strawberries, scripted by Bergman himself with infinite delicacy and compassion, is a poem about old age that wanders through the borderland between the dream world of life and the real world of dreams. A richly rewarding expedition into the labyrinth of the soul."

Newsweek

6   Strawberry fields forever: The family sits down to the midday meal at their country house, where strawberries grow as wildly and intensely as human emotion. Indeed, this is to be the summer that the impassioned Sigfrid (Per Sjöstrand, back row center) snatches Sara away from Isak, whose intellect is both his greatest attribute and fault.

7   One-way window: As he roams through his private dream world, Isak Bork sees characters from the past who cannot see him.

8   Sporting old hats: After Isak realizes that the life he lead lacked substance altogether, he regards the university's praise and his honorary doctorate as one big joke.

6

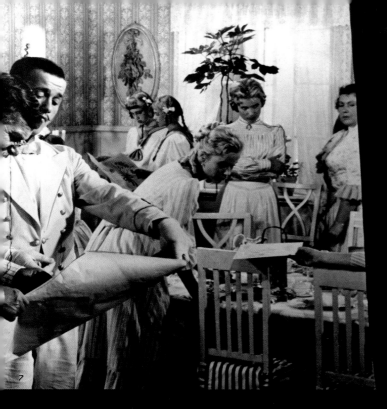

7

VICTOR SJÖSTRÖM (1879–1960)

Born in Sweden, Victor Sjöström spent the first six years of his life in Brooklyn, where his parents lived in the immigrant Scandinavian community. After the death of his mother, he was sent back to Sweden to live with his aunt. He went to school in Uppsala, but left early to join a traveling theater company in Finland. In 1912, he began to appear in films directed by his friend Mauritz Stiller (including *Vampyren*, 1913), and also started directing himself. The two men had a crucial influence on the development of the cinematic art in Sweden, and Swedish cinema would eventually become one of the most artistically powerful in Europe. For the first time in the movies, the forces of nature – volcanoes, the wind and the sea – were used to symbolize spiritual and emotional states. In 1922, Louis B. Mayer hired Sjöström for his Hollywood studio (named MGM from 1924 onwards). Under the name "Victor Seastrom," the Swede directed nine films, including works starring Lillian Gish (*The Wind*, 1928) and Greta Garbo (*The Divine Woman*, 1927). When the talkies gained popularity, Sjöström returned to Sweden; and from then on, with only two exceptions, he restricted himself to acting. Every director who worked with him valued his unique experience; he was a pioneer of American and Scandinavian cinema.

Swedish actor who was famous even in the days of silent film, much of it depicts a more likeable character than Bergman had intended. Thirty-three years later, Bergman noted: "Only now have I realized that Victor Sjöström took the script of my life and made it his own, with his own torment, misanthropy, reclusiveness, brutality, grief, fear, loneliness, chilliness, warmth, asperity and ennui."

With this film, Ingmar Bergman established a new poetics of the cinema. Not unjustly, it's been described as a second surrealism. Yet when Bergman sends his alter ego into the world of dreams, he still draws a line between dream and waking life. In the decade that followed, there would no longer be a clear distinction between the inner and outer worlds of the protagonists. RV

8

257

WITNESS FOR THE PROSECUTION

1957 - USA - 116 MIN. - B & W - COURTROOM DRAMA

DIRECTOR BILLY WILDER (1906–2002)
SCREENPLAY BILLY WILDER, HARRY KURNITZ, LARRY MARCUS, based on the play of the same name
by AGATHA CHRISTIE DIRECTOR OF PHOTOGRAPHY RUSSELL HARLAN EDITING DANIEL MANDELL MUSIC MATTY MALNECK
PRODUCTION ARTHUR HORNBLOW JR. for EDWARD SMALL PRODUCTIONS, THEME PICTURES.

STARRING TYRONE POWER (Leonard Stephen Vole), MARLENE DIETRICH (Christine Vole),
CHARLES LAUGHTON (Sir Wilfrid Robarts), ELSA LANCHESTER (Miss Plimsoll), JOHN WILLIAMS (Mr. Brogan-Moore),
HENRY DANIELL (Mr. Mayhew), IAN WOLFE (Mr. Carter), TORIN THATCHER (District Attorney Myers),
NORMA VARDEN (Emily French), UNA O'CONNOR (Janet McKenzie), FRANCIS COMPTON (Judge).

"I hope we are not to be deprived of the learned and stimulating company of Sir Wilfrid."

Sir Wilfrid Robarts (Charles Laughton) has got the blues. After suffering a heart attack, Britain's most highly regarded defense attorney is sentenced to the nonstop care of an exacting nurse. The overweight Robarts, however, has no intention of giving in to infantilism without a fight. He defies his nanny, who imposes a strict no cigars and cognac diet upon him, which he sees as a death sentence, and takes on a much-needed case to lift his spirits. His client, Leonard Vole (Tyrone Power), has been accused of beating his former benefactress to death. Sir Wilfrid's infallible instincts tells him that the man is innocent; or rather, he is certain he can get the man acquitted of the charges. But victory proves bittersweet. Not only does he help a cold-blooded killer get off the hook, but he also discovers that he has served as a pawn in one of the country's most fantastical crime schemes. In truth, it is the defendant's wife, Christine Vole (Marlene Dietrich), who has been calling the shots the entire time, and as soon as the clever femme fatale steps into the limelight, the

misogynistic barrister is left flailing in the dark. However, an unexpected turn of events suddenly sends the fate of the litigants in a whole new direction ...

A tale like this could have only been penned by the grande dame of mystery, Agatha Christie. As is often the case in her work, the person initially suspected of committing the crime does in fact turn out to be the guilty party. Equally characteristic is the deployment of a perpetrator who is skilled at rebuffing the overwhelming body of evidence against him until shortly before the bitter end.

It's not the least bit surprising that material like this should spark the interest of Billy Wilder. *Witness for the Prosecution* is a study in deception and masquerade, where nothing is as it seems. Wilder himself couldn't have thought up a more brilliantly dumbfounding scenario than that of having the accused party's wife testify against him. Just as in his so-called "black series," fatalistic love and interpersonal ties cast significant doubt upon

1 Prussian perjury: Christine Vole (Marlene Dietrich) is willing to do whatever it takes to get her husband Leonard (Tyrone Power) acquitted of murder.

2 Make a note of it: Sir Wilfrid Robarts (Charles Laughton) presents the court with a watertight piece of evidence.

3 Taking a stand: When the riveting Marlene Dietrich steps into the witness box, the kraut goes wild.

CHARLES LAUGHTON (1899–1962)

He infused many a character with his monumental grandeur. Charles Laughton was Nero, Quasimodo and Henry VIII. His striking face, which the actor himself once described as "an elephant's behind" supplied murderers, cripples, brutes and eccentrics with that certain something. Born into an English family of Scarborough hotel entrepreneurs, Laughton began his theatrical career in 1926. After numerous successes on the London stage, he quickly found his way to silent pictures. It wasn't long before the horror movie *The Old Dark House* (1932) had him packing for Hollywood. Among his most notable pictures are titles like *Mutiny on the Bounty* (1935), *Rembrandt* (1936), *Captain Kidd* (1945), *The Hunchback of Notre Dame* (1939) and *Spartacus* (1960). He was as known for being a glutton as he was for his homosexual and hedonistic tendencies, both on and off screen. Constantly trying to find himself, Laughton put together events in which he performed live readings from works such as the Bible or the writings of Jack Kerouac. He took a single stab at directing for the screen in 1955 with *The Night of the Hunter*. Today, the eerie thriller, starring Robert Mitchum, is considered a cult classic.

"**Laughton, sage of the courtroom and cardiac patient who's constantly disobeying his nurse's orders about cigar-smoking and brandy-drinking, plays out the part flamboyantly and colorfully. His reputation for scenery chewing is unmarred via this outing; he's as robust as ever in making sarcastic cracks and browbeating his nurse and his subordinates.**" *Variety*

matters of individual accountability. But what really makes moviegoers relish the picture is the incomparable Marlene Dietrich as Christine Vole. The German actress, immune to either praise or suspicion, simply plays herself. The character also draws from some of her best-known screen work, playing a former cabaret singer, as she did in *The Blue Angel* (*Der blaue Engel*, 1930), not to mention Wilder's own *Foreign Affair* (1948); in fact, the director took the liberty of editing a shelved Hamburg nightclub scene from *A Foreign Affair* into his 1950s courtroom drama to explain how Christine met her husband to be.

Sir Wilfrid's ridiculous antics supply the film with a jovial counterbalance to Dietrich's angel of death performance. Charles Laughton depicts him as a rock of the British legal system on a par with the Old Bailey, the home of English law and the film's primary location. When the attorney is at work, his

4   The truth is I'm fabulous: Like an elephant in a china shop, Sir Wilfrid gets his way by trampling on everything that stands in his path.

5   If I've told you once, I've told you a thousand times: Miss Plimsoll's (Elsa Lanchester) purpose in life is to nag Sir Wilfrid to death. Being married in real life, Laughton and Lanchester needed little rehearsal to get their bickering down pat.

6   Back in the black: Marlene Dietrich emerges out of the ashes of post-war Germany and blows some soot in the face of Jolly Old England. Dame Agatha couldn't have penned a role more suited for Dietrich's special talents had she tried.

> "*Witness for the Prosecution* is courtroom drama done right. It's intelligent and well acted. The characters are interesting, distinct and full of questions. It's got spins, but spins that make sense. Feel free to leave the bologna in the fridge, because this one's got enough flavor and quality on its own."
>
> *Apollo Movie Guide*

extraordinary range of facial expressions and biting wit can't help but take center stage. Still, his ongoing battle entails more than just ripping the charges against his client to shreds. Waging war on two fronts, he subversively reclaims the right to treat his body as he sees fit while fighting for another man's life. He'll hide cigars in his walking stick or brandy in his thermos; there's nothing he won't do to pull the wool over nurse Plimsoll's eyes and regain command. One simply can't imagine anyone more suitable than Laughton's real-life wife Elsa Lanchester in the role of the penicillin-pushing nemesis who knows just how to push Sir Wilfrid's buttons.

Throughout his work, Wilder made an art form of pitting comedy and drama against one another. However, his virtuoso adaptation of this Agatha Christie play never received the critical recognition it deserved. Nowadays, however, *Witness for the Prosecution* is considered by many to be one of the best courtroom dramas ever made. It is scathingly funny and yet not afraid to go off the deep end. It takes flight with unpredictable twists and turns, and soars thanks to Wilder's impeccable sense of timing. We know that while the road to justice may be plagued with potholes, our destination remains certain with Wilder at the wheel... no matter how bumpy the ride.

THE DEFIANT ONES

♟ ♟

1958 - USA - 97 MIN. - B & W - DRAMA

DIRECTOR STANLEY KRAMER (1913–2001)
SCREENPLAY NATHAN E. DOUGLAS (= NEDRICK YOUNG), HAROLD JACOB SMITH **DIRECTOR OF PHOTOGRAPHY** SAM LEAVITT
EDITING FREDERIC KNUDTSON **MUSIC** ERNEST GOLD PRODUCTION STANLEY KRAMER for CURTLEIGH PRODUCTIONS INC.,
LOMITAS PRODUCTIONS INC., UNITED ARTISTS.

STARRING SIDNEY POITIER (Noah Cullen), TONY CURTIS (John 'Joker' Jackson), THEODORE BIKEL (Sheriff Max Muller),
CHARLES MCGRAW (Captain Frank Gibbons), CARA WILLIAMS (The Woman), LON CHANEY JR. (Big Sam),
KING DONOVAN (Solly), CLAUDE AKINS (Mack), WHIT BISSELL (Lou Gans), CARL SWITZER (Angus).

ACADEMY AWARDS 1958 OSCARS for BEST ORIGINAL SCREENPLAY (Nedrick Young, Harold Jacob Smith),
and BEST CINEMATOGRAPHY (Sam Leavitt).

IFF BERLIN 1958 SILVER BEAR for BEST ACTOR (Sidney Poitier).

"Nigger!
You call me that again,
and I'll kill you!"

The buddy movie, that great forum for co-dependent protagonists at logger-heads with one another, comes from a long-standing cinematic tradition. While *Lethal Weapon* (1987) is perhaps the most salient example of the genre's beloved variation as an unlikely pairing of clashing races, the constellation dates back to *The Defiant Ones* (1958). The film's premise was as simple as its execution was brilliant: two convicts, one black and one white, break loose from a transport truck and set off toward freedom. Chained to each other at the wrists, the two men want nothing more than to liberate themselves from the shackles that bind them. In the meantime, they are compelled to overcome their mutual hatred and work as a unit in order to dodge their advancing pursuers who are aided by hounds.

That their escape was bound to fail couldn't have been a surprise to 1950s audiences. But the crack that bold directors like Stanley Kramer managed to leave in the mold was in addressing racism as a mainstream Hollywood subject matter. It was inconceivable to acquit the convicted felons of the crimes they had committed, but the no way out scenario of chaining the characters together presented Kramer with a golden opportunity to commu-

nicate a humanist message. Both John "Joker" Jackson (Tony Curtis) and Noah Cullen (Sidney Poitier) come from the dregs of society, a society that has made them what they are. Unable to rise above it, the obstinate "nigger hater" Joker tries to market his whiteness as a means of appeasing a lynch mob, but his skin color proves of as little value as Noah's sense of moral superiority. Respect and tolerance mean nothing unless they are followed up by action.

Curtis and Poitier carry almost the entire film themselves. Bound together by an arm's length of shackle, they fight for their lives in the woods and swamps of the American South. When they are confronted by river rapids, they can either try to cross together or let themselves drown. When they are nearly caught in death's clutches at the bottom of a mud pit, their chain is as much a burden as it is a blessing: the deeper it cuts under their skin, the more these two lost souls sense the extent to which they depend on one another – a bit of progress that the current social climate can't undo.

Well into their journey, the fugitives happen upon the house of a single mother, where they manage to remove the manacles. The nameless woman

1 Getting the hounds off their scent: Despite these men's efforts to make a clean getaway, all these guys do is splash a lot of mud around. Tony Curtis and Sidney Poitier as escaped convicts John 'Joker' Jackson and Noah Cullen.

2 Freedom train: Rather than riding solo, Noah gives up his last chance at liberation and prevents Joker from ending up alone on the wrong side of the tracks.

(Cara Williams) tries to seize her last chance at respectable living by bagging the well-built Joker after sending Noah on a collision course with death. But Joker tracks him down so that they may have the chance of collectively tasting the promised freedom. Side by side, their journey comes to an end when their attempted leap onto a moving train falls short and the black man lacks the strength to lift his white buddy abroad the freedom-bound locomotive. Exhausted and in each other's arms, the two lie at the side of the road when Sheriff Max Muller (Theodore Bikel) stumbles upon them moments afterwards. As the images so eloquently show us, actions once again speak louder than words.

Often ridiculed for deliberately weaving messages into his pictures, here Stanley Kramer presents us with a brilliant example of filmmaking free from any traces of melodrama, prepackaged lessons in morality or extra-vagant visuals. Its lasting impact must be attributed to the actors' no-holds-barred performances. Sidney Poitier, at the time the only black leading man on the Hollywood payroll, gives his common crook character an uncompromising credibility. And while Tony Curtis' performance is equally convincing, it was not enough to rid him of his pretty-boy American image; no-one would have guessed that Curtis was the one who insisted on Poitier being billed opposite him, rather than after him, as the studio had originally intended.

Even after the shoot, the destinies of the two actors were to remain intrinsically linked, and the overwhelming critical acclaim earned Oscar nominations for Poitier and Curtis alike. The Academy, however, found the task of choosing among them impossible, and the Oscar for Best Actor went to David Niven for *Separate Tables* (1958).

PB

STANLEY KRAMER (1913–2001)

Branded by critics as the premier voice in the "liberal school of message movies," native New Yorker Stanley Kramer was never praised as a Hollywood legend. To be fair, Kramer didn't set creative standards in American moviemaking. However, he did direct several post-war classics as a result of his compelling social agenda: dramatizing a nuclear threat in *On the Beach* (1959); investigating the Nazi regime and questions of national guilt in *Judgement at Nuremberg* (1961); and comically clashing the haves and the have-nots across racial lines in his remarkably popular *Guess Who's Coming to Dinner* (1967). Aside from his directing work, Kramer also served as producer on a number of pictures, both for Hollywood and independently; the list includes legendary movies like *The Wild One* (1953) with Marlon Brando, and Fred Zinnemann's Western *High Noon* (1952), one of the many projects that earned him a reputation as anti-American. Always wanting to provoke thought rather than moralize, Kramer simply saw himself as a storyteller with his own angle.

3   Gettin' a litte shuteye: Noah sings the old ball-and-chain to sleep …

4   … but wakes him up in a jiffy when he senses the law on their tail.

5   Back on the chain gang: Though they don't know it now, Noah and Joker will fondly remember their time together as the happiest days of their lives – not to mention the freest.

"While he is clawing out this message, Mr. Kramer is also giving us a fast and exciting melodrama, with a man-hunt and chase at its core. By a pattern of crisp, direct cutting and jumping back and forth from the fugitives to their pursuers, among whom there is also a little strife, he keeps the action moving." *The New York Times*

6

6 An indecent proposal: Cara Williams plays a lonely lass who'll stop at nothing to get Joker all to her- self – even if it means sending Noah up the river.

7 Tie me up, tie me down: After falling into the hands of a racist lynch mob, it looks like the convicts' days are numbered. Joker tries to show

a little solidarity with his skin color. But alas, these bigots are color blind when it comes to having fun.

"As 'Joker' Jackson, the arrogant white man chained to a fellow convict whom he hates because of his skin and his need to feel superior, Curtis delivers a true surprise performance. He starts off as a sneering, brutal character, willing to fight it out to-the-death with his equally stubborn companion. When, in the end, he sacrifices a dash for freedom to save Poitier from certain death, he has managed the transition with such skill that audience sympathy is completely with him." *Variety*

TOUCH OF EVIL

1958 - USA - 95 MIN. / 112 MIN. (DIRECTOR'S CUT) - B & W - FILM NOIR, THRILLER

DIRECTOR ORSON WELLES (1915–1985)
SCREENPLAY ORSON WELLES, based on the novel *BADGE OF EVIL* by WHIT MASTERSON
DIRECTOR OF PHOTOGRAPHY RUSSELL METTY EDITING AARON STELL, VIRGIL VOGEL, WALTER MURCH (Director's Cut)
MUSIC HENRY MANCINI PRODUCTION ALBERT ZUGSMITH for UNIVERSAL INTERNATIONAL PICTURES.

STARRING CHARLTON HESTON (Ramon Miguel "Mike" Vargas), JANET LEIGH (Susan Vargas),
ORSON WELLES (Hank Quinlan), JOSEPH CALLEIA (Pete Menzies), AKIM TAMIROFF ("Uncle Joe" Grandi),
JOANNA MOORE (Marcia Linnekar), DENNIS WEAVER (Motel Night Manager), MORT MILLS (Al Schwartz),
MERCEDES MCCAMBRIDGE (Gang Leader), MARLENE DIETRICH (Tanya).

"Come on, read my future for me." "You haven't got any." "What do you mean?" "Your future is all used up."

In Los Robles, a small town on the Texan-Mexican border, a limousine explodes. It belongs to a rich construction magnate. One witness to the attack is Vargas (Charlton Heston), a high-ranking Mexican narcotics detective who just happens to be there on his honeymoon. He offers his assistance to the responsible U.S. Sheriff, Hank Quinlan (Orson Welles), but soon realises that Quinlan is a bigoted racist whose working methods are anything but scrupulous. When Vargas sees Quinlan planting material on a suspect, he resolves to take action. For the Mexican drugs baron Grandi (Akim Tamiroff), this means a welcome opportunity to offer Quinlan a business proposition; for after all, they now have an enemy in common – and Vargas, with his young American wife Susan Vargas (Janet Leigh) is an absurdly easy target.

Touch of Evil was Orson Welles' first Hollywood production after a decade in Europe. As things turned out, it was the last movie he ever made in the States. For after the studios had refused to grant him the final cut on *The Magnificent Ambersons* (1942) and *The Lady from Shanghai* (1947) – disfiguring both films in the process, as Welles saw it – he was subjected to the same humiliating treatment yet again. Shocked by the rough cut, the Universal moguls took the project out of the director's hands, filmed some additional scenes and finally edited the film as they thought fit. Yet even this studio version couldn't completely conceal Welles' signature, and French cineastes in particular hailed the film as a masterpiece. In the U.S. too, it had its fans: Hitchcock's *Psycho* (1960) would hardly have been possible if he hadn't seen the bizarre motel scenes with Janet Leigh and Dennis Weaver in *Touch of Evil*.

1   Tequila sunrise: In the corrupt border town of Los Roblos, Vargas (Charlton Heston) is made to look like a deadbeat scoundrel rather than the lone crusader he actually is.

2   Mrs. Peacock or Mme. Rose: Either way, she's a whore who's seen things that weren't meant for human eyes. Marlene Dietrich as Tanya, the Teutonic tramp.

3   Caning: Law man Quinlan (Orson Welles) has issued a warrant for Vargas' arrest. His crime – sticking his nose where it don't belong.

4   Backroom haberdashery: Quinlan tries to put a lid on Vargas' meddling by working out a deal with Grandi (Akim Tamiroff), a gangster who fronts as a general store owner.

"A tough and lovely film of stunning beauty. The death-throes of a lion. In the words of Gilles Deleuze, the king of kings in this tale of martyrdom is the story of great cinema itself." *Le Monde*

In a certain sense, this movie recapitulates the themes of Welles' previous works. As in *Citizen Kane* (1941), he depicts the collapse of a powerful egomaniac, who forfeits his integrity as he loses touch with the real world. Welles' Quinlan is a fascinating monster, but we can't ignore the tragedy at the heart of his existence: the painful memory of his murdered wife, whose death has never been avenged. The almost totalitarian violence of Quinlan's "lawkeeping" is rooted in his conviction that the law can never produce justice. He despises pettifogging judicial abstractions, preferring instead to trust his own infallible instinct. In this way, he manages to keep a tenuous distance from the lurid decay of the Mexican border town, just as he tames his frustrations with endless bars of chocolate. While Quinlan is a massive patriarch, a relic from times past or passing, his younger rival Vargas is stream-

MERCEDES MCCAMBRIDGE Mercedes McCambridge was born in Joliet, Illinois, in 1916. As the brutal leader of a rocker gang in *Touch of Evil* (1958), she administered drugs to Susan Vargas (Janet Leigh) – but this was not the only androgynous role to which she lent her threatening presence. McCambridge began her career working in radio, where her deep voice was a memorable feature of many plays. This was where she met Orson Welles, whose Mercury Theater she subsequently joined. Her movie career got off to a spectacular start: In Robert Rossen's *All the King's Men* (1949), she played the hench-woman of an unscrupulous political careerist – and promptly won an Oscar as Best Supporting Actress.

Even stranger was her appearance in Nicholas Ray's legendary Western *Johnny Guitar* (1954), in which she led a fascist-style vigilante force to exterminate her rival in love, played by Joan Crawford. The showdown between the two women must be one of the most extravagant closing sequences in Hollywood history. For her small role as Rock Hudson's sister in George Stevens' *Giant* (1956), she was nominated for a further Oscar. Yet Mercedes McCambridge never became a real star, and she was normally cast only in supporting roles. This was undoubtedly due to her un-usual appearance, which hardly fitted the conventional female roles of the period. Tellingly, her most famous film performance was offscreen – as the voice of Linda Blair after she's been possessed by the Devil, in William Friedkin's horror shocker *The Exorcist* (1973).

Mercedes McCambridge died in March 2004 in La Jolla, California.

5

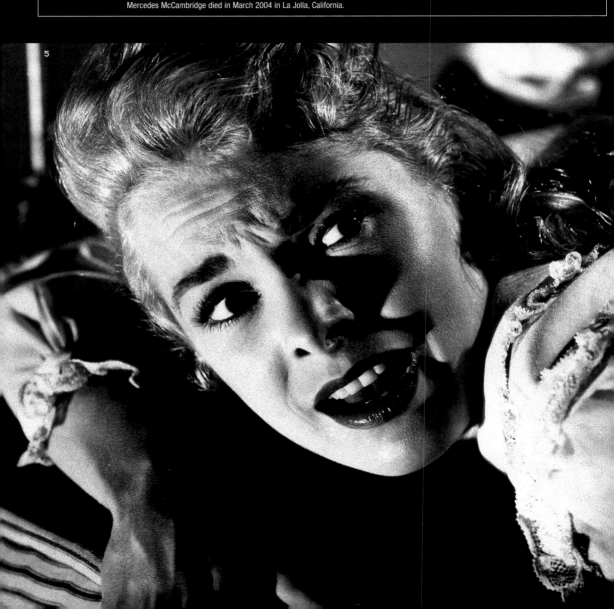

5 Going through hell in a house of ill repute: Vargas'
   wife Susan (Janet Leigh) learns the hard way that
   Quinlan's jurisdiction stretches beyond the borders
   of law and order.

6 Justice for the mighty few: Quinlan falsifies evidence
   whenever he can't seal a conviction with the
   naked truth.

7 Hostages of the honeymoon suite: Vargas thought
   his sojourn in Los Roblos would be one of wedded
   bliss. Now, he'll be happy just to get out of this
   stinking town alive.

lined, dynamic, the embodiment of social progress. Significantly, the Mexican's moral superiority is only once in any doubt: when he himself is under attack. Realizing that Susan is in serious danger, he too resorts to very dubious methods. There's something decidedly hollow about his final victory, as he only prevails by surreptitiously eavesdropping on Quinlan.

With *Touch of Evil*, Welles brought the era of the classical film noir to a worthy end. All of these movies had shared a fundamental doubt about modern man's capacity to understand the world he inhabits. Here, Welles brought this skepticism to a head in a formally spectacular fashion. Extreme camera angles and a distorting wide-angle lens reinforced the eccentric impression made by the film's characters, who seem like parodies at times. Extremely fast tracking shots and an unusual depth of field make it difficult for the viewer to orientate himself within the frame, and the narrative structure of the movie can only be described as labyrinthine. Any hope of discovering the objective truth seems absurdly misplaced here. Los Robles, the shabby border town, is a symbol of chaos, of a world in which Good and Evil began to bleed into one another long ago. At the end of the film, Quinlan – lying in the mud and the garbage by the side of the river – is shot dead by his only friend. Under such circumstances, moral judgment seems out of place; and his former lover Tanya (Marlene Dietrich) says the only decent thing possible: "He was some kind of a man."

UB

"It was named best film at the 1958 Brussels World Fair (Godard and Truffaut were on the jury), but in America it opened on the bottom half of a double bill, failed, and put an end to Welles' prospects of working within the studio system. Yet the film has always been a favorite of those who enjoy visual and dramatic flamboyance." *Chicago Sun-Times*

7

VERTIGO

1958 - USA - 128 MIN. - COLOR - THRILLER, DRAMA

DIRECTOR ALFRED HITCHCOCK (1899–1980)
SCREENPLAY ALEC COPPEL, SAMUEL A. TAYLOR, based on the novel *D'ENTRE LES MORTS* by PIERRE BOILEAU and THOMAS NARCEJAC DIRECTOR OF PHOTOGRAPHY ROBERT BURKS EDITING George Tomasini MUSIC BERNARD HERRMANN PRODUCTION ALFRED HITCHCOCK for ALFRED J. HITCHCOCK PRODUCTIONS, INC., PARAMOUNT PICTURES.

STARRING JAMES STEWART (John "Scottie" Ferguson), KIM NOVAK (Madeleine Elster / Judy Barton), BARBARA BEL GEDDES (Midge Wood), TOM HELMORE (Gavin Elster), KONSTANTIN SHAYNE (Pop Leibel), HENRY JONES (Coroner), RAYMOND BAILEY (Doctor), ELLEN CORBY (Hotel Manager).

"Do you believe that someone out of the past – someone dead – can enter and take possession of a living being?"

The depths of a stairwell beckon from beyond. The ground vanishes, the banister uncoils, and we are overcome by a sense of *Vertigo*. Combining a forward zoom and reverse tracking shot (now sometimes called "contra-zoom" or "trombone shot"), director Alfred Hitchcock creates a dizziness that has gone down as the stuff of legends. As the stairwell springs in and out of proportion, we are thrust into the mind of the protagonist, John "Scottie" Ferguson (James Stewart), a man with a paralyzing fear of heights. A San Francisco police detective, Scottie turns in his badge following a rooftop pursuit that ends in the death of a fellow officer. He blames himself or rather his acrophobia for the incident, convinced that the fatal fall has left him half a man.

Several months pass. Months that for Scottie are a sea of contemplation. Then a phone call promises hope from out of the blue: an old college acquaintance and ship-building tycoon named Gavin Elster (Tom Helmore) wants to meet up and reminisce about old times. However, instead of losing themselves in nostalgic reverie, the businessman offers Scottie a job; Elster's wife, it seems, has been exhibiting signs of psychological instability and

needs to be watched. Scottie initially refuses to get involved, but quickly changes his mind upon laying eyes on her: Madeleine Elster (Kim Novak) – a platinum vision of elegance – is supernaturally stunning, and Scottie just can't look away.

And so begins a hypnotic game of cat and mouse. The private detective discreetly follows Madeleine around San Francisco as she goes about her daily business and journeys to the city's furthest enclaves. Guided by music, these are sequences without dialog and without contact, until one afternoon when Madeleine tries to take her life by jumping into the bay. Scottie dives in after her, but ultimately cannot abate her suicidal tendencies: just days later, a fit of hysteria sends Madeleine running up the stairs of a church bell tower and out of Scottie's life – for now.

Vertigo is the story of a man stricken by a debilitating handicap that prevents him from seeing clearly at higher elevations. The predicament is confounded when Scottie falls in love with an unattainable woman, and loses all sight of reality and literally the ground below. He's a loner and a dreamer, qualities we see heightened through his relationship with his pragmatic con-

1   The fall of man: Scottie (James Stewart) is head
over heels for a suicidal dream girl. Kim Novak as
Madeleine, Hitchcock's ultimate blonde.

2   Image is everything: It's incredible what magic
a gray dress suit and upswept hair can work when
you've got all the right moves.

fidante Midge (Barbara Bel Geddes, of later *Dallas* fame, 1978–1990). And
all these things make him the perfect pawn in this masterful Hitchcockian
chess game.

It seems almost inconceivable that *Vertigo* met with overall disapproval
at the time of its original release. The critics tore it apart and the *New Yorker*
branded it "farfetched nonsense." Elements like the Saul Bass title and
dream sequences most likely estranged the 1950s moviegoer. Both integrate
animation and dissociative color schemes, and qualify as experimental

It was only in the 70s that *Vertigo* gained a second lease on life. Critics
began to praise the film's sleek story, its beautifully composed shots, and it
entered into the canon of great cinema. Although Alfred Hitchcock directed
more than his share of masterpieces, *Vertigo* is beyond compare. With an impact as haunting and captivating as ever, the film exhibits all the laudable
Hitchcockian themes and calling cards theorists once claimed it lacked: from
the master's trademark suspense, where the audience knows more than the
characters, via doppelganger motives, voyeurism, guilt complexes embodied

"Once this movie is under way, it's off into very deep waters. The desperation of Scottie's need to revive Madeleine is both disturbing and moving, a combination you don't expect from a Hitchcock film." *San Francisco Examiner*

3   Dizzy dame: Scottie follows Madeleine to the most remote corners of the Bay Area and discovers nuts among the Sequoias.

4   Breaking the waves and the ice: When they kiss, the moon surrenders its command of the tides.

5   On shore and under the covers: Scottie fishes Madeleine out of the bay, but who will fish him out of the sea of delirium that threatens to drown him?

5

"The female characters in Hitchcocks films reflected the same qualities over and over again: They were blond. They were icy and remote. They were imprisoned in costumes that subtly combined fashion with fetishism."

Chicago Sun-Times

6 Role playing: Scottie convinces Madeleine to confront her nightmarish visions by acting them out. But she breaks character for a parting kiss in the carriage house.

7 39 steps to psychosis: A legendary scene that left cineastes suffering from acrophobia.

8 Dirty blondes play dirty tricks: She changes her hair color, removes her brassiere and voilà – she's a new woman. Kim Novak as brassy redhead, Judy Barton.

9 A dead end: Madeleine's grandmother, Carlotta Valdez, has come back from beyond to take possession of what is rightly hers – Madeleine's soul.

10 On a painful mission: Scottie gets a funny feeling that there's a lotta Carlotta lying around at Mission Dolores.

11 Do it for me, cookie: Scottie wants to transform Judy into the Madeleine he so lovingly remembers.

It is with particular regard to this latter aspect that *Vertigo* emerges as the British filmmaker's magnum opus. As Andreas Kilb argues, it's no secret that Hitchcock was forever molding his vision of the "aloof, mysterious blonde icon," evident in his work with actresses like Ingrid Bergman and Grace Kelly. Yet *Vertigo* takes this single-minded fetish to its zenith. Here, not only Hitchcock, but the characters themselves are doubly driven by the desire to create the perfect blonde. What one can say without robbing the piece of all its mystique is that Madeleine is trained to act as an alluring decoy; and that a woman named Judy turns up in the second half of the film who, apart from her hair color and makeup, is a dead-ringer for Madeleine. And so, after losing the love of his life, Scottie is given the chance to recreate her – using Judy.

HJ

**JAMES STEWART
(1908–1997)**

It's a Wonderful Life (1946), *Winchester '73* (1950) and *Rear Window* (1954) are just three of more than 80 feature films starring James Stewart. What these three masterpieces have in common is that their respective directors were instrumental in shaping Jimmy's career: he made three pictures with Frank Capra, eight with Anthony Mann, and four with Alfred Hitchcock. One of the most remarkable actors ever to grace the screen, Stewart very much deserves his own chapter in its history. At 6'3" he made an art form of lankiness and of never quite knowing what to with his long limbs. This, however, didn't stop him from turning up in the musical *Born to Dance* (1936). Indeed, he felt at home in nearly all genres, appearing in comedies, romances, Westerns, war movies and thrillers alike. He also portrayed a fair share of historical figures, including Glenn Miller and Charles Lindbergh. His list of co-stars is equally impeccable, topped off by names like Edward G. Robinson, John Wayne, Katharine Hepburn, Marlene Dietrich, and a six-foot-three-and-a-half-inch-tall invisible rabbit named *Harvey* (1950). Stewart had an incredible range, always managing to hit on something universal in his acting that was unmarred by histrionics. The son of a Pennsylvania hardware store owner, he got his start in pictures playing shy innocents – usually guys from the countryside – before establishing himself as a leading man in romantic comedies. He freely enlisted in the service during World War II and returned home a highly decorated pilot. From this point on, his screen work took on a darker edge, and his characterizations became more vulnerable and rich with internal conflict. Upon his passing in 1997, the German regional newspaper *Süddeutsche Zeitung* declared him "the last of the cinematic greats ... and the greatest among them."

DRACULA / HORROR OF DRACULA

1958 - GREAT BRITAIN - 82 MIN. - COLOR - HORROR FILM

DIRECTOR TERENCE FISHER (1904–1980)
SCREENPLAY JIMMY SANGSTER, based on the novel *DRACULA* by BRAM STOKER
DIRECTOR OF PHOTOGRAPHY JACK ASHER EDITING BILL LENNY MUSIC JAMES BERNARD PRODUCTION ANTHONY HINDS for HAMMER FILM PRODUCTIONS LIMITED.

STARRING PETER CUSHING (Doctor Van Helsing), CHRISTOPHER LEE (Count Dracula),
MICHAEL GOUGH (Arthur Holmwood), MELISSA STRIBLING (Mina Holmwood), CAROL MARSH (Lucy),
OLGA DICKIE (Gerda), JOHN VAN EYSSEN (Jonathan Harker), VALERIE GAUNT (Vampire), JANINA FAYE (Tania),
BARBARA ARCHER (Inga), CHARLES LLOYD PACK (Doctor Seward), GEORGE MERRITT (Policeman),
GEORGE WOODBRIDGE (Landlord), GEORGE BENSON (Frontier Official).

"It only remains for me now to await the daylight hours when, with God's help, I will forever end this man's reign of terror."

Jonathan Harker's (John Van Eyssen) mission was bound to fail. And lo, the arrogant soul who set forth to put an end to Count Dracula's (Christopher Lee) shameless blood spilling is himself sucked into the world of the undead, only to be purged of his nightly cravings as a stake is driven into heart. And after the man responsible, Dr. Van Helsing (Peter Cushing), frees his former friend's soul, he too goes in search of the legendary vampire. But Dracula always seems to be one step ahead of him, first killing Harker's betrothed, Lucy (Carol Marsh), and then making his way to her sister, Mina Holmwood (Melissa Stribling). With but a glimmer of hope, Van Helsing and Mina's husband Arthur (Michael Gough) try to stop the terror at its source, venturing to Dracula's castle for a final showdown amongst the living and the dead ...

While it may not have been clear to anyone at the time of the picture's world premiere, Terence Fisher's *Dracula* adaptation was a cinematic revolution. Hammer Film Productions Limited, riding on the coattails of Fisher and screenwriter Jimmy Sangster's sleeper, the revisionist horror picture *The Curse of Frankenstein* (1957), commissioned the two men to go grave digging at the tombs of other genre classics. Still, no-one expected their take on Bram Stoker's *Dracula* to alter the course of the vampire's big-screen future, or redefine the parameters of movie horror altogether.

This boon owes much to the fact that striking details of Stoker's novel were either played down, distorted or omitted in the story's previous black-and-white film incarnations, such as Friedrich Wilhelm Murnau's *Nosferatu*

"I know that the boundaries of what is considered 'bad taste' have broadened considerably since we made *Dracula*. But even by 1958 standards I don't think it warranted such epithets." *Jimmy Sangster*

"The cornerstone of the Hammer Films legend ... *Dracula*'s status, certainly in Anglo-horror fandom, is sacrosanct and its importance near-mythic."

Science Fiction, Horror and Fantasy Film Review Database

he Vampire (Nosferatu – Eine Symphonie des Grauens, 1922) or Tod Browning's *Dracula* (1931). Hammer Film's *Dracula* restored blood to its natural vermilion, annihilated the undead in plain sight, and – much to the chagrin of he upholders of propriety and disturbed viewers everywhere – shamelessly had married women lusting after the bloodthirsty brute. The picture served as a precursor to the splatter sub-genre that soon hit the scene.

Sangster and Fisher's film effectively revamped the vampire. Leagues emoved from the aristocratic Bela Lugosi portrayal in the Browning masterpiece, actor Christopher Lee took center stage as a base bloodsucker with an nsatiable sexual appetite and charisma to match. Practically begging for it, emale victims fell at the count's feet and the vampire bite was at long last depicted as an act of sexual climax: when Lee, the sex-crazed Dracula,

stormed his castle's apartments with bloodstained lips to rip a vampire bride (Valerie Gaunt) from Harker's neck – he readily dropped his human mask to expose the character for the monster he was.

To balance Christopher Lee's sexually aggressive, powerhouse performance, Sangster and Fisher cast Peter Cushing in the role of the precision fired rationalist Van Helsing. From Harker's death on, the flesh and blood opponent makes his way into almost every shot and presents the perfect counterpoint to Lee's exonerated beast – a brilliant pairing first seen on screen in Hammer Film's *The Curse of Frankenstein*. Breathtaking set pieces and locations emerged as yet another of the production company trademarks. At the same time, even when *Dracula* is supposed to take place in Romania's Klausenberg or Germany's Ingolstadt (curiously just a short car

1   Sucker! Dracula (Christopher Lee) longs for but a taste of Mina Holmwood's (Melissa Stribling) blood. His sexual appetite, however, is insatiable.

2   Faster than a bat outta hell: Dracula strikes his vampire bride (Valerie Gaunt) just before she sinks her teeth into Jonathan Harker, the count's mortal guest.

3   The avenger: Dr. Van Helsing (Peter Cushing) protects the pint-sized Diana Rigg look-alike, (Janina Faye as Tania), from the creatures of the night with a religious trinket.

"Thanks to Technicolor, the red really comes into its own. It's there on Dracula's teeth and lips, on his victims' necks and on the stake that pierces the vampire's breast."

Karsten Prüßmann: Die Dracula-Familie

PETER CUSHING (1913–1994)

Three roles secured him a place in the golden circle of horrific suspense. Briton Peter Cushing played the title character in Hammer Film's *The Curse of Frankenstein* (1957), Dracula's nemesis Dr. Van Helsing in the company's follow-up project *Dracula / Horror of Dracula* (1958) and Sherlock Holmes in *The Hound of the Baskervilles* (1959). These films marked the beginning of a fruitful collaboration between the actor and Hammer Films, closing the book on Cushing's unremarkable career as a stage and TV mimic.

Following his studies at London's Guildhall School of Music and Drama, Cushing got his start in Hollywood show-business with adventure films like *The Man in the Iron Mask* (1939) and comedies like *A Chump at Oxford* (1940). But it wasn't long before that the actor bid the USA adieu to try his hand at theatrical life in London's West End. Stints in pictures like Laurence Olivier's *Hamlet* (1948) and *Moulin Rouge* (1952) came shortly thereafter, followed by his Hammer breakthrough. By the end of the decade Cushing had been pigeonholed in screen horror, a slot that the deeply religious actor would never escape. Oodles of obscure Hammer productions kept his schedule full: *Dracula A.D. 1972* (1972), *The Legend of the 7 Golden Vampires* (1974) etc. Professional life beyond Hammer included B-movie fantasies like *At the Earth's Core* (1976), as well as George Lucas' box-office smash *Star Wars* (1977) in which he played the villainous Grand Moff Tarkin. Still, having had his fill of second-rate celluloid, Cushing dramatically cut down on his screen engagements in the 1980s, but did seize the opportunity to prove his flair for comedy in the spy spoof *Top Secret!* (1984). His final retreat from pictures came at the end of the 80s. In 1989, Cushing was distinguished as an Officer of the British Empire, but sadly lost his life to cancer in Canterbury, England just a few years later.

Dracula from an unstoppable reign of terror. Then again, isn't the prospect of killing the undead a contradiction in terms?

5   Careful, he bites: Dracula doesn't bother to wipe up after a little midnight snack, before going back for seconds.

6   It's hammer time! Arthur Holmwood (Michael Gough) accompanies Dr. Van Helsing on his crusade to defeat the vampire. Christopher Lee and Peter Cushing went on to star together in numerous subsequent Hammer Studios productions.

riage ride away from one another in this piece of cinematic folklore), the meticulous art direction couldn't scream Victorian England any louder if it tried.

For both budget and technically related reasons, Jimmy Sangster was compelled to fudge a few plot elements from Bram Stoker's book. The real estate agent Harker is rewritten as a vampire slayer; and mental institution director Dr. Seward (Charles Lloyd Pack) is turned into the Holmwoods' family doctor – conveniently allowing for the mental institution to be scrapped. Other amendments to the vampire legend were made to forego costly special effects: Dracula is denied all his traditional means of transmutation and expedient travel, never appearing on screen as a bat or a wolf; instead, he simply seems to appear out of thin air when coveting his victims.

As a marketing strategy *Dracula* was retitled *Horror of Dracula* for the American market prior to its international release. In his autobiography, *Do You Want It Good or Tuesday?* Sangster cheekily says of the decision, "I can only assume that it was in case the American cinemagoer didn't know who Dracula was and the distributors wanted to make it clear that this was a horror movie." Be that as it may, the film spawned numerous Hammer follow-up projects and industry rip-offs. While none of these recreated the grandeur of this first *Dracula* remake, they did succeed in cementing an image of the character still evident in the story's greater collective. The only nasty side effect is that, despite many valiant attempts and other notable accomplishments, actor Christopher Lee never entirely escaped the fangs of his once beloved screen persona.   ES

6

IT HAPPENED IN BROAD DAYLIGHT

Es geschah am hellichten Tag / El cebo

1958 – WEST GERMANY / SWITZERLAND / SPAIN - 99 MIN. - B & W - CRIME FILM

DIRECTOR LADISLAO VAJDA (1906–1965)
SCREENPLAY FRIEDRICH DÜRRENMATT, HANS JACOBY, LADISLAO VAJDA **DIRECTOR OF PHOTOGRAPHY** HEINRICH GÄRTNER
EDITING HERMANN HALLER **MUSIC** BRUNO CANFORA **PRODUCTION** LAZAR WECHSLER, ARTUR BRAUNER for
PRAESENS-FILM AG, CCC FILMKUNST GMBH, CHAMARTÍN PRODUCCIONES Y DISTRIBUCIONES.

STARRING HEINZ RÜHMANN (Commissioner Matthäi), MICHEL SIMON (The Peddler, Jacquier),
EWALD BALSER (Professor Manz), GERT FRÖBE (Mr. Schrott), BERTA DREWS (Mrs. Schrott),
SIGFRIT STEINER (Detective Feller), SIEGFRIED LOWITZ (Inspector Heinzi), HEINRICH GRETLER
(Police Commandant), MARÍA ROSA SALGADO (Frau Heller), ANITA VON OW (Annemarie Heller).

"Such a devil cannot possibly exist."

Child murderers have always been an object of particular revulsion and dread. Sometimes they dominate the headlines for days on end; and sometimes they haunt us for a lifetime.

It Happened in Broad Daylight (Es geschah am hellichten Tag) is a forgotten classic. A German / Swiss / Spanish co-production, it focuses on Commissioner Matthäi (Heinz Rühmann), a kindly, good-natured police detective who is put in charge of the case of a murdered eight-year-old girl just before his retirement. The main suspect is a peddler (Michel Simon), but Matthäi doesn't believe he's guilty. Then the man hangs himself in his cell in despair, and it looks like an open-and-shut case. But the elderly cop is plagued by doubts, and he decides to pursue his own private investigation. He has promised the parents he will find the culprit, and if Matthäi's suspicions turn out to be well founded, the killer still poses a threat.

The murder, and others like it, took place in Eastern Switzerland. Matthäi rents a gas station on a country road there, and waits. It's a hopeless strategy, but Matthäi believes that sooner or later the nameless monster will put in an appearance. The policeman's only clue is a drawing by the child victim, who, it seems, had met her killer on several occasions: the picture depicts an enormous man with a black car. As this isn't enough to catch the killer, Matthäi hatches a monstrous idea: he hires a housekeeper and uses her little daughter as bait. For months on end he watches and waits, forgetting that it's impossible to keep an eye on a child from dawn till dusk. And when the trap finally snaps shut, it's almost too late …

Sean Penn's remake, The Pledge (2000) starred Jack Nicholson and had a very different ending: the murderer dies in a car accident, and the cop descends into madness after years of waiting in vain. Penn was faithful to the

"Gert Fröbe plays the murderer like the Kasper character in German puppet theater. The red-haired giant Rübezahl stands in his plushy bedroom; in the sewing-basket are the socks his wife has darned for him; jars of marinated fruit line the walls. With a faint smile, he stares almost blissfully at Kasper's stupid, friendly face. Rübezahl does conjuring tricks for children, and under his jacket he always keeps a knife." *Der Tagesspiegel*

4

1   Trick or treat: Child killer Mr. Schrott (Gert Fröbe) has got a heart of gold – when it suits him.

2   Vigilantes hold a midnight vigil: Commissioner Matthäi (Heinz Rühmann) has trouble preventing the outraged villagers from turning into a lynch mob.

3   Sure as Sherwood: Traveling salesman Jacquier (Michel Simon) lays low in the forest while devising ways to clear his name of the crimes.

4   Could you run that by me again? Sometimes Inspector Heinzi (Siegfried Lowitz) can't make head or tail of the schemes his boss cooks up.

5   Teasing the killer out of hiding: Inspector Heinzi wins the trust of a little girl who supplies him with the first clue to the killer's identity – a drawing.

novel by the famous Swiss author Friedrich Dürrenmatt, who had substantially reworked the storyline in his final screenplay for the original movie. But *It Happened in Broad Daylight* can hardly be accused of excessive optimism: in one of his few straight roles, Heinz Rühmann, the roly-poly German screen idol, plays a character of deep moral ambiguity. In order to catch the killer, Matthäi abuses the trust of an unsuspecting mother and her child, thereby becoming a kind of ruthless seducer himself. And as for Gert Fröbe … he became known as the very archetype of a terrifying sex fiend. And indeed, his

performance is every bit as memorable as Peter Lorre's in Fritz Lang's *M* (*M – Eine Stadt sucht einen Mörder*, 1931). At first, all we're shown of him is a black shadow; then we see his huge fleshy fingers, cramping in panic as his domineering wife humiliates him; finally, this massive man appears full-size – and with his gruesome Punch and Judy Show, he beguiles tiny Annemarie (Anita von Ow), Matthäi's "bait." Fröbe's career never really recovered from this role.

The subject of the movie is as topical as it ever was, although Sean Penn's treatment is more "modern," as it places the Commissioner's struggle

GERT FRÖBE
(1913–1988)

After an early career as a stage violinist and set painter, Gert Fröbe made his screen acting debut as the emaciated Otto Normalverbraucher in the post-war satire *Berliner Ballade* (1948). There followed a host of minor films. As Fröbe put on more and more weight, he came to symbolize Germany's "economic miracle" of the 1950s. Then he developed a remarkable international career. The James Bond producers Broccoli and Saltzman had noticed his performance in *It Happened in Broad Daylight* (*Es geschah am hellichten Tag / El cebo*, 1958). As Auric Goldfinger in *Goldfinger* (1964), he became the epitome of the nasty Teuton, the charming-but-bestial villain, or – as the English papers put it – "the man you love to hate." Lauded by all and sundry as Bond's best enemy, he was also one of the few German actors to make a name for himself abroad. In his private life, he was known to be a likable chap, but few moviegoers noticed it. Fröbe, who never wanted to lose his German accent, accepted the image he had acquired. In more than 100 movies, he mainly had to content himself with playing very minor roles, but some run-of-the-mill productions were enriched by his fine character acting. His best-known German films included Fritz Lang's *The Thousand Eyes of Dr. Mabuse* (*Die 1000 Augen des Dr. Mabuse / Le Diabolique docteur Mabuse / Il diabolico Dr. Mabuse*, 1960) and *Der Gauner und der liebe Gott* (1960). The rest of the world enjoyed his jokey performances in *Those Magnificent Men in Their Flying Machines* (1965) and *Chitty Chitty Bang Bang* (1968). In 1968, Gert Fröbe died in Munich of a heart attack.

6 Giving pointers: To set a trap for the killer, the overly ambitious Matthäi convinces little Annemarie (Anita von Ow) to help him bait the killer. His plan, however, ends up endangering the girl's life.

7 You should be ashamed of yourself: Annemarie's mother (María Rosa Salgado) is outraged by Matthäi's reckless behavior. And so is he.

"The cast is uniformly excellent. Rühmann gives a thoroughly convincing performance away from his comic parts. Michel Simon in a relatively short role as the peddler is topnotch, and Gert Fröbe impresses as the perverted killer." *Variety*

with his conscience in the foreground of the film. But it's the almost unbearably tense atmosphere of the older movie that makes *It Happened in Broad Daylight* the best German film of the post-war period. Its disturbing effect also has a lot to do with its location: the pristine world of the Swiss mountains, a kind of Garden of Eden in the sugary German *Heimatfilme* that emerged after the horrors of World War II. Switzerland is the land of alpine horns, chocolate and Heidi — and the Hungarian director makes cleverly suggestive use of those ambivalent motifs. The music deceptively promises safety where none exists, and the chocolate is used to entice innocent children. In the idyllic picture-postcard world of an unspoiled natural paradise lurks the threat of bestial human wickedness. And not even Matthäi will succeed in taming it.

PB

THE 400 BLOWS
Les quatre cents coups

1958/59 - FRANCE - 101 MIN. - B & W - DRAMA

DIRECTOR FRANÇOIS TRUFFAUT (1932–1984)
SCREENPLAY FRANÇOIS TRUFFAUT, MARCEL MOUSSY DIRECTOR OF PHOTOGRAPHY HENRI DECAË EDITING MARIE-JOSÈPHE YOYOTTE
MUSIC JEAN CONSTANTIN PRODUCTION FRANÇOIS TRUFFAUT, GEORGES CHARLOT for LES FILMS DU CARROSSE, SÉDIF PRODUCTIONS.

STARRING JEAN-PIERRE LÉAUD (Antoine Doinel), CLAIRE MAURIER (Gilberte Doinel, the mother), ALBERT RÉMY (Julien Doinel, the father), GUY DECOMBLE ('Petite Feuille', the French teacher), PATRICK AUFFAY (René Bigey), ROBERT BEAUVAIS (Principal), PIERRE REPP (English teacher), LUC ANDRIEUX (Sports teacher), DANIEL COUTURIER (Mauricet), RICHARD KANAYAN (Abbou).

IFF CANNES 1959 BEST DIRECTOR (François Truffaut).

"Your mother, your mother ... Well? What's wrong with your mother?" "She's dead, Monsieur!"

When the Nouvelle Vague celebrated its breakthrough at the Cannes Film Festival in 1959, reporters and photographers flocked around the 14-year-old Jean-Pierre Léaud. His performance as a neglected kid in *The 400 Blows* had impressed the critics – and moved them. At his side was the director François Truffaut, himself only 27, but already a notoriously belligerent film critic for *Arts* and *Cahiers du cinéma*. A year previously, he had been barred from the festival because of his polemical writings; now he was there to pick up the prize as Best Director.

Moviegoers also reacted ecstatically to the film, Truffaut's first full-length feature. *The 400 Blows* approached its topic with unprecedented honesty, directness and compassion. It tells the tale of an unhappy childhood

in Paris; and essentially, it was Truffaut's own story. He did nothing to embellish that story, or to romanticize his protagonist.

Young Antoine Doinel is no more an angel than his parents are devils. He skips school and heads for the Pigalle to watch movies with his buddy René (Patrick Auffay). To avoid the teacher's wrath, he forges notes and invents ever more drastic excuses; once, he even claims his mother has died. Antoine's parents are mainly preoccupied with themselves. Bored with her life as a housewife, his mother (Claire Maurier) has taken a lover. Antoine's father (Albert Rémy) tolerates this for the sake of a quiet life, and devotes all his time to his hobby: rally racing. This leaves little room for Antoine, who has in any case seen long since seen through the adults' hypocrisy. When he

"The boy actor, who had never faced a movie camera before Truffaut found him, plays faultlessly and with pure, unsentimental appeal, mostly in his own unrehearsed words and gestures." *Time Magazine*

1   Kennel club: In his first feature-length film, François Truffaut recounts his isolated childhood.

2   A child star with staying power: Jean-Pierre Léaud (age 14) won instant accolades for his portrayal of Truffaut's alter ego, Antoine Doinel.

3   Count them on your fingers: Léaud went on to perform in four more Truffaut pictures over the next 20 years.

4

4 Extended slumber party: Antoine says good
   riddance to his neglectful parents and sets up
   camp with his friend René (Patrick Auffay).

5 Out of line: Following in the footsteps of young
   Truffaut, Antoine endures a regimented life in
   a reform school. Even here, he sticks out like a
   sore thumb.

functions, he's ignored; when he misbehaves, he's punished. It's not just that
the adults fail to understand Antoine, it's just that they are loveless. Truffaut's
film depicts a boy who is quite painfully alone.

Catastrophe strikes when Antoine steals a typewriter from his father's
office, intending to sell it for cash. His dad catches him and calls the cops.
Antoine spends the night in a police cell, shoved in amongst crooks and
hookers. Eventually he lands in a reform school for juvenile delinquents,
somewhere out in the sticks.

For all the bitterness of the events it depicts, *The 400 Blows* is an as-
tonishingly optimistic film. The tone of the movie oscillates between melancholy and exuberance. Like a secret ally, the camera accompanies Antoine
and René on their adventures in Paris, and it succeeds almost miraculously
in capturing the specific flavor of what it feels like to be young. These black-
and-white Dyaliscope images convey the luminous intensity of adolescent
experience, a vital spontaneity and innocent curiosity that most adults have
lost forever.

CAHIERS DU CINÉMA   Probably no other film journal has had such a decisive influence on the history of the movies: *Cahiers du cinéma*, founded in Paris in 1951 by Jacques Doniol-Valcroze, Lo Duca and André Bazin, was not just a major contributor to the development of modern film criticism and theory, but also played a key role in the development of the cinema itself. In the 50s, uncompromising young critics such as François Truffaut, Jean-Luc Godard, Jacques Rivette and Claude Chabrol made the *Cahiers* the leading voice for a renewal of the French cinema. Calling for a *politique des auteurs*, these so-called Young Turks demanded a cinema of personal artistic expression; they wanted to see films that reflected the filmmaker's own, unique vision. As examples of what an *auteur* looked like, the *Cahiers* critics pointed to Hollywood directors such as Howard Hawks and Alfred Hitchcock, or to French individualists such as Jean Renoir and Robert Bresson – and they lambasted the respected representatives of the established French cinema. This *cinéma de qualité* they found sterile, clichéd, unoriginal and fixated on the script.

Several *Cahiers* authors regarded their critical writings as a necessary prelude to their own filmmaking activity. And so, at the end of the 50s, Truffaut, Godard, Chabrol and others exchanged the desk for the director's chair, and the Nouvelle Vague was born. Since then, the journal has gone through numerous changes. After May '68, the *Cahiers* was heavily influenced by Marxist ideas for a number of years. Now more docile politically, and with a smart new look, the *Cahiers du cinéma* has maintained its reputation as an intellectual forum for passionate *cinéastes*.

"Truffaut has responded to his doubters and detractors in the only way that carries conviction: by offering us a very fine film." *Le Monde*

Though *The 400 Blows* was a key film of the Nouvelle Vague, most present-day viewers will agree that it's far less radical in its form than – for example – the work of Jean-Luc Godard. What was new about this movie was the unforced episodic narrative structure and the unprejudiced view of its characters, who are always more than mere marionettes of the screenplay. Above all, it was the autobiographical aspect of this film that would ensure its seminal influence on the *cinéma d'auteur*. The movie's final scene has also inspired a host of filmmakers. In the middle of a soccer match,

Antoine manages to escape from the reformatory. He runs and runs until he reaches the sea, then suddenly turns to the camera and pauses. The frame freezes, and the film ends with a close-up of the boy gazing straight out at us. Not that this was to be audiences' last encounter with Antoine Doinel: over the 20 years that followed, Léaud went on to play Truffaut's alter ego no fewer than four times. It was a collaboration that would eventually go down in the history of cinema.

JH

6   Civil servant: When Antoine's father hands him over to the authorities, the boy learns that a man's first and foremost duty is to the state and not to his family.

7   Clouds in my coffee: This is the closest Antoine will ever come to having anything handed to him on a silver platter.

8   French fashion trends: Antoine tries to avoid taking an additional *400 Blows* by sporting a tough-guy fedora. The film was the first big hit of the Nouvelle Vague and started a major cult of its own.

HIROSHIMA, MON AMOUR

Hiroshima, mon amour / Nijushi – jikan no joji

1959 - FRANCE / JAPAN - 90 MIN. - B & W - DRAMA

DIRECTOR ALAIN RESNAIS (b. 1922)
SCREENPLAY MARGUERITE DURAS DIRECTOR OF PHOTOGRAPHY SACHA VIERNY, TAKAHASHI MICHIO EDITING HENRI COLPI, JASMINE CHASNEY, ANNE SARRAUTE MUSIC GIOVANNI FUSCO, GEORGES DELERUE PRODUCTION SAMY HALFON, ANATOLE DAUMAN for ARGOS FILMS, COMO, PATHÉ ENTERTAINMENT, DAIEI STUDIOS.

STARRING EMMANUELLE RIVA (the Actress), EIJI OKADA (the Japanese), BERNARD FRESSON (the German), STELLA DASSAS (the Mother), PIERRE BARBAUD (the Father).

"Hi – ro – shi – ma ... that's your name."

A young French actress (Emmanuelle Riva) is in Hiroshima, making a film about peace. There she meets a local architect (Eiji Okada), and although they are both happily married, they spend the night together. The following morning, he asks her to stay, but she refuses: filming has finished, her work is done, and she wants to get back to Paris. So the couple have only one last day together, a few hours in which the woman will tell of her first love: a German soldier she had met with secretly in her home town of Nevers during World War II. And as she tells the tragic story, her memories merge with the present – and with her burgeoning love for the Japanese man.

Hiroshima, mon amour was Alain Resnais' first full-length feature film. And like *Night and Fog* (*Nuit et brouillard*, 1955), his documentary about the Nazi death camps, this is a film that deals with the possibility of memory and the presence of the past. It was a subject that Resnais would take up again in *Last Year in Marienbad* (*L'Année dernière à Marienbad* / *L'anno scorso a Marienbad*, 1961) and *Muriel, or The Time of Return* (*Muriel ou Le Temps d'un retour* / *Muriel, il tempo di un ritorno*, 1963).

Resnais had originally planned to make a documentary film about the atom bomb with Chris Marker; but after they had viewed the films that already existed on the topic, Marker dropped out, and Resnais abandoned the idea of a documentary. Both filmmakers were members of the left-leaning Rive Gauche group, which was closely associated with the writers of the Nouveau Roman. So Resnais teamed up with Marguerite Duras and they developed the idea of a film that would combine documentary with fictional material: a love story, set in Hiroshima.

Resnais struggled to find new forms of cinematic expression that would permit a more adequate approach to the situation of human beings in their particular place and time. At the same time, he wanted to demonstrate the impossibility of representing reality. And so he turned to the

1 Love in the time of cholera: A French actress (Emmanuelle Riva) meets a Japanese architect (Eiji Okada) in Hiroshima and rises from the ashes like a phoenix.

2 Turning and returning: The atrocities of war hang like a cloud over Hiroshima and permeate the psyche of all who set foot in the city.

3 Between two fronts: Alain Resnais' first feature was scripted by Marguerite Duras, and mixes Nouveau Roman narrative with the Nouvelle Vague style of filmmaking.

4 Summer of love '59: Both the intimate and public aspects of the cross-cultural romance caused quite a bit of hoopla among audiences worldwide.

"After *Hiroshima, mon amour*, everything must change, for the cinema and the individual. This is a film that remakes the conscience of the individual." *Le Monde*

formal vocabulary of modern literature, and the influence of Duras is clearly visible in the pictorial language and narrative structure of *Hiroshima, mon amour.*

The famous 15-minute opening sequence clearly expresses Resnais' skeptical attitude towards the traditional forms of documentary and fictional film, and it is as provocative as it is magically sensual. Images of the couple making love, made almost abstract by the camera's proximity, are radically combined with pictures showing the destruction of Hiroshima and its inhabitants. Close-ups of intertwined bodies, caressing hands and beautiful skin are followed by mutilated corpses, maimed hands and terrible burns. Sheer horror invading the most intimate and private space, in images that attempt to grasp what really happened in Hiroshima.

EMMANUELLE RIVA Before Alain Resnais discovered her for *Hiroshima, mon amour* (*Hiroshima, mon amour / Nijushi – jikan no joji*, 1959), Emmanuelle Riva (b. 1927 in Cheniménil, France) was a theater actress. Her performance in Resnais' film drew a lot of attention, and suddenly she was one of the female stars who shaped a new image of womanhood in the films of the Nouvelle Vague. Riva was extremely selective about the films she appeared in. She often played women who were self-confident, sensual and sensitive, and she lent these characters an indefinable air of tragedy. In *Hiroshima, mon amour*, she spoke much of her text off-screen, and her impressive voice was subsequently often deployed in this way. Among the many remark-able films she took part in up to the mid-60s, three were outstanding. In Jean-Pierre Melville's *The Forgiven Sinner / Leon Morin, Priest* (*Léon Morin, prêtre*, 1961), she had her most complex role to date, as an attractive widowed atheist whose faith is restored by a priest (Jean-Paul Belmondo). As the titular heroine of Georges Franju's *Thérèse Desqueyroux* (1962), she played a young woman who tries to escape her suffocating existence in a country mansion by attempting to murder her husband. For this role, she was named Best Actress at the Venice Film Festival in 1963. And with the same director, she gave a compelling performance as the Princess de Bomes in the Cocteau adaptation *Thomas the Imposter* (*Thomas, l'im-posteur*, 1964). After this, she concentrated mainly on her theater work. She was still to be seen quite regularly on screen, but less often than before, and mainly in smaller roles.

The French woman has seen these pictures in documentaries, feature films and exhibitions. Her off-screen voice tells us of this. But again and again, her Japanese lover retorts that she has seen nothing of Hiroshima. The filmed images, whether fictional or documentary, are empty, because they cannot communicate the subjective experience; when turned into an image, a living memory is pinned down as a thing of the past. But by interspersing the pictures of bomb victims with the thoughts and physical presence of the couple, Resnais revives these images and makes it possible to connect with them at a personal, subjective level. And in doing so, he creates a sequence of extraordinary poetic power.

In *Hiroshima, mon amour*, Resnais develops a filmic structure that links collective tragedy with individual experience. The film has certain points of intense focus, but its plot remains sketchy, or fragmentary. Yet it has a dynamism all of its own, thanks in no small part to the camera work, which is characterized by numerous rapid tracking shots. Sacha Vierny filmed in Nevers and Takahashi Michio in Hiroshima. Cross cut, these sequences seem to dissolve space and time. Contrasts and oppositions arise throughout the film, and the viewer is forced to create his own synthesis, thus participating in the film's creation. Love and death, past and present, remembering and for-getting, fiction and documentation: Resnais' dialectical construction reveals his skepticism about rigid terms that essentially signify nothing but them-selves. This is why none of the characters have names. In one conversation, the Japanese man takes on the role of the dead German. At the end of the film, the Frenchwoman calls him "Hiroshima" and he calls her "Nevers." UB

BREATHLESS
À bout de souffle

1959 - FRANCE - 88 MIN. - B & W - CRIME FILM, LOVE STORY

DIRECTOR JEAN-LUC GODARD (b. 1930)
SCREENPLAY JEAN-LUC GODARD, FRANÇOIS TRUFFAUT DIRECTOR OF PHOTOGRAPHY RAOUL COUTARD
EDITING CÉCILE DECUGIS, LILA HERMAN MUSIC MARTIAL SOLAL PRODUCTION GEORGES DE BEAUREGARD for IMPÉRIA, LES FILMS GEORGES DE BEAUREGARD, SOCIÉTÉ NOUVELLE DE CINÉMATOGRAPHIE.

STARRING JEAN-PAUL BELMONDO (Michel Poiccard / Laszlo Kovacs), JEAN SEBERG (Patricia Franchini), DANIEL BOULANGER (Police Inspector), JEAN-PIERRE MELVILLE (Parvulesco), HENRI-JACQUES HUET (Antonio Berrutti), VAN DOUDE (Journalist), CLAUDE MANSARD (Used-Car Dealer), RICHARD BALDUCCI (Tolmatchoff), JEAN-LUC GODARD (Informer), LILIANE DAVID (Liliane).

IFF BERLIN 1960 SILVER BEAR for BEST DIRECTOR (Jean-Luc Godard).

"C'est vraiment dégueulasse."

At the end of the 50s, the new French cinema thrilled the young and shocked the Establishment. The stars of *Breathless* were the dream couple of this Nouvelle Vague: Jean-Paul Belmondo as the car thief Michel – a cocky French youth with sensual lips and a boxer's nose, a would-be tough guy who's modeled himself on Humphrey Bogart, and Jean Seberg as his partner Patricia, an American student in Paris – crop-haired, blonde, gazelle-like, dressed in pants and T-shirt, selling the *New York Herald Tribune* in the middle of the Champs Élysées.

Their story is quickly told. Michel shoots a traffic cop, more by accident than by design. He goes into hiding in Paris, where an old buddy still owes him some money. More importantly, he wants to see Patricia again, so he can talk her into running off to Italy with him to Cinecittà. But Patricia is less than bowled over by Michel's daydreams of *la dolce vita* under the southern sun. She wants to pursue a career as a journalist, and she's also expecting Michel's child. His situation becomes ever more perilous, and when the police start taking an interest in Patricia too, she makes a fateful decision: she betrays Michel, in order to force him to flee – and to prove to herself that she doesn't love him. But he stays in Paris, where he is eventually shot dead in the street.

This brief plot summary is enough to show that *À bout de souffle* was also a homage to the U.S. cinema. And although many people in France were fascinated by American movies, the phenomenal success of Jean-Luc Godard's first full-length feature can hardly be explained by reference to its cinephile plot. (The original idea for the film had come from François Truffaut, Godard's friend and former colleague at the legendary film journal, *Cahiers du cinéma*.) But moviegoers loved *Breathless* more for *how* it told its story than for the story it told.

In fact, Godard's film marked a fundamental break with the principles that guided the French "quality" cinema of the day. Instead of having a script worked out to the final detail, Godard allowed his actors to improvise. Instead of carefully honed dialog, he had them speak the jokey slang of the streets. He turned the rules of dramaturgy on their head, so that "dramatic high-

points" such as the policeman's death were over within seconds, while comparatively inconsequential episodes were drawn out to a surprising length (the 15-minute bedroom sequence, for example). Then there was the abrupt editing, the jump cuts, the deliberately disorienting breaches of the sacrosanct "180-degree rule" … All of this was a frontal attack on the cinematic illusion, as was Belmondo's ironic address to the audience: "If you don't like the sea, if you don't like the mountains, if you don't like the city, then you can kiss my ass." A joke, certainly; but it was also a sly appeal to the audience to join in Godard's game and to participate in his reflection on the nature of cinema.

Perhaps most importantly of all, *À bout de souffle* was not made in the studio but in the heart of Paris, on its boulevards and in its alleys, in real apartments, bistros and bars. Godard's cameraman was Raoul Coutard, a former photo-reporter with an appetite for experiment. His raw black-and-white pictures captured the life of the city with a positively sexy directness.

He used as little artificial light as possible and deployed extremely light-sensitive film, and he did without tripods and tracks, using a hand-held camera and sometimes filming from a wheelchair. The city became the secret star of the film, alongside Belmondo and Seberg.

Many of this movie's innovations have long since become part of commercial cinema's stock-in-trade. If this makes *Breathless* seem less radical today, it's still lost nothing of its freshness, rebellious charm, and infectious spontaneity. In 1960, moviegoers reacted ecstatically. Belmondo's role spawned a horde of young male imitators, so that the noun *le belmondisme* entered the French language. At the end, Michel lies grimacing on the street before uttering his famous last words to Patricia: "This is really sick …" ("C'est vraiment dégueulasse"). He may have failed to realize his dream of turning life into a movie, but this movie made him a cinematic icon. Belmondo's Michel achieved posthumous immortality.

JH

DANIEL BOULANGER   He was probably the most interesting-looking bit-part actor of the Nouvelle Vague. Daniel Boulanger was born in Compiègne in 1922, and his actual métier was scriptwriting. His acting roles display the same kind of black humor as his screenplays. In *Breathless* (*À bout de souffle*, 1959), the bald Boulanger played the grim-faced police inspector who shoots Jean-Paul Belmondo in the back. He also made some memorable appearances in films by François Truffaut. As the erotomaniac gangster in *Shoot the Piano Player* (*Tirez sur le pianiste*, 1959/60), it's he who shoots Charles Aznavour's lover; and in *The Bride Wore Black* (*La Mariée était en noir*, 1967), he finishes off the bridegroom with a shotgun – on the steps of the church. Boulanger's career as a screenwriter was notable for his long-lasting collaboration with director Philippe de Broca. Together, they wrote the scripts for de Broca's elegant early comedies, *The Games of Love* (*Les Jeux de l'amour*, 1960), *Five Day Lover* (*L'Amant de cinq jours / L'amante di cinque giorni*, 1960) and *The Joker* (*Le Farceur*, 1961). Boulanger also worked on the scripts to de Broca's two most successful films: *Cartouche* (1962) and the turbulent adventure movie *That Man From Rio* (*L'Homme de Rio / L'uomo del Rio*, 1963).
Many other prominent directors have since profited from Boulanger's wit, his feeling for tempo and his talent for dialog, including Claude Chabrol, Louis Malle, Jean Becker, Marcel Ophüls and Alain Corneau.

"A fascinating communication of the savage ways and moods of some of the rootless young people of Europe (and America) today."

The New York Times

1 Two legends for the price of one: Car thief Michel Poiccard (Jean-Paul Belmondo in his most memorable role) tries to integrate his Hollywood idol's screen persona into his daily life. Here's lookin' at you, Bogey.

2 Savage love: Michel and Patricia (Jean Seberg) have a sexual chemistry that continues to capture the imaginations of moviegoers worldwide.

3 A bang-up job: Improvising along with the actors, director Jean-Luc Godard and cinematographer Raoul Coutard simply shot footage at will, often spontaneously deciding on Paris locales as they happened upon them.

4 Pleased as punch: Michel's mug-shot is in all the papers and he gets to dress up in costume as a result. He'll take fame in any form.

5 Heaven and earth: Belmondo and Seberg's light and carefree love scene is as captivating today as it was nearly half a century ago. Then, it was just about the raciest thing to have ever appeared on the major European screen.

SOME LIKE IT HOT

1959 - USA - 120 MIN. - B & W - COMEDY

DIRECTOR BILLY WILDER (1906–2002)
SCREENPLAY BILLY WILDER, I. A. L. DIAMOND, suggested by a short story by ROBERT THOEREN and M. LOGAN
DIRECTOR OF PHOTOGRAPHY CHARLES LANG JR. EDITING ARTHUR P. SCHMIDT MUSIC ADOLPH DEUTSCH
PRODUCTION BILLY WILDER for THE MIRISCH CORPORATION, ASHTON PRODUCTIONS.

STARRING MARILYN MONROE (Sugar Kane Kowalczyk), TONY CURTIS (Joe / Josephine), JACK LEMMON (Jerry / Daphne),
JOE E. BROWN (Osgood Fielding III), GEORGE RAFT ("Spats" Colombo), PAT O'BRIEN (Mulligan),
NEHEMIAH PERSOFF (Little Bonaparte), JOAN SHAWLEE (Sweet Sue), GEORGE E. STONE (Toothpick Charlie),
EDWARD G. ROBINSON JR. (Johnny Paradise).

ACADEMY AWARDS 1959 OSCAR for BEST COSTUMES (Orry-Kelly).

Josephine: "You're NOT a girl! You're a GUY! Why would a guy wanna marry a guy?" Daphne: "Security!"

Chicago, 1929. After accidentally witnessing a mob massacre, fly-by-night musicians Jerry (Jack Lemmon) and Joe (Tony Curtis) decide that a change of scenery might be good for their health. They get a gig with an all-girl band headed south for Florida, shave their legs to blend in with the crowd, and say arrivederci to the city's trigger-happy hoods.

Life as the weaker sex presents each of the boys with unforeseen snags: Joe alias "Josephine" loses his heart to a liquor-loving, ukulele-strumming singer named Sugar Kane (Marilyn Monroe) and wants nothing more than to liberate himself of both dress and drawers. Jerry, on the other hand, takes to his feminine side a little too well: calling himself "Daphne" and exuding natural charm, Jerry catches the eye of octogenarian tycoon Osgood Fielding III (Joe E. Brown), and can't shake the aging playboy off his skirt. But when murderous Chicago mafioso "Spats" Colombo (George Raft) turns up on the scene, there's suddenly one beau too many in what was supposed to have been a "ladies only" club.

You might wonder what prompted Billy Wilder to shoot the picture many consider to be his best comedy in black and white. For wouldn't Technicolor's dazzling effects do better in bringing out the contours of a story about men caked in rouge? Perhaps, but *Some Like It Hot* is more than just a drag comedy; it's a salute to the dawn of cinema, Hollywood gangster pictures, screwball comedies of the 1940s, and that special brand of Marx Bros irreverence. These old-fashioned ingredients, when shaken up in the Wilderian cocktail mixer, make for a high-octane concoction that strips us of all inhibitions and has us laughing ourselves silly over its overtly sexual subtext.

If your last viewing of *Some Like It Hot* predates puberty, be prepared for a real eye-opener: racy double-entendres about free love, homosexuality and impotence – as fresh today as they were fifty years ago – pop up throughout the film's seemingly innocent dialog. The film censors must have been deaf, dumb and blind to miss the connotations of remarks like Sugar's demure "I-always-get-the-fuzzy-end-of-the-lollipop." And no less audacious

> ## "Both Curtis and Lemmon are practicing cruel deceptions – Curtis has Monroe thinking she's met a millionaire, and Brown thinks Lemmon is a woman – but the film dances free before anyone gets hurt. Both Monroe and Brown learn the truth and don't care, and after Lemmon reveals he's a man, Brown delivers the best curtain line in the movies."
> *Chicago Sun-Times*

is how Wilder pits glaring opposites like sex and money, life and death, appearance and reality, as well as mobsters and music against one another.

It is, without question, a comedy is born out of contradiction and role-reversal. The virile Joe, for example, must dress up as an allegedly impotent and near-sighted oil baron to strike it big with Sugar; but rather than putting the moves on her, he lets an intimate evening on board Osgood's yacht inspire her to do the job for him. And thus by seeing to it that his protagonists are constantly compelled to don various disguises, Wilder transforms what should be a fight for survival into a never-ending laugh-attack. It is a dynamic that waxes doubly ironic when the prospects of a honeymoon with Osgood *à la* "he wants to go to the French Riviera but I'm kinda leaning towards Niagara Falls" make Jerry / Daphne wish he were dead.

Some Like It Hot was a legendary endeavor from start to finish; from the shimmering sheer dress Marilyn wears while singing "I Wanna Be Loved By You" right up until Osgood's unfazed "Nobody's perfect" in reaction to Daphne's true identity. And the long journey to this immortal last line was even more of an adventure than the fittings with Academy Award-winning costume designer Orry-Kelly; for working with Marilyn Monroe entailed a crazy shooting schedule that supplied Billy Wilder and Tony Curtis with a lifetime of anecdotes: there was simply no telling whether she'd show up on the set; and when she would, she'd need forty takes for a single line of dialog like "Where's that bourbon?" At her mercy, Curtis and Lemmon were left standing for hours on end in high-heels, and Wilder himself claimed to have suffered a nervous breakdown as a result of his leading lady's unreliable work

1   Last tango in platforms: Jerry alias Daphne (Jack Lemmon) celebrates his engagement to Osgood Fielding III (Joe E. Brown) with the dance of death.

2   You're blocking my sun: While posing as the shortsighted heir to the Shell-Oil fortune, Joe (Tony Curtis) tries to get Sugar (Marilyn Monroe) to share her own special set of riches with him. Her chaperone, however, is a real drag.

3   Now make a wish and blow out the candles: Cuz da mob iz gonna blow da livin' daylights outta youz if ya don't, seeeee?

4   How's about a little goodnight kiss? Now, nighty night and don't let the Chihuahuas bite.

"When we talked about it we decided that they should join the girls' band as an absolute question of life and death. Otherwise it would seem that at any point in the picture they could remove their wigs and skirts and say to the girls that they love 'Look, no problem, we're guys and you're gals and we love you'." *Billy Wilder*

5 Girls will be girls: Nothing like sneaking a slug of whiskey when mother hen isn't looking.

6 I wanna be loved by you: Sugar Kane does some field research to help find a cure for impotence.

7 The Great Depression hits home: Like so many other qualified men, Jerry and Joe are out of work

and flat out of luck. Looks like Santa Claus might not be the only one putting those old Christmas stockings to good use.

8 Rock candy: Joe can barely keep his mind on his sax with all that sweetness kicking about on stage.

9 In hot water: To look at the two of them, who would ever believe that Tony Curtis could ever have compared locking lips with this blonde to kissing Hitler? Not Curtis, that's for sure. These days he denies ever having said it.

ethic. Years later, the director was singing a very different tune, deifying Monroe for her electric presence and the perfect sense of comic timing she demonstrated here.

Be it scripted subtext or revisionist interpretation, *Some Like It Hot* can also be seen as a commentary on the tragic sex goddess' off-screen life: misguided by romantic ideals and driven to drink by irresponsible partners, Sugar longs to find a sensitive, understanding man. Was it just coincidence that the spectacled heir to Shell Oil she falls in love with resembled Monroe's real-life intellectual husband Arthur Miller? For indeed a sentimental heart-note lies beyond the picture's general lunacy and Wilder's cynical overtones: pouring her heart out in song, Sugar is granted the magical kiss she's been yearning for all along, when Joe, dressed as a woman, marches across the stage and reveals his true feelings for her. Now that Joe has gained insight into how "the other half lives," he can no longer toy with Sugar's emotions.

Marilyn Monroe's tragic death in 1962 was far removed from the celluloid happy endings so many of her characters knew. But her story and her appeal transcend them all.

PB

TONY CURTIS (b. 1925) His candid autobiography tells of a Jewish kid in Brooklyn who didn't have it easy, but managed to soar to the top thanks to his naturally good looks. Indeed, Hollywood whole-heartedly opened its gates to Bernard Schwartz's winning appearance, and the name his Hungarian immigrant parents bestowed on him quickly fell by the wayside. Curtis' initial successes in low-caliber period pieces like *Son of Ali Baba* (1952) had him pigeonholed as the Hollywood Dream Factory's first teen idol, and presented James Dean with a bit of competition. But Curtis was seldom cast as the heartthrob, acting instead in epics like *Spartacus* (1960) and *Taras Bulba* (1962) as the on-screen son to stars like Kirk Douglas, Burt Lancaster, Yul Brynner and Cary Grant. Stanley Kramer's racial drama *The Defiant Ones* (1958) gave him his first break at character acting, and the *The Boston Strangler* (1968) was his second and last attempt at making headway in that field. His knack at comedy was responsible for the greatest hits and most regrettable misses of his circa 120 films. And when he wasn't in front of the camera, the tabloids kept Tony Curtis in the public eye: his numerous marriages to actresses like *Psycho's* Janet Leigh and Germany's Christine Kaufmann as well as his long battle with drugs were highly publicized. Fast cars and beautiful women were always among Curtis' greatest loves. And today, the proud father of eight is also the father of a Hollywood legacy thanks to his equally famous daughter, Jamie Lee Curtis.

BEN-HUR

✝✝✝✝✝✝✝✝✝✝✝✝

1959 - USA - 213 MIN. - COLOR - HISTORICAL EPIC

DIRECTOR William WYLER (1902–1981)
SCREENPLAY KARL TUNBERG, based of the novel *BEN-HUR: A TALE OF THE CHRIST* by LEW WALLACE
DIRECTOR OF PHOTOGRAPHY ROBERT SURTEES EDITING JOHN D. DUNNING, RALPH E. WINTERS MUSIC MIKLÓS RÓZSA
PRODUCTION SAM ZIMBALIST for MGM.

STARRING CHARLTON HESTON (Judah Ben-Hur), JACK HAWKINS (Quintus Arrius), HAYA HARAREET (Esther),
STEPHEN BOYD (Messala), HUGH GRIFFITH (Sheik Ilderim), MARTHA SCOTT (Miriam), CATHY O'DONNELL (Tirzah),
FRANK THRING (Pontius Pilate), FINLAY CURRIE (Balthasar), MINO DORO (Gratus), CLAUDE HEATER (Jesus).

ACADEMY AWARDS 1959 OSCARS for BEST PICTURE (Sam Zimbalist), BEST DIRECTOR (William Wyler),
BEST LEADING ACTOR (Charlton Heston), BEST SUPPORTING ACTOR (Hugh Griffith),
BEST CINEMATOGRAPHY (Robert Surtees), BEST EDITING (Ralph E. Winters, John D. Dunning),
BEST MUSIC (Miklós Rózsa), BEST ART DIRECTION (William A. Horning, Edward C. Carfagno, Hugh Hunt),
BEST COSTUMES (Elizabeth Haffenden), BEST VISUAL EFFECTS (A. Arnold Gillespie, Robert MacDonald),
BEST SOUND EFFECTS (Milo B. Lory), and BEST SOUND (Franklin Milton).

"I tell you, the day Rome falls there will be a shout of freedom such as the world has never heard before."

In the 26th year of our Lord, the Roman province of Judea is in turmoil. The winds of revolt stir up the empire, and the sermons of an awe-inspiring rabbi in the little village of Nazareth are drawing ever-larger crowds.

Suspicious of any hint of subversion, Rome sends reinforcements to Jerusalem. Messala (Stephen Boyd), the man appointed commanding officer of the Roman legions, grew up in the Jewish holy city as the son of a high-ranking official. The first person to welcome his homecoming is a childhood friend named Judah Ben-Hur (Charlton Heston), a well-respected and influential businessman. Sadly, the years have made strangers of them: Messala wants nothing more than to serve the Emperor Tiberius and implores Judah to disclose the names of the rebel ringleaders; Judah's allegiance, however, is to his people, and he refuses to betray them.

Messala doesn't have to wait long to act against the Jews and spite Ben-Hur. The day after their encounter, proconsul Gratus (Mino Doro) arrives in Jerusalem and a dislodged roof tile from Judah's palatial home injures the official as he rides by. Messala has Judah's family arrested in a flash: his mother Miriam (Martha Scott) and sister Tirzah (Cathy O'Donnell) are incar-

cerated, and Judah is sentenced to the slave galleys with little prospect of survival. Miraculously, he survives his excruciating labors. Tormented by a blistering thirst, he and the other prisoners are hauled through Nazareth, where a carpenter's son lets Judah drink from the elixir of life ...

Three years go by, and Judah finds himself chained to the oars of a slave-powered Roman warship under the command of consul Quintus Arrius (Jack Hawkins). Stationed in the Mediterranean, the vessel's mission is seek out and destroy Macedonian pirates. When battle is joined with some pirates on the open water one day, the imperial ship is rammed, and Judah slips his chains, escapes from the galley and saves Quintus Arrius. To show his gratitude, the Roman consul adopts Judah as his son. Galley slave number forty-one is reborn as Roman citizen Ben-Hur, raising himself up from hard labor-er to star chariot driver. After several years of fame and fortune in the capital city, Ben-Hur heads home to settle scores with Messala.

With a reputation that precedes him, the undefeatable charioteer from the great circus at the Roman arena challenges Messala to a race: nine laps in battle chariots, with four horses harnessed to each cart. It is a deadly com-

1   Your own personal Jesus: Charlton Heston as the godly Coliseum chariot driver Judah Ben-Hur.

2   Battleship Potemkinus: A countless number of men will lose their lives slaving away in these galleys. But not to worry, Hollywood can always replenish them with another round of extras.

"Great credit goes to producer Zimbalist, scenarist Tunberg and director Wyler, but the greatest belongs to Wyler. His wit, intelligence and formal instinct are almost everywhere in evidence, and he has set a standard of excellence by which coming generations of screen spectacles can expect to be measured." *Time Magazine*

3   Pony express: Judah challenges his archenemy to a Roman-style drag race. Heston trained for months to pull off the spectacular sequence without a stuntman. His competitor obviously trained less.

4   Manischewitz makes meshugga: Behold a set of Jews who are about to mix some ancient traditions with some newer ones this high holiday season. From right: Judah's right-hand-man Simonides (Sam Jaffe), Judah's mother Miriam (Martha Scott), Simonides' daughter Esther (Haya Harareet) and Judah's sister Tirzah (Cathy O'Donnell).

petition without rules, and not everyone makes it home in one piece. Messala dies trying, but a sadistic bit of glory is left to be his: just as the consul takes his final breath, he tells the victorious Ben-Hur that although Tirzah and Miriam have survived the Roman dungeons, they have both contracted leprosy, a then incurable disease.

Judah finds Miriam and Tirzah living as outcasts in the Valley of the Lepers, but Tirzah's days are numbered. Ben-Hur now realizes that avenging his enemy did not afford him the peace of mind he had anticipated. But

stories once again abound of the miraculous rabbi who preaches of love and forgiveness on the hill outside the city. Miriam and Tirzah want to hear one of the sermons, but the Roman Pontius Pilate robs them of the chance when he sentences the man called Jesus of Nazareth to death by crucifixion. Death, however, cannot stifle the man's message, and as Jesus' mortal life comes to an end, thunder and lightning tear across the sky bringing forth a downpour that cures Miriam, Tirzah and all the lepers of their ailments. The miracle also has a cathartic effect on Judah, who at last finds inner peace.

5 Chalice from the palace: Messala (Stephen Boyd) and Judah have no idea what damage drinking can do to a friendship.

6 Jesus Christ Superstar: Or is it a precursor to Woodstock? To maintain the sense of mystery, director William Wyler only shows Jesus (Claude Heater) from his best side – the rear.

7 I work and I slave and what thanks do I get? Messala sentences loyal subject Ben-Hur to hard labor aboard the war galleys. His survival will require nothing short of a miracle.

8 I haven't got time for the pain: What these guys need for their tired and achy joints is a good Ben-Gay rubdown. But alas, Judah gets stuck rowing unmerrily down the stream for three years until a twist of fate sets him free.

"Although many viewers tend to believe that this is a fact-based story, it is a quintessentially American fiction that could as easily have been set in the American Revolutionary war as in the Holy Land during the time of Christ." *Apollo Movie Guide*

MIKLÓS RÓZSA (1907–1995)

In 1934, 27-year-old Miklós Rózsa received some friendly, career-shaping advice from well-established composer and colleague Arthur Honegger, who convinced him that his future lay in scoring motion pictures. The son of a Budapest entrepreneur, Rózsa started off writing orchestra and chamber music. He went to London, where he landed his first job in cinema, composing the score to *Knight Without Armour* (1937) directed by Jacques Feyder and starring Marlene Dietrich. The film's producer, fellow Hungarian Alexander Korda, was so taken by his work that he put him under contract. The Korda production *The Thief of Bagdad* sent both men to Hollywood, and Rózsa was soon working for some of the industry's largest studios. It wasn't long before he'd rooted himself as one of the premier fixtures in his field, earning his first of three Oscars in 1945 for Alfred Hitchcock's *Spellbound*. His scores were the first to be pressed and sold as records – a further testament to his greatness. The flip side to his success is that Rózsa thought he had been pegged as a specialist in the scoring of period pieces. And considering some of the highlights of his resumé, including *Quo vadis?* (1951), Richard Thorpe's *Ivanhoe* (1952), and Joseph L. Mankiewicz's *Julius Caesar* (1953), there was little question as to who would be asked to compose *Ben-Hur* (1959) when MGM announced their intention to remake it. Full-orchestra scores went out of fashion in Hollywood during the earlier 1960s, and Rózsa put his academic roots to good use, becoming a music professor University of Southern California. The last picture he worked on was Carl Reiner's detective caper comedy *Dead Men Don't Wear Plaid* (1981).

By 1959, Hollywood's own empire was faltering. Television was the enemy, and the number of its disciples was increasing rapidly. Ready to do whatever it took to get audiences to return to the cinema, the big-name studios planned a counterattack that promised to deliver a larger-than-life movie-going experience flooded with dazzling images, wide-screen dimensions, exotic locales, a host of stars, and sets and costumes of unprecedented opulence. With its 365 speaking parts, 50,000 extras and 15-million-dollar budget, *Ben-Hur*, was not only the most ambitious of this wave of epic films (which also included Mervyn LeRoy's *Quo vadis?* (1951), Henry Koster's *The Robe* (1953), and, in 1956, Cecil B. DeMille's *The Ten Commandments*), but also the most acclaimed. It was one of the box-office sensations of the decade and became the first picture to win a total of eleven Oscars, a record not matched until

James Cameron's *Titanic* (1997). Unfortunately, *Ben-Hur*'s gold standard was far costlier than anticipated: while shooting was still in progress, produce Sam Zimbalist died of what is widely believed to have been a stress-induced heart attack. At the time, the movie's enormous budget had threatened to send the failing Metro Goldwyn Mayer filing for bankruptcy, but its enormous popularity with audiences supplied the studio with a manifold return on its invest ment. Still, *Ben-Hur* would end up being the zenith of such spectaculars, for there was no denying that the inordinate effort productions like these demanded made them an unviable means of saving the studio system.

On the other hand, *Ben-Hur*'s story was already a proven cinematic success. Lew Wallace's novel of the same was an instant bestseller when it was published in 1880. The piece was subsequently adapted for the stage and ther

8

9　March of dimes: Rest assured, they're marching
for a good cause – world domination.

10　Live from Las Vegas: After a brief stint on the
stage of the MGM Grand, Messala packs up his

things and moves on to bigger and better things at
Caesar's Palace.

resurrected in 1925 as a sensational silent film by director Fred Nibo. Banking
on the "you can never have too much of a good thing" Hollywood mentality, the
1959 remake drew from all the magic of the original and enhanced it by means
of the 65mm Technicolor camera, a stereo soundtrack and all imaginable
technical innovations of the day.

A filmgoing experience that supplies everything the eye could possibly
want, Ben-Hur's chariot race in Jerusalem remains one of the cinema's most
recognized and revered sequences. An entire year was required to bring the
nine-minute scene to the screen. One of the great ironies of this meticu-

an Oscar for his work, wasn't responsible for the sequence's staging. The job
was the task of Andrew Marton and Yakima Canutt. The latter also served
as the picture's stunt director and had risen to screen fame for his death-
defying pass beneath director John Ford's moving Stagecoach (1939).

Several uncredited names on the Ben-Hur production team went on to
become some of the industry's movers and shakers: second unit director
Sergio Leone is known today for his own Ancient World epics; and set
designer Ken Adam, on staff with the production's art department, ventured
off to more covert arenas, waging war as the most prominent art director of

"And then the furious chariot race! The cameras are so close to the horses and charioteers that it simply takes one's breath away. Seldom before has any film scene achieved such a heartstopping tempo, such active suspense. This is pure cinema, at the height of technical perfection." *Die Welt*

LOOK BACK IN ANGER

1959 - GREAT BRITAIN - 115 MIN. - B & W - DRAMA

DIRECTOR TONY RICHARDSON (1928–1991)
SCREENPLAY NIGEL KNEALE, JOHN OSBORNE, based on his play of the same name
DIRECTOR OF PHOTOGRAPHY OSWALD MORRIS EDITING RICHARD BEST MUSIC JOHN ADDISON, CHRIS BARBER
PRODUCTION HARRY SALTZMAN for WOODFALL FILM PRODUCTIONS, ORION.

STARRING RICHARD BURTON (Jimmy Porter), CLAIRE BLOOM (Helena Charles), MARY URE (Alison Porter), EDITH EVANS (Mrs. Tanner), GARY RAYMOND (Cliff Lewis), GLEN BYAM SHAW (Colonel Redfern), PHYLLIS NEILSON-TERRY (Mrs. Redfern), DONALD PLEASENCE (Hurst), JANE ECCLES (Miss Drury), S. P. KAPOOR (Kapoor).

"I learned at an early age what it is to be angry. Angry!"

An angry young man became a spokesman for an entire generation. Thousands of young Britons were thrilled by his furious tirades against the government, the Church and the middle classes. Yet the actual target of his fury is a single individual: his own wife. Alison (Mary Ure) stands at her ironing board and takes it all until she can take no more. Jimmy Porter (Richard Burton) takes pleasure in pouring scorn on her privileged upbringing, which has long since ceased to offer her any protection at all. The young couple live in a shabby garret, and the eloquent young cynic has left university without a degree. Mentally torturing this defenseless woman appears to be the only thing that gives his life any meaning at all. And she can't bring herself to tell him she's expecting a baby.

"Why do you try so hard to be unpleasant?" It's Alison's friend Helena (Claire Bloom) who asks the obvious question, even if Jimmy doesn't actually give her a serious answer. But Helena does succeed in persuading Alison to leave the hell her marriage has become. Helena is the stronger of the two – strong enough to stand up to the ranting tyrant, yet too weak to resist his charm for very long. For that's the secret of Jimmy Porter: his blind rage is magically attractive. In dull, dusty post-war Britain, Jimmy Porter was a new zeitgeist waiting to happen. John Osborne's stage debut had its premiere in 1956, and it immediately established him as a leading figure among the "angry young men" of the time. The critic Kenneth Tynan celebrated it as "the best young play of its decade," describing it as "A Streetcar named Desire seen through the eyes of Stanley Kowalski." In parallel with this theater revolution, Tony Richardson's first film introduced a new era in the British cinema. Grim and gray this "kitchen-sink realism" may have been, but it achieved new heights of thrilling psychological intensity.

1

"*Look Back in Anger* seems to stem from the 'people are no damn good' school of thought. Though of varying temperaments, these characters have all resigned themselves to life as it would have them, betraying their true longings with steely British resolve. It's a bleak world to inhabit, and makes for disturbing entertainment. Luckily, all the actors are incredible, especially Burton, who rips through the movie like a limey chainsaw, and Mary Ure as Alison, whose fragile beauty echoes her lost, forlorn performance."

Apollo Movie Guide

2

1 Would you shut up already?! Helena Charles (Claire Bloom) can't take much more of Jimmy Porter's (Richard Burton) booming presence.

2 Sugar shock: Outside of his own four walls, candy vendor Jimmy is a regular sweetheart. Here he's pictured with wife Alison (Mary Ure) and roommate Cliff (Gary Raymond).

3 Boogie-woogie bugle boy of Company B: Jimmy's jazzy passion is proof positive that music tames the savage beast.

4 Glutton for punishment: Alison can't live with Jimmy, but she can't live without him.

"The fury and hate that John Osborne was able to pack into a flow of violent words in his stage play 'Look Back in Anger' are not only matched but also documented in the film Tony Richardson has made from that vicious play." *The New York Times*

Look Back in Anger brilliantly captures the atmosphere of the English Midlands. Raindrops thrash against the windows, and dark masses of humanity trudge to church, accompanied by Jimmy's curses. In the scenes shot outdoors — Jimmy runs a candy stall and plays the trumpet in the city's jazz clubs — Richardson shows himself to be a scion of the documentary film school that produced most of the country's top post-war directors. In the interiors, Richardson turns the limitations of the small-scale theatrical format to his advantage. The camera makes a couple of Jimmy and Helena long before they discover their love for another — and the same thing happens with Alison and Cliff (Gary Raymond), the patient, long-suffering friend and flatmate of this infernal duo. The film suggests that both of these partnerships might well have a lot going for them. But that's not the way love works; like Osborne's drama, love is a play of polarities, contrast and differences. Hele-

6

5 The mirror has – at least – two faces: John Osborne need not worry. The movie version of *Look Back in Anger* by no means made an ass of him or his play. Claire Bloom as Helena, the woman who brings up the rear.

6 Truth among thieves: Helena convinces Alison friend to leave the tyrannical Jimmy. After Alison takes her advice, Helena inadvertently snatches him herself. Well, as the old saying goes, "finders keepers, losers weepers."

na, too, comes to realize this; Alison resumes her place in Jimmy's life after having a miscarriage. In Jimmy's logic, she has acquired sufficient experience in the pain of human existence, and now the two of them – a couple once more – can turn their attention hesitantly to the future.

In order to make the film, Richardson and Osborne founded the Woodfall production company. The money was put up by Harry Saltzman, who would later be a producer on the James Bond movies. Richardson was worried that the unique presence of Richard Burton would "unbalance" the film, and his worries were not unfounded. The Welsh star's immense talent had been squandered in various second-rate Hollywood epics, and now his powerful voice and physical presence dominated every scene he was in. In truth, Jimmy's menacing dominance is an essential element in Osborne's play, for it embodies a crisis in the central character's masculinity. In full flight from personal failure, Jimmy seeks refuge in politics, and the existence of social injustice serves to morally legitimize his sexual despotism. It's no wonder, then, that later generations of angry young women would decry Osborne's play as misogynistic.

PB

HARRY SALTZMAN (1915–1994)

Harry Saltzman was one of the most important producers in the post-war British cinema. He was born into a family of circus artistes in 1915, in the Canadian province of Quebec. After serving with the Royal Canadian Air Force during World War II, he took on a position as the producer of a TV show. Together with the dramatist John Osborne and the director Tony Richardson, he founded Woodfall Film Productions, and there followed several milestones of the Free Cinema movement: *Look Back in Anger* (1959) with Richard Burton, *The Entertainer* (1960) with Laurence Olivier and *Saturday Night and Sunday Morning* (1960) with Albert Finney. Shortly thereafter, he acquired the rights to Ian Fleming's James Bond novels, thus proving himself to be a real producer with an instinct for money-spinners. As Eon Productions, Harry Saltzman and his partner Albert R. Broccoli produced nine Bond films, from *Dr. No* (1962) to *The Man with the Golden Gun* (1974). Practically at the same time, his next company, Lowndes Productions, was developing the Harry Palmer series, conceived as a kind of "anti-Bond," and starring Michael Caine. The first movie in the Palmer series was *The Ipcress File* (1965). In 1975, Saltzman sold his shares in James Bond to United Artists. Broccoli complained that Saltzman was eventually only interested in the technical side of the big-budget Bond productions. After this, Saltzman – a polyglot and a chain-smoker – increasingly withdrew from the film business. In 1988, however, he surprised the moviegoers one last time by producing Emir Kusturica's *Time of the Gypsies* (*Dom Za Vesanje*).

7 She takes a lickin' and keeps on kickin': Alison is not the person Jimmy should be venting his aggression on, but she's practically the only one who'll listen.

8 The mouse that roared: Even when Cliff makes his voice heard, he's still no match for Jimmy, and thus no real help to Alison.

9 Let sleeping dogs lie: Jimmy and Mrs. Tanner (Edith Evans) are ready to bury the past.

> "Stage plays sometimes struggle on the movie screen, but *Look Back in Anger* is beautifully choreographed and filmed by director Tony Richardson. The luscious black-and-white photography almost appears as colour when compared to the lousy English weather – it's a perfect match." *Apollo Movie Guide*

THE MISFITS

1960 - USA - 124 MIN. - B & W - DRAMA

DIRECTOR JOHN HUSTON (1906–1987)
SCREENPLAY ARTHUR MILLER DIRECTOR OF PHOTOGRAPHY RUSSELL METTY EDITING GEORGE TOMASINI
MUSIC ALEX NORTH PRODUCTION FRANK E. TAYLOR for SEVEN ARTS.

STARRING CLARK GABLE (Gay Langland), MARILYN MONROE (Roslyn Taber), MONTGOMERY CLIFT (Perce Howland),
THELMA RITTER (Isabelle Steers), ELI WALLACH (Guido), JAMES BARTON (Old guy at the bar),
ESTELLE WINWOOD (Woman Collecting for the Church), KEVIN MCCARTHY (Raymond Taber).

"Anything is better than wages."

It's a fact of life that you can't teach an old dog new tricks and it goes double for cowboys. Facing facts, however, doesn't come easy to young divorcée Roslyn Taber (Marilyn Monroe), who is appalled by the prospect that lonesome dove Gay Langland (Clark Gable) would capture a herd of wild Mustangs in this day and age. He tries to defend his position, but to no avail. For the fate of these animals is not to be tamed, but to be slaughtered for dog food.

In one of the most poignant scenes in John Huston's modern-day Western The Misfits, and one that epitomizes how obsolete a once gallant way of life has become, Gay stands in the middle of the Nevada Prairie, trying to hold onto Roslyn and a profession that has come to represent a despicable pack of lies. Only tomorrow will the magnitude of his actions start to sink in.

Arthur Miller's screenplay was based on a semi-autobiographical short story he'd published in a 1957 edition of Esquire. Having divorced his first wife, Miller set up camp in Reno, soon making the acquaintance of two cowboys and saddling up to their way of life. It is therefore hardly surprising that the passages detailing the lifestyle of Gay, Perce (Montgomery Clift) and Guido (Eli Wallach) are some of the finest in the script. Like dusty winds of desolation, their nomadic lifestyle whistles through our ears as they drift from one seasonal job to another, and one rodeo to the next. They are among the men of the West who abstained from the security of a wage-paying job in the name of personal freedom — only to discover that personal freedom was a mirage.

Occupying only a minor role in his original short story, Miller elevated Roslyn to a stature suitable for his leading lady and then wife, Marilyn Monroe. Many interpreted the naive and fragile character to be a written apotheosis of the legendary sex symbol. This would explain some of the more exalted dialog uttered by Gable, such as when he likens her smile to a

sunrise. That may be true, but *The Misfits*, the last film Monroe completed reads more like a crass epitaph that spotlights the glamour girl's every contradiction.

In an attempt to break with her blonde bombshell image and establish herself as a serious actress, Monroe had been taking regular classes with coaches Lee and Paula Strasberg of the Actors' Studio in New York. The Stanislavskian instruction she received aimed to help actors find points of correspondence between themselves and their role, thus enabling the character to emerge naturally. Despite this, her performance in *The Misfits* comes across as haphazard and erratic. Relying on wild gesticulation and her trademark little-girl-lost manner of speaking, she seems bent on prying out more depth and meaning than the character has to offer. For the fact was that even

"At face value, *The Misfits* is a robust, high-voltage adventure drama, vibrating with explosivly emotional histrionics, conceived and executed with a refreshing disdain for superficial technical and photographic slickness in favor of an uncommonly honest and direct cinematic approach." *Variety*

4

1 Sunset boulevard: Marilyn Monroe always did smile like the dawn, but by the time *The Misfits* started filming, both her and Clark Gable's glory days were far behind them.

2 Where cowboys go to die: Seeking refuge from a life of rodeos, alcohol and neuroses, Perce (Montgomery Clift) joins up with Gay and Roslyn.

3 The Michelin Man: Gay builds a barricade out of old tires to trap the mustangs.

4 Opposites attract: But the abrasive Gay and delicate Roslyn have got their work cut out for them as far as lasting relationships go.

after Miller's alterations to the story, the script was still heavily weighted toward the men. As such, all of Roslyn's relationships – be it her romance with Gay or her friendships with Perce and Guido – are rather muddled and somewhat unmotivated, if not altogether out of place.

The shoot must have been as torturous for its leading lady as it was for everyone else involved. Most of the time, the actress was incapacitated. She'd either arrive late on the set – or not at all – and had constant trouble remembering her lines. This aside, her six-year marriage to Miller had come to a bitter close. At one point, filming was postponed for two weeks when Monroe had to be hospitalized for her pill-popping habit and psychological instability. Ironically, the actress' finest moments in *The Misfits* are full of the sort of glib naturalness for which she was most revered, as seen during a jaunty dance sequence with Guido and at a ball game.

Still, Monroe was not the only cast member fighting demons. Montgomery Clift had been seriously injured in a car accident that left his face permanently scarred (a fact referred to in the movie when Perce tells his mother

MONTGOMERY CLIFT   Montgomery Clift (b. 1920 in Oklahoma, Nebraska, d. 1966 in New York) made his first appearance on Broadway at the age of thirteen, having already displayed inordinate talent with an amateur repertory company as a young child. He remained a successful stage actor for ten years before heading for Hollywood. Debuting as John Wayne's freethinking, adopted son in Howard Hawks' Western *Red River* (1948), his character presented the harsh, capitalist cowboy with a formidable opponent. Clift was most often seen playing vulnerable or fragile characters, either fraught with emotional trauma or burdened by moral dilemmas. In Fred Zinnemann's *The Search* (1948) Clift portrayed an American G.I. who helps a child boy find his mother after surviving Auschwitz; Alfred Hitchcock ordained him a man of the cloak in *I Confess* (1953), the story of a Catholic priest who discovers a murderer at a confessional and refuses to reveal the killer's identity, even when he himself becomes a suspect in the crime. Hitchcock, Hawks and Zinnemann were just a few of the great directors Clift had the fortune of acting for; other names include William Wyler, George Stevens, Elia Kazan, John Huston, Vittorio De Sica and Joseph Mankiewicz.
Nevertheless, numerous personal problems always overshadowed his career. Trapped as a victim of the Hollywood closet, and marred for life in a car accident, he quickly became dependent on drugs and alcohol. The once great Method actor was more or less professionally washed up by the time the 60s rolled around. Indeed, his life was to end on a tragic note in 1966, when it was claimed by a heart attack.

5   Sex drive: Gay must kiss the illusion of the Great
      American West goodbye, but is granted personal
      happiness with Roslyn in return.

"Alongside Clark Gable, Marilyn Monroe demonstrates that she is a truly great actress. Her performance escapes all definition; it's drawn from a new and surprisingly profound depth of intuition."

Der Tagesspiegel

that the wounds he incurred at a rodeo have nearly healed). Once considered a genius of method acting, Clift's real-life accident had left him an alcoholic.

Nonetheless, unlike Monroe he managed to muster up a high-caliber performance despite his neuroses, perhaps even using them to his advantage. The actor's disabilities arguably helped him bring out the emotional depth in Perce, who is a character unable to come to terms with his father's sudden death and his mother's ensuing remarriage.

The picture's uncontested star, however, is Clark Gable. Gay Langland, the cowboy who frees himself of his own lies, was the best part he'd had in years, if not decades. It was also to be his last. Sadly, Gable died of a heart attack shortly after shooting had wrapped. His on-screen vigor in *The Misfits* makes his real life fate seem virtually unbelievable. The personification of triumph, Langland indeed captures the stallion – "cause a cowboy's gotta do what a cowboy's gotta do" – but ends up setting him free out of love for Roslyn. Although the two of them ride off into the warm sunset of an uncertain future, Marilyn Monroe biographer Norman Mailer is right in saying that "it is Gable alone who exits a saint."

LP

6   On the ball: Even in her final picture, Marilyn Monroe's girlish whimsy took the screen by storm.

7   Chasing the gravy train: Try though it may, corporate America just can't take the romance out of wrangling wild horses.

8   All of them, misfits: Nomads Guido (Eli Wallach), Isabelle (Thelma Ritter), Gay and Roslyn don't have any gold to show for the rainbows they've chased.

"Visually, the pounding wild-horse chase and the magnificent battle between man and beast that ends the chase are hung like a grand insane mirage against the glittering salt flats." *Time Magazine*

LA DOLCE VITA – THE SWEET LIFE

La dolce vita

1959/60 - ITALY / FRANCE - 177 MIN. - B & W - DRAMA

DIRECTOR FEDERICO FELLINI (1920–1993)
SCREENPLAY FEDERICO FELLINI, TULLIO PINELLI, ENNIO FLAIANO, BRUNELLO RONDI DIRECTOR OF PHOTOGRAPHY OTELLO MARTELLI
EDITING LEO CATOZZO MUSIC NINO ROTA PRODUCTION GIUSEPPE AMATO, ANGELO RIZZOLI for RIAMA FILM, PATHÉ CONSORTIUM CINÉMA, GRAY-FILM.

STARRING MARCELLO MASTROIANNI (Marcello Rubini), ANITA EKBERG (Sylvia), ANOUK AIMÉE (Maddalena), YVONNE FURNEAUX (Emma), ALAIN CUNY (Steiner), WALTER SANTESSO (Paparazzo), ADRIANO CELENTANO (Singer), LEX BARKER (Robert), ALAIN DIJON (Frankie Stout), ANNIBALE NINCHI (Marcello's Father), NADIA GRAY (Nadia), NICO (Partygoer).

ACADEMY AWARDS 1961 OSCAR for BEST COSTUMES (Piero Gherardi).

IFF CANNES 1960 GOLDEN PALM (Federico Fellini).

"Rome is simply marvelous. A kind of jungle – humid and beautiful, loud at times, peaceful at others – it's a place where you can hide behind the foliage."

"Scandalous!" The cries of the Italian press were heard far and wide: *La dolce vita* was a wanton, permissive, blasphemous piece of celluloid and nothing short of appalling. The Vatican condemned it to the last circle of hell, and the in-crowd turned up their noses. Federico Fellini was spat at and even challenged to a duel. With *La dolce vita*, the filmmaker immersed himself in a world of stars and hopefuls, artists and intellectuals, and supplied his audience with superficiality and decadence instead of the traditional content and good morals. As Fellini saw it, desire had won out over reason, speechlessness over communication, and filth over purity …

A stone-carved Jesus glides over the rooftops of Rome, sanctifying arms outstretched. Suspended by cables, the gigantic statue is being flown to the Vatican via helicopter, followed by a second chopper in which reporter Marcello (Marcello Mastroianni) and photographer Paparazzo (Walter Santesso) keep a close eye on the action. The two men are tabloid journalists, riff-raff propagators of the flashbulb storm that hits the city whenever a movie star struts down a runway. Their notebooks are always within arm's reach in case they spot an aristocrat canoodling with his mistress at a nightclub. Paparazzo chomps at the bit for a potential photo opportunity of Rome's A-listers – preferably with their pants down. The suave Marcello, however, is discrete in his approach, offhandedly ensnaring his quarry while as he shadows them from one haunt to the next. The chic cafés of the Via Veneto are his second home, the heart of the action and a breeding ground for young ladies itching to get discovered.

Marcello is not an impartial observer, more an active member of the lofty company he keeps tabs on. Accompanied by Maddalena (Anouk Aimée), a local billionaire's daughter, he gallivants through the night until sunrise, then rushes off to the side of a Hollywood glamour girl (Anita Ekberg), giving her a personal tour of all Rome has to offer … He'll attend a palace soirée, and promenade with blue bloods across the expanse of the princely estate. At an outdoor party where starlets and movie producers fill the dance floor, Marcello's the one who puts a sizzle in their step, only to watch from the sidelines as the night nearly ends in an orgy. Sunset comes and goes, and he completes the circle at a gathering hosted by his intellectual buddy Steiner (Alain Cuny), bringing a tone of calm to the evening while rediscovering his calling in life as a writer – only to let it slip through his fingers once more.

By openly depicting sexuality to an extent that had been virtually unheard of until then – from a barefooted Anita Ekberg getting down and dirty

2

"This sensational representation of certain aspects of life in contemporary Rome, as revealed in the clamorous experience of a free-wheeling newspaper man, is a brilliantly graphic estimation of a whole swath of society in decay and a withering commentary upon the tragedy of the over-civilized." *The New York Times*

1   Couldn't aspire to anything higher: The statuesque Anita Ekberg soaks up the sweet life during a midnight bath in Rome's Trevi Fountain.

2   Passing up the paparazzi: And wouldn't you know it, the man that coined the term 'paparazzi' was none other than former tabloid journalist gone film director, Federico Fellini.

3   Sweets for the sweet: Within minutes, this sober pair will be utterly drunk on life and ready to brave the shallows.

to the sound of young Adriano Celentano's wild rock'n'roll stylings to Nadia Gray baring it all at a party to the pack of hungry eyes – Fellini's film was immediately the target of a heated debate. The outcome: even in the more remote provinces, audiences lined up in their thousands to see a three-hour picture that would normally have only run in art house cinemas. *La dolce vita* instantly became Federico Fellini's greatest hit, regardless of its episodic narrative structure and the absence of an exciting storyline. Marcello is the film's sole connecting thread, leading us through a labyrinth of nightly escapades across Rome.

The film's opulent visuals meant that it was often compared to a painting, deemed either a "portrait of society" or "Baroque fresco." Much of that in fact is the result of Swedish actress Anita Ekberg's performance. Her nighttime dip in Rome's Trevi Fountain is one of the most illustrious images ever to grace the screen; her viewing of St. Peter's Dome in a slinky priest-like garment created a furore among the Catholic churchmen sensitive to the use of symbols. Ekberg, in fact, was a sensation throughout Rome even before shooting commenced, and Fellini made shrewd use of her celebrity status. He drew from actual tabloid anecdotes – the slap Ekberg takes from

4 Wiggle and jiggle your way across the dance floor: Fellini's depiction of high society's decadence-till-dawn mentality awakens images of the Fall of Rome.

5 Caught up in the glamour: An ordinary woman loves the unexpected media attention she is showered with. Little does she suspect her husband's suicide and the murder of their children is the reason for it. Without a doubt, Fellini's criticism of the media has even more clout today than it did then.

6 Undulating Undine: A former 'Miss Sweden,' the real life Anita Ekberg also lost her heart to Italy's capital city. Shortly after the shoot of *La dolce vita* wrapped up, she relocated there permanently.

7 Va-va-va-voom! A woman, dressed in her own rendition of the holy cloth, awaits Marcello at the top of the cathedral. It was one of the many scenes that shocked the Vatican, especially considering that St. Peter's Square can be spotted in the background.

8 Maestro Mastroianni: *La dolce vita* marked the beginning of a collaboration between Mastroianni and Fellini that spanned several decades and six films. As the director's on-screen alter ego, the suave actor plays Marcello Rubini, a man desperately trying to escape the frustrations of life as a tabloid journalist.

"**... an allegory, a cautionary tale of a man without a center.**"
Chicago Sun-Times

her on-screen husband (Lex Barker) was directly lifted from a public incident with her real life spouse – and shamelessly blurred the distinctions between real life people and film characters. Likewise, he had numerous aristocrats and models portray themselves, thus hoping to get the episodes to play as naturally and authentically as possible. His choices paid off. The German newspaper *Die Welt* wanted to know why there was so much controversy surrounding the film, claiming that Fellini had simply spliced together a chronicle of scandals to unmask Rome's nitty-gritty demimondes.

What *La dolce vita* does succeed in unmasking is the inter-dependency of the media and media sensations, and journalists and stars. The former needs material to write about, and the latter needs the publicity in order to exist in at all. Long before this habitual feed-off became a point of public interest with regard to World Trade Center attacks in 2001, Fellini began to ask himself whether an event without media attention can be regarded as an event *per se*. It is precisely this question which still makes the film read like something hot off the press.   NM

NINO ROTA
(1911–1979)

It all started with a bus stop. This was the site where Fellini was to happen upon a fellow caught up in his own thoughts and waiting for a line that normally took a totally different route. Fellini wanted to inform him of his error, but the gentleman's desired bus stopped right in front of them before he got the chance. The event left a lasting impression on Fellini, who was convinced that he had met someone capable of performing magic. Although the particulars of the account vary – sometimes the director placed the bus stop at Rome's Via Po, sometimes in front of Cinecittà Studios – this is allegedly how Fellini got to be friends with composer Nino Rota just after the end of World War II. Their genial relationship gave rise to many a magical moment in cinematic history. Be it Gelsomina's lament in *The Road* (*La strada*, 1954) or the circus march in *8 1/2* (*8 1/2 / Otto e mezzo*, 1962) Nino Rota's music was, as one critic wrote, very much an invisible player within a film's narrative. Nino Rota Rinaldi was born into a Milano family of musicians in 1911. It wasn't long before he was deemed a prodigy and schooled in classical music throughout Italy and abroad in American conservatories. He started out composing orchestra and choir pieces, before trying his hand at film scoring in the early 1940s. By the time he scored Alberto Lattuada's *Without Pity* (*Senza pietà*, 1948) it became clear just what the distinguishing factors of Rota's music were: he had a knack for pursuing known melodies, transforming them, and integrating existing snippets here and there. Later, for example, he was awarded an Oscar for scoring, Francis Ford Coppola's *The Godfather – Part II* (1974), a project largely inspired by the musical compositions he created for Eduardo de Filippo's *Fortunella* (1957).

Rota produced dozens of readily recognizable melodies. His music seesawed between pathos and irony, and it was not unheard of for melancholy bars to suddenly switch into something snappier, or for a loud note to subside into an extended undertone. He collaborated with big name directors like Luchino Visconti, King Vidor, and René Clément. Nonetheless, his lifelong partnership with Fellini is the stuff of legend. Starting with *The White Sheik* (*Lo sceicco bianco*, 1952), Rota wrote the music to all Fellini's pictures for the remainder of his life. The two men would sit together at the piano with Rota composing and testing out combinations, while Fellini provided feedback. This was to be the birthplace of some of the cinema's most magical music. *The Orchestra Rehearsal* (*Prova d'orchestra*, 1978) was the last project they would work on together. Nino Rota died in Rome the following year. He was one of the 20th century's most influential film composers.

PSYCHO

1960 - USA - 109 MIN. - B & W - PSYCHO THRILLER

DIRECTOR ALFRED HITCHCOCK (1899–1980)
SCREENPLAY JOSEPH STEFANO, based on the novel of the same name by ROBERT BLOCH
DIRECTOR OF PHOTOGRAPHY JOHN L. RUSSELL EDITING GEORGE TOMASINI MUSIC BERNARD HERRMANN
PRODUCTION ALFRED HITCHCOCK for SHAMLEY PRODUCTIONS INC.

STARRING ANTHONY PERKINS (Norman Bates), JANET LEIGH (Marion Crane), VERA MILES (Lila Crane),
JOHN GAVIN (Sam Loomis), JOHN MCINTIRE (Al Chambers), MARTIN BALSAM (Milton Arbogast),
LURENE TUTTLE (Mrs. Chambers), SIMON OAKLAND (Doctor Richmond), PATRICIA HITCHCOCK (Caroline),
MORT MILLS (Policeman).

"Mother, she's just a stranger!"

It's what you might call a *twisted* fate. Marion Crane's (Janet Leigh) illicit affair with the married Sam Loomis (John Gavin) awakens deviant impulses within her. Entrusted with 40,000 dollars in company funds, she promptly invests in the future, making off with a sum that will allow her to start a new life with Joe. But the cops are on to her, and Marion thinks twice about executing her plan. The choice, however, isn't hers: a storm forces Marion to seek sanctuary at a remote motel, where a relaxing shower ends as a bloodbath. The murderess, it seems, suspected the overnight guest of making advances toward her son, the motel's introverted manager Norman Bates (Anthony Perkins), and decided to nip danger in the bud. Attempting to cover up his mother's regrettable actions, Bates wipes the scene clean, stuffs Marion's corpse into her car, and sinks the vehicle in a swamp – forty grand and all.

Then the real investigation begins. Despite all their hard work, the gruesome twosome don't get to close shop just yet. Sam, Marion's sister Lila (Vera Miles) and a private detective named Arbogast (Martin Balsam) come in search of the missing woman and the stolen funds. Sticking his nose in the wrong place, Arbogast is also disposed of by the deranged old lady, who apparently resides in the seclusion of the familial estate overlooking the motel. After Sam and Lila wise up to the horrors of the Bates' mansion, they are dumbfounded to learn from the authorities that Mrs. Bates has been dead for a good ten years ...

Psycho is undoubtedly Hitchcock's boldest film – although the critical uproar of the time, fixated on a close up of a toilet bowl, seemed to miss the point. Tauntingly, the master of suspense plays with the viewer's expectations time and again: mercilessly killing off his leading lady in the first third of the picture, and introducing plot elements like the suitcase of money that amount to nothing more than red herrings. Arguably, the entire plot is a network of setups and visual suggestions meant to keep the audience unnerved until the

"What makes *Psycho* immortal, when so many films are already half-forgotten as we leave the theater, is that it connects directly with our fears: Our fears that we might impulsively commit a crime, our fears of the police, our fears of becoming the victim of a madman, and of course our fears of disappointing our mothers." *Chicago Sun-Times*

curtain falls. And the seamless manner in which these subversive images undermine the story and suck it into the background makes *Psycho* more reminiscent of an experimental art-house piece than a Hollywood blockbuster. The most striking example of this is the shower scene, where a total of 70 camera shots fill forty-five seconds of scream time – the hard cuts between shots and Bernard Herrmann's screeching score viscerally tuning us to each stab of the killer's knife. The scene was so shocking that Hitchcock

abstained from the further inclusion of similarly violent displays in the rest of the film for he clearly already had the audience just where he wanted them.

Equally remarkable is how ingeniously the filmmaker and cinematographer John L. Russell come up with excuses not to reveal the face of Norman's mother until just before the end. We never suspect that Arbogast's stairwell death is shot from a bird's eye for anything other than artistic reasons.

1 Who? *Moi?* Mama's boy Norman Bates (Anthony Perkins) fears the gaze of foreign eyes – especially when they belong to his attractive hotel guests.

2 Heartbreak hotel: The Bates' Mansion, a set-piece replica of an existing building, is among the most readily recognizable homes ever to grace the screen. The original is located in the 6th circle of hell.

3 Behind bars and closed doors: All the conniving Marion Crane (Janet Leigh) ever wanted in life was to run off and elope with lover Sam Loomis (John Gavis). And she would have, had it not been for one little, but fatal, mistake. But then you only get to make one now darling, don't you?

JANET LEIGH (b. 1927)

Jeanette Helen Morrison, born in Merced, California, was just 15 years old when she finished high school and began her studies in music and psychology. Her rise to fame is something of a Hollywood fairy tale: actress Norma Shearer apparently saw her while vacationing at a ski resort where Janet's father was working. Soon the young woman was cast in films opposite some of the industry's biggest names, including Robert Mitchum in *Holiday Affair* (1949), James Stewart in *The Naked Spur* (1953), John Wayne in *Jet Pilot* (1957), and both Charlton Heston and Orson Welles in *Touch of Evil* (1958). With *Psycho* (1960), Alfred Hitchcock supplied her with her most memorable role: Marion Crane, a heroine who is murdered before the first half of the picture is over. The part earned Leigh an Oscar nomination. John Frankenheimer's classic political drama *The Manchurian Candidate* (1962) proved to be one of the last high-caliber Hollywood films she would appear in; playing the girlfriend of the brainwashed Bennett Marco (Frank Sinatra), Leigh relies on her particular brand of aloof understatement to help him get his life back on track. From 1951 to 1962, the actress was married to favorite co-star Tony Curtis. They had two daughters, Kelly and Jamie Lee Curtis, both of whom followed in their parents' professional footsteps. Janet made a recent appearance in front of the camera at the side of daughter Jamie Lee in *Halloween H20 – 20 Years Later* (1998), the eighth installment in the horror film series made popular by Janet Leigh's world-famous child.

Psycho's narrative takes just as many experimental liberties. Much like in a television drama, lengthy dialog clarifies plot and subtext. Of prime importance is Norman and Marion's conversation at the motel, in which a bond is established between the killer and his victim. It is here that the viewer learns of Norman's interest in taxidermy, with the stuffed birds themselves acting as an eerie congress of witnesses: no amount of money can make them divulge the grizzly acts they've seen. These petrified beasts, and the peephole that Norman uses to spy on Marion as she undresses, are reminders of the camera's voyeuristic nature.

Everywhere we turn, *Psycho* confronts us with visual analogies of watching and being watched: from the eye-like shower drain into which Marion's blood disappears, to the smirking toilet seat that stares us down in one of the final shots. And there is no misunderstanding the accompanying dialog: "They're probably watching me. Well, let them. Let them see what kind of person I am. I hope they are watching. They'll see. They'll see and they'll know."

It's more than just a coincidental choice of words Hitchcock placed in Bates' mouth. In truth, the soliloquy is as much a personal confession on the part of the director as of its speaker. At the peak of his career, Hitch couldn't have picked a more poignant moment to make it. For beyond the façade of terror, what is *Psycho* if not a great master's artistic manifesto?

SH

4   Drowned out screams: How many cuts does it take to kill Marion Crane? Hitchcock used approximately seventy. Urban legend would have you believe that renowned cinema graphic artist, Saul Bass, staged *Psycho's* shower scene. But it's a bloody lie!

5   Checking in and checking out: Norman is among the few hotel managers who hate having guests.

6   Don't tell mama: Mother will be livid if she finds out who's been sleeping in one of Norman's beds.

SATURDAY NIGHT AND SUNDAY MORNING

1960 - GREAT BRITAIN - 89 MIN. - B & W - DRAMA

DIRECTOR Karel Reisz (1926–2002)
SCREENPLAY ALAN SILLITOE, based on his novel of the same name DIRECTOR OF PHOTOGRAPHY FREDDIE FRANCIS
EDITING SETH HOLT MUSIC JOHN DANKWORTH PRODUCTION TONY RICHARDSON, HARRY SALTZMAN for
BRYANSTON FILMS LTD., WOODFALL FILM PRODUCTIONS.

STARRING ALBERT FINNEY (Arthur Seaton), SHIRLEY ANN FIELD (Doreen Gretton), RACHEL ROBERTS (Brenda),
HYLDA BAKER (Aunt Ada), NORMAN ROSSINGTON (Bert), BRYAN PRINGLE (Jack), ROBERT CAWDRON (Robboe),
EDNA MORRIS (Mrs. Bull), ELSIE WAGSTAFF (Mrs. Seaton), FRANK PETTITT (Mr. Seaton).

"What I'm out for is a good time; All the rest is propaganda!"

In the English industrial town of Nottingham, young Arthur Seaton (Albert Finney) earns his living in the factory, like his father and grandfather before him. He still lives with his parents in a working-class part of town. When Friday evening comes, Arthur puts on a tie, empties a tin of Brylcreem into his air and heads for the pub. A good time means drinking, chasing women, and fighting at the drop of a hat. Like John Travolta in *Saturday Night Fever* (1977), he lives for the weekend, and his motto could have been written by The Who: "Hope I die before I get old." Arthur is having an affair with Brenda (Rachel Roberts), who's married to his workmate Jack (Bryan Pringle); far from being bothered by this fact, Arthur's glad of it, for it means she can't tie him down. When Brenda gets pregnant, she turns to Arthur's Aunt Ada (Hylda Baker), a backstreet abortionist; but it doesn't work out, and Brenda decides to keep the baby. When her husband gets wind of all this, Arthur Seaton suffers a bad beating. Eventually, Arthur meets young Doreen Gretton (Shirley Ann Field); soon, they're a couple, and they plan to get married. In the final scene, they visit a new housing development outside Nottingham. For

"James Dean has been resurrected as a member of the English working class." *Der Spiegel*

1 Oh, what a night! Party animal Arthur Seaton (Albert Finney) just can't stand Sundays.

2 A game of blue-collar tag: It's uncanny how urban slums on both sides of the Atlantic can look so similar – apart from a few minor variations like the skin color of the residents.

3 Feel like sharing? Arthur tells Jack (Bryan Pringler) that his wife has been cheating on him with someone they both know very well.

4 The way to a man's heart is through his stomach: And this cook (Rachel Roberts as Brenda) has several customers she intends on serving.

5 Saturday's child works hard for a living: But tonight, Doreen Grettan (Shirley Ann Field) intends to forget all her troubles and cares.

5

Doreen, it means a step up the social ladder and a better life: for Arthur, it's the end of his career as a weekend rebel.

The film embodies and examines some of the social fears and fantasies of the 1950s. There's the rage at lives wasted in wage-slavery, a feeling clearly articulated in Arthur's off-camera commentaries. And there's the nostalgic depiction of traditional working-class culture as it begins to decline: Arthur's local is divided into two sections – one for the old men, who sit together singing songs, and one for the young'uns, getting raucous drunk to the noisy accompaniment of a skiffle group. *Saturday Night and Sunday Morning* observes the rise of a new mass culture and the Americanization of Europe by means of TV; while Arthur does his best to talk to his dad, the old

man is attempting to escape his quotidian existence through "the window on the world."

Along with Tony Richardson and Lindsay Anderson, director Karel Reisz was one of a group of British documentary filmmakers who compiled film programs for the National Film Theatre (the cinema of the British Film Institute). The fictional movies of this "Free Cinema" group dealt with young people from the British working class, their monotonous manual jobs, the cramped conditions in which they lived, and – by way of contrast – their ability to let go and enjoy themselves in the clubs and under the influence of alcohol. Reisz and his colleagues filmed on location on council estates and in factories, and their protagonists spoke the language of the streets. All this

6   Anything but a Sunday drive: Doreen and Arthur just love playing bumper cars.

7   Would you be mine? Could you be mine? Albert Finney makes a proposal a girl just can't say no to.

"Finney is the quintessential British rebel." *Manchester Guardian*

KAREL REISZ (1926–2002)

British feature and documentary filmmaker Karel Reisz was born in Ostrava, Czechoslovakia in 1926. Shortly before the Germans invaded and occupied the country in March 1939, he escaped to Britain in a Quaker transport. His Jewish parents were deported and died in Auschwitz. Towards the end of World War II, Reisz became a pilot with the Royal Air Force. After the war, he studied chemistry at Cambridge, became a teacher and wrote articles for *Sight and Sound* and *Sequence*. In 1953, he published *The Technique of Film Editing*, which is still regarded as a standard work. From 1955 until 1958, Reisz worked for the Ford Motor Company, made advertising films and was active as a producer. He then directed a prizewinning documentary funded by Ford: *We are the Lambeth Boys* (1958).

His best-known films include *Isadora* (1968), a biopic about the dancer Isadora Duncan, starring Vanessa Redgrave, and the John Fowles adaptation *The French Lieutenant's Woman* (1981), starring Meryl Streep and Jeremy Irons. In Hollywood, this renewer of the British cinema stayed true to his social and political principles with *The Gambler* (1974) and *Who'll Stop the Rain / Dog Soldiers* (1978). Karel Reisz died in London at the age of 76.

was a manifestation of the filmmakers' desire to make movies that also functioned as documentary records of their time. The Free Cinema movement was a powerful attempt to establish a new, socially critical and determinedly political British cinema.

For all that, the director of *Saturday Night and Sunday Morning* does preserve a critical distance from the angry young man whose tale he tells. Though the audience immediately identifies with this witty, sarcastic, one

chic outsider, it soon becomes clear that Arthur Seaton will never succeed in breaking the chains of his blue-collar origins.

This working-class hero was embodied by the newcomer Albert Finney. His uncompromising egoism was something quite new in the British cinema of the time, and it played a large part in the movie's success: "What I'm out for is a good time. All the rest is propaganda."

SPARTACUS

�

1960 - USA - 197 MIN. - COLOR - HISTORICAL EPIC

DIRECTOR STANLEY KUBRICK (1928–1999)
SCREENPLAY DALTON TRUMBO, based on the novel of the same name by HOWARD FAST
DIRECTOR OF PHOTOGRAPHY RUSSELL METTY, CLIFFORD STINE **EDITING** ROBERT LAWRENCE **MUSIC** ALEX NORTH
PRODUCTION EDWARD LEWIS for BRYNA PRODUCTIONS, UNIVERSAL PICTURES COMPANY.

STARRING KIRK DOUGLAS (Spartacus), LAURENCE OLIVIER (Marcus Licinius Crassus), JEAN SIMMONS (Varinia), CHARLES LAUGHTON (Gracchus), PETER USTINOV (Lentulus Batiatus), TONY CURTIS (Antoninus), JOHN GAVIN (Julius Caesar), NINA FOCH (Helena Glabrus), HERBERT LOM (Tigranes), JOHN IRELAND (Crixus), JOHN DALL (Glabrus), CHARLES MCGRAW (Marcellus), JOANNA BARNES (Claudia Marius), WOODY STRODE (Draba), JOHN HOYT (Caius).

ACADEMY AWARDS 1960 OSCARS for BEST SUPPORTING ACTOR (Peter Ustinov), BEST CINEMATOGRAPHY (Russell Metty), BEST COSTUMES (Bill Thomas, Valles), BEST ART DIRECTION (Alexander Golitzen, Eric Orbom, Russell A. Gausman, Julia Heron).

"When a free man dies, he loses the pleasure of life. A slave loses his pain."

Two armies confront one another in combat on a plain: in the distance, a sea of men draped in vermilion capes march in the name of the Roman Empire; close by, a dirt-colored ocean of slaves seems to rise out of the ground against them. Two forces, the rebels and the rulers, come face to face in a moment of truth. The slave leader, Spartacus (Kirk Douglas) was once a warrior at a gladiator academy in Capua. He and his fellow gladiators managed to escape, and together they swept through Italy freeing slaves who joined up with them. Intent on shipping out of the country, they are forced to face the Roman legions led by Marcus Licinius Crassus (Laurence Olivier) who stand between them and the sea.

Spartacus is based on the slave revolt of 73–71 B.C. that sent shockwaves through the Roman Empire. Master director Stanley Kubrick (best

known for his 1968 *2001: A Space Odyssey*) created a magnificent epic, a film of monumental emotions and awe-inspiring images that peak in the decisive battle scene, a sequence that remains unequalled in the genre.

Kubrick tells the story on two levels, one private, the other political. The first follows Spartacus' personal story: from his back-breaking labors in a mine, via Lentulus Batiatus' (Peter Ustinov) gladiator academy where he is trained to be a cut-throat warrior, to the moment when he is sent off to fight in a one-on-one death match for the privileged amusement of the elite. It is here that he meets the enslaved Varinia (Jean Simmons), with whom he falls in love.

The story's political strand focuses on intrigues in the Roman Senate, where the elderly Gracchus (Charles Laughton) attempts to block the unscrupulous young Crassus' rise to power. The latter, however, seizes upon the

1   Roman gladiola: Ace warrior Spartacus (Kirk Douglas) builds a reputation as a freedom fighter and emerges as the Roman Empire's answer to Moses.

2   Private congress: Roman General Crassus (Laurence Olivier) tries to claim a few spoils of war for himself. Jean Simmons as Spartacus' eternal flame Varinia.

3   All we have to do, is take these lies and make them true: A stampede of slaves flees Lentulus Batiatus' gladiator academy, proving that sometimes the sandals do not make the man.

"At the time of its first release in 1960, *Spartacus* was hailed as the first intellectual epic since the silent days. Seen three decades later, *Spartacus* still plays like an extraordinary epic, and its intellectual strength is still there." *Chicago Sun-Times*

battle against the slaves as the opportunity he has been looking for to appoint himself Rome's first consul. The private and the political planes are most strikingly merged in the superb parallel montage sequence in which Spartacus and Crassus prepare their men for battle, the dialog switching back and forth between them.

British actors Laughton, Olivier and Ustinov (as the director of the gladiator academy who unexpectedly joins in the scheme) have a field day with the sly malice and nefarious intrigues that went on in the Senate. Playing op-

posite them is the American Kirk Douglas, an athletic freedom fighter who carries the world on his shoulders. Douglas was also involved behind the scenes on the production team. With his own Bryna production company at the helm, Douglas saw to it that the man originally signed to direct *Spartacus*, Anthony Mann (*Bend of the River*, 1951), was replaced by the 30-year-old Stanley Kubrick, who had worked with Douglas three years before on the anti-war film *Paths of Glory* (1957). The young producer also made sure that screenwriter Dalton Trumbo's name appeared in the titles rather than the

4   Spear me the drama: Spartacus rises up against Crassus in an attempt to impale the Roman Empire.

5   Homo erectus: In a sequence axed from the original cinematic release, the crass Crassus asks young Antoninus (Tony Curtis, left) if he could use a private tutor.

SIR LAURENCE OLIVIER (1907–1989)

"Acting is a masochistic form of exhibitionism. It's not quite the occupation of an adult." Thus spoke the typically wry Sir Laurence Olivier, the man considered the greatest actor of his day. Olivier's name is inseparable from the great Shakespearean plays he performed, and synonymous with classic British culture. The son of an Anglican minister, Olivier played Brutus at the age of nine in a school play, and at 14, he held the title role in the "The Taming of the Shrew" at the Stratford Shakespeare festival. Over the course of a theatrical career spanning five decades, he staged 34 of the bard's works, 22 of which he performed more than 100 times. Shakespeare is also at the heart of Olivier's film career. Olivier's three Shakespearean screen adaptations, *Henry V* (1944), *Hamlet* (1948) and *Richard III* (1955), remain the most striking examples of his acting and directing genius. *Henry V* garnered him a special Oscar for achievements in producing, directing, and acting. Two more came shortly thereafter, when *Hamlet* was named best picture and Olivier best actor. He received his last Academy Award at the age of 72 as an honorary distinction for lifetime achievement.

Film critic Leonard Maltin called his "the first serious Shakespeare adaptation ever to grace the screen." Sir Laurence acted in more than 80 films, including William Wyler's version of Emily Brontë's *Wuthering Heights* (1939) and the Hitchcock thriller *Rebecca* (1940). He gave the audience a run for their money in *Marathon Man* (1976) as a sadistic Nazi dentist bent on drilling death into Dustin Hoffman. Hoffman put himself through two consecutive sleepless nights to look convincingly deranged for the scene. Olivier's remark on his Method technique was simply: "Why not try acting, dear boy? It's much easier."

pseudonym he was usually forced to use. *Spartacus* was the first film in ten years that accomplished this task. Both Trumbo and Howard Fast, the communist author of the original novel, had been blacklisted by the McCarthyist House un-American Activities Committee and were openly criticized by Hollywood. Seen in this light, the film's behind-the-scenes politics give another dimension to the tale of slavery and freedom.

Spartacus was seldom shown in its entirety during its initial release in 1960. National advisory boards censored scenes from both U. S. and German versions. The homosexual element was wiped out of the German version, and with it the scene in which Crassus asks the enslaved Antoninus (Tony Curtis) to reveal his sexual preference by having him choose between oysters and snails. In the anglophone world, a handful of scenes considered particularly violent were left on the cutting room floor. It was only in the 1990s that a fully restored version of Stanley Kubrick's masterpiece was made available for viewing.

HJK

THE APARTMENT

⬆⬆⬆⬆⬆

1960 - USA - 125 MIN. - B & W - TRAGICOMEDY

DIRECTOR BILLY WILDER (1906–2002)
SCREENPLAY BILLY WILDER, I. A. L. DIAMOND DIRECTOR OF PHOTOGRAPHY JOSEPH LASHELLE EDITING DANIEL MANDELL
MUSIC ADOLPH DEUTSCH Production BILLY WILDER for THE MIRISCH CORPORATION.

STARRING JACK LEMMON (C. C. Baxter), SHIRLEY MACLAINE (Fran Kubelik), FRED MACMURRAY (J. D. Sheldrake),
RAY WALSTON (Mr. Dobisch), DAVID LEWIS (Mr. Kirkeby), WILLARD WATERMAN (Mr. Vanderhoff),
DAVID WHITE (Mr. Eichelberger), JACK KRUSCHEN (Dr. Dreyfuss), JOAN SHAWLEE (Sylvia),
HOPE HOLIDAY (Mrs. MacDougall).

ACADEMY AWARDS 1960 OSCARS for BEST PICTURE FILM (Billy Wilder), BEST DIRECTOR (Billy Wilder),
BEST ORIGINAL SCREENPLAY (Billy Wilder, I. A. L. Diamond), BEST EDITING (Daniel Mandell),
and BEST ART DIRECTION (Alexander Trauner, Edward G. Boyle).

IFF VENICE 1960 BEST ACTRESS (Shirley MacLaine).

"You see, I have this little problem with my apartment."

He's just the way you imagine a bookkeeper to be: neat, tidy, polite and punctual. When he arrives home from a hard day at work, he airs his living room, clears the dirty dishes from the coffee table – and gathers up the empty bottles of booze. And while mild-mannered C. C. Baxter (Jack Lemmon) is by no means a drinker, he suffers from another type of dependency with equally far-reaching consequences. For Consolidated Life Insurance's favorite clerk has agreed to let his bigwig bosses use his New York apartment as a bachelor pad so that he can climb the rungs of the slippery corporate ladder.

The deal, however, is not without side-effects. Baxter is forced to spend many a frosty winter night out on the cold New York streets, and has earned himself a reputation among his neighbors as a party animal and cold-blooded heartbreaker. Then one fine day Baxter's superiors reward him for being a team player, hauling him out of the 19th floor's anonymous catacombs and into a comfy, cozy single-room office on the 27th story, complete with name plate on the door.

If it weren't for his apartment, C. C. Baxter would be nothing more than a drip. His name says it all; he never places first or second, and has had to make do with a third-rate life as a solid C, a double C. It is only thanks to his own variation on the sure-fire "sleep your way to the top" business strategy that the sky is suddenly the limit. Offering his services to department execs

across the board, his ship comes in when company head honcho Mr. Sheldrake (Fred MacMurray) asks the humble bookkeeper to pencil him in for an evening of adultery chez C. C. But Baxter finds himself in an emotional pickle after discovering that Sheldrake's mistress is none other than sassy elevator girl Fran Kubelik (Shirley MacLaine), the woman of C. C.'s dreams ...

There are movies that are universally recognized as cinematic masterpieces and those that one can see again and again, as if they were old friends. Experts are torn as to whether The Apartment has secured a spot in the first category, but few would deny it membership in the second. In 1933, just after the Nazi rise to power, the Viennese filmmaker Billy Wilder left Berlin to take his place among the Hollywood greats. Often collaborating with fellow screenwriter I. A. L. Diamond, Wilder wrote and directed some of the finest comedies ever to come out of Tinseltown; in addition to The Apartment, Wilder and Diamond are responsible for classics like Some Like It Hot (1959) and Irma la Douce (1963, also starring Jack Lemmon and Shirley MacLaine). For The Apartment, the duo penned a beautifully constructed story full of snappy dialog, about a hopeless zero and a putative power broker. The picture's intentional ambivalence as to which party is more morally reprehensible makes it all the more enjoyable. There's always plenty of room for priceless misunderstandings that have Baxter taking the fall for his

1 Well, we can just about tie things up: Mr. Sheldrake (Fred MacMurray) welcomes C. C. Baxter (Jack Lemmon) into the executive club.

2 A classic case of prom night jitters: Even in C. C.'s own apartment, the radiant Miss Kubelik (Shirley MacLaine) holds all the cards.

3 Like a kid at Christmas: C. C. has just been promoted and has every reason to celebrate. Doesn't he?

"The Apartment captured one of the singular images of early '60s America: the immense office in which the human workers appear completely subordinate to the dehumanizing mechanisms of conformity and efficiency."

TV Guide

4 Twister and other party games: C. C. and his neighbor, Dr. Dreyfuss (Jack Kruschen, right), try to revive an unconscious Miss Kubelik.

5 A busy little bee: Accountant C. C. Baxter (Jack Lemmon) is a drone in the Consolidated Life Insurance hive – but not for long.

6 Truth serum: Elevator operator Fran Kubelik (center) discovers an incriminating thing or two about executive boyfriend J. D. Sheldrake over a glass of eggnog at the company Christmas party.

superiors' shady dealings and his neighbors thinking he's a philandering scoundrel.

Billy Wilder's favorite leading man Jack Lemmon simply wins our hearts as Baxter. He's a patsy you just can't help but love – an overgrown kid in a bowler who gets giddy about his promotion and has a weakness for gin rummy. Despite conspiring with the wicked and covering for their treachery, his good nature absolves him from any harsh judgment. Shirley MacLaine's Fran Kubelik is very much his female counterpart, a brilliant fireball of contradictions: as boyish as she is sexy, as witty as she is no-nonsense, and charmingly vulnerable all the while.

The Apartment is not just an ironic analysis of what it means to be good or bad. It is more a gentle satire about the modern workplace, hypocrisy and dogged ambition. Right from the start, the camera equates the sea of office cubicles with lay hen battery cages. This is a world in which nobody matters, and to escape it Baxter conducts business in a manner he himself finds despicable. Those who have broken out of the anonymous 19th floor and found their way to the higher echelons lie, cheat, swindle and abuse their power for sex. That the film manages to so subtly communicate all this without compromising any of the story's levity or entertainment value speaks volumes about the genius of Billy Wilder. HJK

SHIRLEY MACLAINE (b. 1934)

She's "American cinema's grande dame of naive" (*Süddeutsche Zeitung*), and a genuine, good-natured soul you can't help but love. Delivering one of the most memorable lines in Oscar history upon her first and sole Best Actress win (*Terms of Endearment*, 1983), Shirley MacLaine said, "I really deserve this." And considering her numerous nominations for the title, including *The Apartment* (1960), there wasn't much room to argue. She started dancing at the age of two and landed a leading role in a Broadway musical when she was twenty. Shortly thereafter, Shirley was lighting up Hollywood. It was Alfred Hitchcock who cast her in her first motion picture, *The Trouble with Harry* (1955). But the woman born Shirley Beatty – Warren Beatty's big sister – got her real breakthrough with *The Apartment*, allegedly rattling the nerves of notorious perfectionists director Billy Wilder and co-star Jack Lemmon by trying to improvise. Clearly, it couldn't have been so bad working with Shirley or the two men wouldn't have given it another go three years later with *Irma la Douce* (1963). It was her girlish whimsy and knucklehead charm that had her winning audiences' hearts time and again as the irresistible hooker with a heart of gold in *Some Came Running* (1958), *Irma La Douce* and *Sweet Charity* (1969). And that youthful glow has added a certain magic to her more recent, saltier performances in pictures like *Postcards from the Edge* (1990) and *Carolina* (2003); that, at least is what Nicolas Cage's character thought in *Guarding Tess* (1994), in which he plays bodyguard to her mature ex-first lady and succumbs to her charms – hook, line, and sinker.

PEEPING TOM

1960 - GREAT BRITAIN - 101 MIN. - COLOR - PSYCHO THRILLER

DIRECTOR MICHAEL POWELL (1905–1990)
SCREENPLAY LEO MARKS DIRECTOR OF PHOTOGRAPHY OTTO HELLER EDITING NOREEN ACKLAND MUSIC BRIAN EASDALE, ANGELA MORLEY, FREDDIE PHILLIPS PRODUCTION MICHAEL POWELL for ANGLO-AMALGAMATED PRODUCTIONS, MICHAEL POWELL (THEATRE).

STARRING KARLHEINZ BÖHM (Mark Lewis), MOIRA SHEARER (Vivian), ANNA MASSEY (Helen Stephens), MAXINE AUDLEY (Mrs. Stephens), BRENDA BRUCE (Dora), ESMOND KNIGHT (Arthur Baden), PAMELA GREEN (Milly, the model), MARTIN MILLER (Doctor Rosan), BARTLETT MULLINS (Mr. Peters), JACK WATSON (Chief Inspector Gregg).

"Whatever I photograph – I always lose!"

Whenever the movies show us eyes in close-up, we're confronted with questions about the nature of visual perception and filmic representation. When the open razor sliced through the eye in Buñuel and Dalí's *An Andalusian Dog* (*Un Chien andalou*, 1929), it also cut through the audience's habits of perception, which had been formed in the theater at a safe distance from the stage. Many spectators found the notorious sliced-eyeball scene literally impossible to watch, for what they were seeing was their own still-innocent moviegoer's eye, attacked as they wallowed in the cinematic illusion. *Peeping Tom* operates in the same field of visual trespass, although it intrudes on the spectator's senses less harshly than the surrealist shocker.

The film begins with a close-up of a human eye – closed, as if the person it belongs to were dreaming. Then it snaps opens like a camera shutter and stares horror-struck from the screen. This eye is a filmic emblem. It introduces a complex constellation of perceptions, in which the spectator will participate in a highly unusual manner. The eye that fills the screen also stares at the spectator like a camera lens, returning his interested gaze. The watcher is being watched: the spectator – a voyeur, a Peeping Tom – is himself under observation.

In a separate introductory section before the titles sequence, a slow zoom draws the spectator into the lens of a 16-millimeter amateur film camera, half-hidden under a young man's coat. Then the point of view changes: we're now walking towards a prostitute; the camera's crosshairs disfigure the frame. The streetwalker takes us with her to her room. We have become the eye of the camera. And as the woman undresses, the camera moves slowly towards her. Terrified, she raises her hands to her face, and screams. And the camera keeps rolling.

For almost 20 years, critics either ignored *Peeping Tom* or vilified it. From a contemporary perspective, it's hard to understand why. Not until 1979 was the film rehabilitated, when Martin Scorsese and Paul Schrader presented it at the New York Film Festival and placed it on a list of their "guilty pleasures." Better late than never, one might say; but for Michael Powell, it was definitely too late. Since the London premiere of *Peeping Tom* in 1960, his reputation had been ruined. The critics had simply been unable or unwilling to understand the film, ignoring the clear thematic parallels between the eye (of the camera) and the "I" of the killer, the director and the spectator. "I, the eye:" it's this that provides the key to the conflict-ridden personality of Mark

1. Make love to the camera: It's about the only thing Mark Lewis (Karlheinz Böhm) shares a tender moment with.

2. Smile for the birdie: Helen Stephens (Anna Massey) is horrified to discover what lies beyond Mark's bashful veneer. Her disgust, however, is tempered by concern.

3. Self-inflicted punishment or just posing? Mark serves as his own stand-in to calculate the perfect angle for photographing mortal fear.

4. Jack the rip-roaring photographer: Like most men in his field, Mark only selects a certain type of individual to partake in his art projects — namely, prostitutes, cover girls, and actresses.

"Martin Scorsese once said that this movie, and Federico Fellini's *8 1/2*, 'contain all that can be said about directing.' The Fellini film is about the world of deals and scripts and show biz, and the Powell is about the deep psychological process at work when a filmmaker tells his actors to do as he commands, while he stands in the shadows and watches." *Chicago Sun-Times*

Lewis (Karlheinz Böhm), the shy, film-obsessed assistant cameraman whose traumatic childhood made him a voyeur and a murderer.

The little 16-mm film camera that accompanies Mark everywhere he goes is literally a deadly weapon. When he has found a victim, he moves towards her, filming all the while; then he flips up a leg of the tripod, which he has converted into a deadly stiletto, and stabs. And it's not enough for him to see and film the death struggle of his petrified victims: he also confronts them with their fear by holding up a parabolic mirror, so that the victims can see themselves dying. As he says to Helen (Anna Massey) at one point: "Do

you know what the most frightening thing in the world is?" The answer, we learn, is fear itself.

Helen, a novice author of children's books, is the only human being he can trust. The pathologically shy son of a renowned psychologist, Mark had himself been the victim of an inhuman form of voyeurism, for his father's lust for knowledge had known few limits: in a long series of experiments on fear, he had placed the boy in nightmarish situations and filmed his reactions.

Night after night, Mark watches his own homemade snuff movies, but they can solve his conflicts or straighten his twisted soul. The victims'

5   Oh, they got me! Mark collapses at Helen's side and dies while she lies unconscious on the floor. If Helen thought Mark was shocking before, she's in for a rude awakening.

6   Neatly partitioned lifestyle: Mark's darkroom and archives are set off from the rest of his apartment. Even though she hasn't seen them yet, Helen senses that Mark's artsier shots might not exactly suit her taste.

7   Needle point: Mark tweaks his tripod to hold his victims in place while 'capturing' what he believes is the ultimate in authenticity on film.

KARLHEINZ BÖHM

Karlheinz Böhm was an exceptionally versatile and multifaceted actor, and his finest performances were all distinguished by a certain quality of alertness and powerful concentration. The son of the famous conductor Karl Böhm, he was born in Darmstadt, Germany, in 1928. He was much loved for his performance as the Emperor Franz Joseph in the three notoriously kitschy "Sissi" films of the 50s. His partner in these movies was the young Romy Schneider as the Empress Sissi herself. She and Böhm spent their lives trying to escape the image they had acquired in the process: "the pink marzipan piglet image," as Böhm memorably put it. Both of them wanted to be seen as the excellent character actors they were, and Böhm believed he had achieved this goal in Michael Powell's *Peeping Tom* (1960). However, the film was torn to pieces by shortsighted critics. Böhm went to Hollywood and signed a three-year contract. He didn't like it there; after only four films, he returned to Germany, where the social upheaval of '68 left its mark on him politically. He worked a lot in the theater before he landed up with Rainer Werner Fassbinder. His roles in *Martha* (1973) and *Faustrecht der Freiheit* (1975) finally brought him the change of image he had been seeking for so long. In 1981, his life and career took another surprising turn, when he appeared on the German TV show "Wetten dass ..." ("I bet you ..."). Seven million people were watching as he wagered that not even half of them would contribute a single Deutsche Mark to an emergency charity project for starving people in the Sahel-Sahara zone. Böhm won his bet; and with the 1.7 million Marks sent in by viewers, he went to Ethiopia and founded the aid organization "Menschen für Menschen" (People for People). Since then, he has been managing the organization and soliciting charitable contributions on its behalf, so that new aid projects can be initiated every year.

final terror is finally just a sequence of film in a rattling projector. It's never enough. In order to free himself from his trauma and lend some meaning to his life through the medium of his "art," Mark ultimately chooses to kill himself – and to leave a photographic record of his own extinction. He attaches his murderous apparatus to a cupboard and walks towards it. On the short path to his death, he captures the story of his own life in a series of photos shot with a self-timer: from the abused boy he has always remained to the

book to be accepted for publication. No doubt she had had something rathe different in mind.

Peeping Tom is a film that does what it sets out to do, staring un flinchingly into the abyss of the soul and the cinema, and reflecting upor what it sees there. It is neither self-consciously avant-garde nor timidly subject to the dictates of taste, following only its own dramaturgical laws And as a study of filmmaking itself, *Peeping Tom* has a positively timeles

PURPLE NOON
Plein soleil / Delitto in pieno sole

1960 - FRANCE / ITALY - 116 MIN. - COLOR - THRILLER, LITERARY ADAPTATION

DIRECTOR RENÉ CLÉMENT (1913–1996)
SCREENPLAY RENÉ CLÉMENT, PAUL GÉGAUFF, based on the novel *THE TALENTED MR. RIPLEY* by PATRICIA HIGHSMITH
DIRECTOR OF PHOTOGRAPHY HENRI DECAË EDITING FRANÇOISE JAVET MUSIC NINO ROTA PRODUCTION RAYMOND HAKIM, ROBERT HAKIM for PARIS FILM, PARITALIA, TITANUS.

STARRING ALAIN DELON (Tom Ripley), MAURICE RONET (Philippe Greenleaf), MARIE LAFORÊT (Marge Duval),
ERNO CRISA (Riccordi), ELVIRE POPESCO (Mrs. Popova), FRANK LATIMORE (O'Brien), BILLY KEARNS (Freddy Miles),
LILY ROMANELLI (Housekeeper), AVE NINCHI (Signora Gianna), NERIO BERNARDI (Agency Director).

"Vous me tuez ... Vous voilà riche."

Why should only others enjoy the good life? What kind of man do you have to be to share the luxurious lifestyle of the rich and beautiful? In the same year that Federico Fellini's *La dolce vita* (1959/60) conquered the movie theaters, another film approached the topic from its darker side. If Fellini's alter ego Marcello Mastroianni was in danger of losing his identity amongst the starlets and the pleasures of the senses, Tom Ripley has no identity to lose; and so he takes somebody else's, after murdering the previous owner.

Clément's film is also set in Rome, in and around the Via Veneto. The
~~Americans Phili~~ ~~Greenleaf (Ma~~ ~~ce Ronet) and Tom Ripley (Alain Delon)~~

enjoy the Italian lifestyle in the most expensive and exclusive cafés. Money is no obstacle, for Philippe's old man, a filthy-rich tycoon, is paying for everything. In fact, Philippe's father has hired Tom to persuade his son to come home. But the good-for-nothing Philippe is having none of it. Tom envies him his monthly checks, his worry-free life and the love of his beautiful girlfriend Marge (Marie Laforêt). When Mr. Greenleaf Sr. declares the mission has failed, what had been a vague idea becomes an actual plan: Tom kills his snobbish companion and takes on his identity. The footloose survival artist Tom Ripley becomes Philippe Greenleaf, the cosmopolitan
~~son of a millionaire~~

"Against some sparkling backgrounds of the blue Thyrrhenian Sea, a fishing port on the Gulf of Salerno and the three-shaded avenues of Rome, French director René Clément has done the incongruous thing of unfolding a murder thriller that is as fascinating as it is dazzlingly beautiful." *The New York Times*

2

This cold-blooded murder is only a preview to Tom's real task and vocation: the masquerade, which is always on the verge of being uncovered. He imitates Philippe's voice, forges his signature, and types letters on the dead man's typewriter. Further precautions are necessary: Tom has to change hotel constantly, avoid unwanted encounters and commit a second murder – for Philippe's pal Freddy Miles (Billy Kearns) has seen through his little game. Getting rid of the body turns out to be a literally massive problem; but no-one will ever pin the murder on Tom Ripley, for everyone knows that the killer was named Philippe Greenleaf.

Mediterranean savoir-vivre, the sun reflected on bronzed bodies, and the music of Fellini's composer Nino Rota: this is the deceptively pleasant face of an exceptionally intense psycho thriller that explores the dark abyss of the human soul. Who is Tom Ripley? Is it narcissism, greed or sheer immorality that drives him to merge his identity with that of another man? Is there a homoerotic element in all this? Certainly, Marge remains a strangely pale and undefined figure in comparison to the two men.

Much more revealing is an embarrassing scene at the start of the film, when Philippe discovers Tom posing in front of a mirror, dressed in Philippe's clothes. It's an intellectual pleasure to compare this movie with Patricia Highsmith's novel and the successful remake, *The Talented Mr. Ripley* (1999). In each movie version, we meet a different Ripley, a different Philippe, a different Marge. In Minghella's version, Matt Damon is a Ripley

1 That glint in his eye: And who should be is the wiser? In one of his first major roles, Alain Delon commits a little murder under the sun.

2 Starboard side: Wealthy playboy Philippe Greenleaf (Maurice Ronet) and his charming girlfriend Marge Duval (Marie Laforêt) make Tom go green with envy.

3 The last supper: Philippe initially gets a real kick out of Tom's plan, but the fun doesn't stop there.

4 The deed is done: Tom takes command of the helm, disposing of the physical evidence and assimilates his corpse's lucrative identity upon reaching shore.

"Hollywood has forgotten that the creepiest movies are those that quietly crawl under your skin, making you look at your neighbor and nervously wonder what's going on in his head. Modern thrillers are all action and gore, but the 1960 French film *Purple Noon*, which has just been re-released, is a thriller of the old school, its horror unfolding slowly with every quiet conversation." *The Washington Post*

**PATRICIA HIGHSMITH
(1921–1995)**

Alfred Hitchcock once claimed he had never been able to work well with writers who specialized, as he did, in horror, thrills or suspense. He was referring in particular to his adaptation of Patricia Highsmith's first novel, *Strangers on a Train* (1951). His scriptwriter Raymond Chandler struggled to make anything of the novel, which he described as silly and lacking in credibility, and was later replaced. Despite this difficult birth, it eventually became one of Hitchcock's best films, focusing on a fatal male friendship and a bizarre theory: two people agree to perform each other's murders. While the Hitchcock film only hinted at possible homoerotic undertones, Anthony Minghella's version of *The Talented Mr. Ripley* (1999) was considerably less hesitant in this respect.

A native Texan, Patricia Highsmith was always more popular in Europe than in the USA. Many of Highsmith's psychologically insightful novels – there are more than 20 of them – are set in her adopted home country of France. They inspired numerous film adaptations, particularly by French and German directors. Wim Wenders took *Ripley's Game* and made *The American Friend* (*Der amerikanische Freund / L'ami américain*, 1977), with Dennis Hopper playing Tom Ripley. Hans W. Geissendörfer adapted two of her novels: *The Glass Cell* (*Die gläserne Zelle*, 1977) and *Edith's Diary* (*Ediths Tagebuch*, 1983), followed by Claude Chabrol with *Cry of the Owl* (*Le Cri du hibou*, 1987). Filmmakers clearly loved Patricia Highsmith's work, something she acknowledged with detached amusement. The Queen of Crime died in Locarno in February 1995.

6

5 The Reverse Heimlich Maneuver: Tom makes sure an eyewitness won't live to see the light of day.

6 Erotic yet expendable: In director Clément's hands, Marge's character is little more than a hot body.

7 He plays her like a violin: But as a guitar player, Marge remains oblivious to Philippe's grim fate.

8 Decanter and deflower her: With the 'transformation' complete, Tom takes possession of all that is rightfully his. And Marge just comes with house.

driven by fears and dark instincts; in *Purple Noon*, Alain Delon's Ripley is cool, unruffled and elegant. Quietly conscious of his own superiority, he can bear with equanimity the humiliations visited upon him by Philippe. And although each of his two murders may have been due to a momentary lapse of self-control, the deceptions that follow are planned right down to the tiniest detail. Highsmith's Ripley was a seductive swindler who simply couldn't be caught – much to the pleasure of her readers, who looked forward to the Rip-

ley novels that would follow. In this respect, René Clément, one of the most celebrated directors of the post-war French cinema, was a little less brave than the novelist. Yet although the ending does disap-point, it is served up with the same almost unbearable suspense as the rest of the film. In 1996, *Purple Noon* was re-released by Martin Scorsese.

PB

THE HORROR CHAMBER OF DR. FAUSTUS / EYES WITHOUT A FACE

Les Yeux sans visage

1960 - FRANCE / ITALY - 88 MIN. - B & W - HORROR FILM

DIRECTOR GEORGES FRANJU (1912–1987)
SCREENPLAY PIERRE BOILEAU, PIERRE GASCAR, THOMAS NARCEJAC, CLAUDE SAUTET, based on the novel of the same name by JEAN REDON DIRECTOR OF PHOTOGRAPHY EUGEN SCHÜFFTAN EDITING GILBERT NATOT MUSIC MAURICE JARRE PRODUCTION JULES BORKON for CHAMPS-ÉLYSÉES PRODUCTIONS, LUX FILM.

STARRING PIERRE BRASSEUR (Doctor Génessier), EDITH SCOB (Christiane), ALIDA VALLI (Louise), FRANÇOIS GUÉRIN (Jacques), ALEXANDRE RIGNAULT (Inspector Parot), BÉATRICE ALTARIBA (Paulette), JULIETTE MAYNIEL (Edna), CHARLES BLAVETTE (L'homme de la fourrière), CLAUDE BRASSEUR (Inspector), MICHEL ETCHEVERRY (Forensic surgeon).

"You shall have a proper face."

The clinic of Dr. Génessier (Pierre Brasseur) is only a short distance from Paris. He's an ambitious surgeon, famed as a specialist in skin transplants, but no-one realizes his terrible secret: since his daughter Christiane (Edith Scob) was disfigured in an accident, Génessier has sworn to do everything he can to restore her beauty. With the help of his assistant Louise (Alida Valli), he lures young women to his remote villa, where he anesthetizes them and sets to work. In an operating theater concealed in the basement of his house, he removes their facial skin and transplants onto his daughter. To no avail

When this film was released, almost everyone disliked it. Many critics accused Georges Franju of a severe lapse of taste, while others missed the aggressive social criticism of his previous films and lamented that he had wasted his talent on a mannered horror movie. Nonetheless, *Eyes Without a Face* was soon hailed as a classic of the genre. With this fascinating film, Franju, the former co-founder of the legendary Cinémathèque Française, succeeded in making film history a source of inspiration for his own unique cinematic vision. It's still an extremely disturbing film, not least thanks to Eugen Schüfftan's camerawork. His brilliant black-and-white photography

"One of the greatest horror films ever made, and one of the most bizarre."

Edinburgh University Film Society

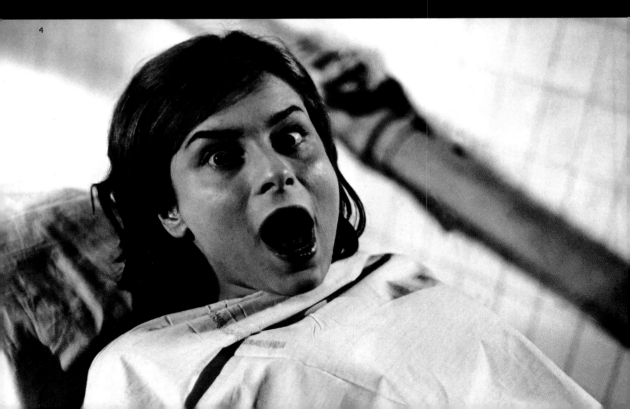

5

1 Nip and tuck: Everything about Christiane (Edith Scob) is smooth as porcelain – even though she's 100% plastic.

2 Medicine man or witch doctor? Workaholic, Dr. Génessier (Pierre Brasseur) cleanses his conscience by restoring his daughter to her former state of glory. The task, however, has him washing his hands in blood.

3 Need a lift? Christiane still harbors hopes of reuniting with her fiancé, but he wrote her off for dead long ago.

4 Silence, lamb! A routine checkup with Dr. Génessier leaves young ladies with more than they bargained for.

5 Face pokers: Dr. Génessier and his assistant Louise (Alida Valli) wear expressions as enigmatic as the human masks they create.

is worthy of comparison with the great works of German Expressionism. It lends Génessier's villa an eerie life of its own, transforming it into a weird labyrinth from which there is apparently no escape. The stair-rails cast their barred shadow on everyone who enters this house; they are the prisoners of Génessier's madness. As is his daughter, who floats through her father's house like a ghost, her ravaged face hidden behind a white porcelain mask. Its permanently sad expression seems to foretell her fate.

Christiane's mask is also one manifestation of the film's central formal characteristic: much of its tension arises from the interplay between the visible and invisible, the exposed and the hidden. Franju skilfully evokes a nightmarish atmosphere without explicitly showing what Génessier does – until some time into the film … When the surgeon does suddenly insert his scalpel into the face of one young girl, it has the shocking intensity of the sliced eye in Dalí and Buñuel's surrealist classic *An Andalusian Dog*

"A horrifying brew of terror and allegorical poetry … The author's most impressive work to date."

6 A plea against plastic surgery: The more artificially beautiful Christiane becomes the more fragile she seems. Eat your heart out, Michael Jackson!

7 The children's hour: Although Christiane longs to be a 'good girl,' there's just no way she'll ever be good enough.

(*Un chien andalou*, 1929). Franju, like his famous predecessors, is gleefully provocative. A sober series of close-up photos shows Christiane's perfectly-restored face; and then we see how the grafted skin grows mottled, starts to peel, and eventually – after two weeks – drops off.

The horror of these two sequences unmasks Génessier: not only is he a murderous physician who has betrayed his Hippocratic oath, but his fatherly love is shown to be a brutal obsession. In attempting to equip his daughter with a new face, he is also erasing her identity. Frankenstein-like, he wishes to recreate her as an ideal woman – and in the end, he suffers a terrible punishment for his hubris. Tellingly, though, it's not the police who finally bring Génessier to his knees. Deceived by his respectable façade, they withdraw after making enquiries. So it's left to Christiane to put a stop to her father's crimes and to free herself from her prison. She stabs Génessier's assistant with the scalpel and helps the last victim to flee. Her final act is to free the dogs Génessier has been using in his skin-grafting experiments. Let loose from their cages, they attack their tormentor and tear him to pieces. Christiane walks free into the night.

JH

EUGEN SCHÜFFTAN

Eugen Schüfftan, born in Wroclaw (Breslau) in 1893, studied art and architecture before turning to the cinema. He began as a special-effects specialist, inventing the famous Schüfftan technique, which made it possible to reflect models or painted backdrops into real scenes. This was method used, for example, by Fritz Lang for his impressive futuristic visions in *Metropolis* (1926). Soon after this, however, the technique was replaced by simpler methods. Today, Schüfftan's work as a cinematographer seems more important. For Robert Siodmak and Edgar G. Ulmer, he made the legendary Berlin film *Menschen am Sonntag* (1929), before emigrating to France. There, he changed his name to Eugène Shuftan and made a name for himself as a master of light, with his work on movies such as Marcel Carné's *Port of Shadows* (*Quai des brumes*, 1938). He went on to consolidate this reputation with Georges Franju's *Head Against the Wall / The Keepers* (*La Tête contre les murs*, 1959) and *The Horror Chamber of Dr. Faustus / Eyes Without a Face* (*Les Yeux sans visage*, 1960). Towards the end of his career, he worked mainly in the U.S., where he changed his name yet again to Gene Shufton. In the States, he was able to capitalize on the reputation he had built up in Europe. Robert Rossen's study of a pool-shark (*The Hustler*, 1961, starring Paul Newman) won him an Oscar for Best Cinematography (Black-and-White). His monochrome photo-graphy for Rossen's *Lilith* (1964) was no less i

"Narrow and haunted, *Eyes Without a Face* is a truly French-style film fantasy, and will forever inhabit one of those dark recesses of the realm of the imaginary." *Le Monde*

INDEX OF FILMS

IMPRINT

This edition published by Barnes & Noble Publishing, Inc.,
by arrangement with TASCHEN GmbH

2006 Barnes & Noble Books

© 2006 TASCHEN GmbH

M 10 9 8 7 6 5 4 3 2 1

ISBN 0–7607–8082–X

PHOTOGRAPHS

defd and CINEMA, Hamburg
BRITISH FILM INSTITUTE, London
BIBLIOTHÈQUE DU FILM (BiFi), Paris

PROJECT MANAGEMENT
EDITORIAL COORDINATION
DESIGN

PETRA LAMERS-SCHÜTZE, Cologne
STILISTICO and THIERRY NEBOIS, Cologne
SENSE/NET, ANDY DISL and BIRGIT REBER, Cologne

TEXTS

ULRIKE BERGFELD (UB), PHILIPP BÜHLER (PB), DAVID GAERTNER (DG),
STEFFEN HAUBNER (SH), JÖRN HETEBRÜGGE (JH), KATJA KIRSTE (KK),
HEINZ-JÜRGEN KÖHLER (HJK), OLIVER KÜCH (OK), PETRA LANGE-BERNDT (PLB),
NILS MEYER (NM), ECKHARD PABST (EP), LARS PENNING (LP),
STEPHAN REISNER (SR), BURKHARD RÖWEKAMP (BR), ERIC STAHL (ES),
MATTHIAS STEINLE (MS), RAINER VOWE (RV)

TECHNICAL EDITING

DAVID GAERTNER, Berlin

ENGLISH TRANSLATION

PATRICK LANAGAN (introduction and texts), SHAUN SAMSON (texts and captions) for
ENGLISH EXPRESS, Berlin

EDITING
PRODUCTION

DANIELA KLEIN for ENGLISH EXPRESS, Berlin and JONATHAN MURPHY, Brussels
TINA CIBOROWIUS, Cologne

PRINTED IN CHINA